PRACTICAL BUSINESS ETHICS

PRACTICAL BUSINESS ETHICS

WARREN A. FRENCH
University of Georgia

JOHN GRANROSE
University of Georgia

Prentice Hall
Englewood Cliffs, New Jersey 07632

Library of Congress Cataloging-in-Publication Data

French, Warren A., 1941–
    Practical business ethics / Warren A. French, John Granrose.
      p.   cm.
    Includes index.
    ISBN 0-02-338863-3
    1. Business ethics.   2. Business ethics—Case studies.
  I. Granrose, John. II. Title.
  HF5387.F74   1995
  174'.4—dc20   93–50588
                                          CIP

Editor: Natalie Anderson
Production Supervisor: Helen Wallace
Production Manager: Francesca Drago
ETM Manager: Kurt Scherwatzky
Text Design: A Good Thing, Inc.
Cover Design: Curt Tow Design

Copyright © 1995 by Prentice-Hall, Inc.
A Division of Simon & Schuster, Inc.
Englewood Cliffs, New Jersey 07632

Printed in the United States of America

10 9 8 7 6 5 4 3 2 1

ISBN 0-02-338863-3

Prentice-Hall International (UK) Limited, *London*
Prentice-Hall of Australia Pty. Limited, *Sydney*
Prentice-Hall Canada Inc., *Toronto*
Prentice-Hall Hispanoamericana. S.A., *Mexico*
Prentice-Hall of India Private Limited, *New Delhi*
Prentice-Hall of Japan, Inc., *Tokyo*
Simon & Schuster Asia Pte. Ltd., *Singapore*
Editora Prentice-Hall do Brasil, Ltda., *Rio de Janeiro*

*To the future research of William Kurtines
and Marvin Berkowitz. May they break down barriers!*

PREFACE

In teaching business ethics, our experience has shown that many students enter the course with a particular mindset. That mindset is that they know what is right or wrong, and no teacher or text can convince them otherwise. We have found over time that such mindsets can be changed but rarely by the instructor advocating a particular ethical theory.

We believe that though we may have arrived at our own personal stances with respect to ethics, our task is not to try to convince others that we have found "truth." Rather, our task is to provide readers with background knowledge and guidelines that will enable them to test their own ethical positions in business situations. How we achieve these goals is described in the Introduction.

Each of the ten chapters of the text is followed by three cases. The cases depict ethical situations that have actually occurred for the firms and individuals mentioned. The theme of each case matches the theme of the chapter in which it is contained. The task laid out for the reader is to establish a process for resolving conflicts over the ethical issues described by each case. Also contained within the chapters are the issues which the Conference Board has designated as the most serious ethical problems facing business. There are twenty-seven of these issues, and they, along with other moral issues, are spread through the book.

Toward the end of establishing a process for resolving conflicts, we have made conflict resolution the focal point of the text. The title of our text, *Practical Business Ethics*, contains a term, *practical*, that connotes a workable procedure. This procedure is composed of three components:

1. Any workable ethical stance has to be grounded in theory. Intuition alone just does not work. Theory gives legitimacy to ethical arguments and provides a logical framework for analyzing positions and arriving at positions. We have outlined two approaches to ethical theory. The first is an overview of the traditional deontological and consequentialist views. The second is the analysis of ethical reasoning according to stages of moral development. These approaches, which constitute the first six chapters, give the reader options to choose from.

2. The last four chapters center on the process of conflict resolution. As we mention in the text, rarely does a person win an ethical argument. Lasting conflict resolution usually results from a position with which both parties can live. Thus the last four chapters provide the reader with the groundwork for negotiating ethical concerns.

3. Underlying the presentation of ethical theory and the process of conflict resolution are guidelines for arriving at practical positions. Four guidelines are offered as tests to check if positions are truly viable. These tests or guidelines are described in the first six chapters and used in the last four chapters.

This three-component process is simply an attempt to synthesize some of the more important contributions from the literature in ethics, moral development, and conflict resolution so as to apply the knowledge from those disciplines to resolving ethical problems.

Most of us tend to forget much of what we have been exposed to in academic courses. On this assumption, we are more interested that our readers incorporate the process outlined in this text into their lives rather than memorize different moral philosophers' theories of ethics.

Acknowledgments

We wish to extend our thanks to the following persons, whose helpful comments improved this text: Professor Ben Abramowitz, University of Central Florida, Orlando; Professor David Newell, Washington College, Chestertown, Maryland; and Professor Stephen Snyder, University of West Florida, Pensacola.

This text has been in various draft forms since 1978. While there may be much to criticize in it, we have noticed one thing about the process it outlines. The students who have used it seem to think it works.

Warren A. French
John Granrose

CONTENTS

Chapter 2   Exploitation   41

Chapter 3   Custom, Convention, and Courtesy   61

Chapter 4   The Letter of the Law Versus the Spirit of the Law   81

PRACTICAL BUSINESS ETHICS

INTRODUCTION

General Goals

We believe it is important to clarify goals or objectives at the beginning of any major project. Hence, we shall list and explain certain general goals that we have had in mind in preparing *Practical Business Ethics*. We base these goals on two related studies published by the Hastings Center: *Ethics in the Education of Business Managers*[1] and *The Teaching of Ethics in Higher Education*.[2] The development of sound moral judgment in business situations depends on six kinds of capabilities and skills, and we believe that the study of business ethics, directed by these goals, can help in this process.

1. Stimulating the Moral Imagination

It is tempting for both the business student and practitioner to suppose that legal and economic factors totally determine rational business decisions. We want the reader of this book to see that "human beings live their lives in a web of moral relationships, that a consequence of moral positions and rules can be actual suffering or happiness, and that moral conflicts are frequently inevitable and difficult."[3] We want the reader to develop a greater ability to imagine himself or herself "in the other person's shoes," to notice hidden assumptions in our thinking about moral dilemmas that arise in business, and to recognize that the moral dimensions of a business situation are important—even when they are somewhat vague or difficult to quantify.

2. Moral Identification and Ordering

The ability to identify, to order, and to set priorities about the moral factors in a situation requires cultivation. A business manager makes use of a similar process

1

when he or she sorts out and orders the economic factors that bear on a decision. The cases and points of view presented in this text are intended to help the reader, through repeated practice and reflection, to identify ethical issues quickly and to begin to analyze them rationally rather than just emotionally.

3. Moral Evaluation

Notoriously, there are several different and conflicting schools of thought about how issues of moral right and wrong are to be settled. The major viewpoints described in the following pages can be applied to specific cases within each chapter. By the conclusion of this book, the reader may expect to have advanced toward a position on ethics that will be coherent and consistent on the one hand and applicable to business situations on the other. Not all readers will arrive at the same position, but this should not be surprising. Neither will the authors try to support one theory of moral evaluation over another. The goal will be for the reader to come to appreciate the pros, cons, and applicability of each major theory in business situations. The choice of a personal (or corporate) position on ethics is an issue for the reader of this volume, not for the writers.

4. Tolerating Moral Disagreement and Ambiguity

For the most part, the people described in the chapters' cases in this text believed that they were morally justified in choosing their actions. By including particular cases in our book, we do not mean to suggest that these persons acted correctly. Rather, the actions taken by the individuals and firms cited in the cases are presented because they present conflicts about moral values and judgments. The inevitable disagreements that will arise during group discussion of the cases should result in an increased tolerance for both disagreement and ambiguity on the part of those who work carefully through each chapter.

5. Integrating Managerial Competence and Moral Competence

The purpose of studying and discussing cases concerning business ethics should not be simply to recognize moral dilemmas and be able to analyze them. Once the skills of recognition and analysis have been developed, the reader must tackle the additional problem of using those skills in a business situation to negotiate a resolution to the conflict. Both moral and managerial competence are required and must be integrated. Managerial competence is developed through experience as well as through formal training. Moral competence, by contrast, is usually assumed as a given. The essential skill here is to develop a combination of moral and managerial competence so that moral decisions may be transformed into institutional practices.

Such integration may result in somewhat different sets of practical skills, depending of course on one's role in the business community. The problems faced by a chief executive officer will differ from those faced by a middle manager, and the skills required to accommodate the moral concerns of each employee in a company will be different. Also, the response to a moral issue in a small business may well differ from the response in a large corporation.

6. Eliciting a Sense of Moral Responsibility

A course focusing on value conflicts in business must at some point address the underlying question in all moral dilemmas: "Why be moral anyway?" The reader of this book who fails to raise this question may well be tempted to evade his or her responsibilities with the glib conclusion, "It doesn't really matter after all." Beyond exploring these fundamental questions of responsibility, there may be relatively little that can be done by any book, course, or teacher to create a sense of moral responsibility if none exists in a person to begin with. Perhaps all that can be expected is that whatever level of commitment to morality itself already exists can be built upon, applied to business situations in some coherent and explicit way, and, to some small and limited extent, be deepened or made more sophisticated. In some situations, the reasoning used by others in discussions of these cases may influence the development of a personal sense of responsibility. In any case, we list this sixth goal separately from the first five since it is the most fundamental—and in many ways the most elusive.

About Case Studies

We believe that the case study approach has proven itself to be the most stimulating and productive method of helping both students and business people develop the skills necessary to cope effectively with the moral or ethical dilemmas that arise in the competitive business world. And we believe that actual cases, rather than fictitious ones, provide the best starting point. This belief is reinforced by the conclusions of the Hastings Center study in *Ethics and the Education of Business Managers.*[4] That report strongly suggests that case studies be used as the crux of courses devoted to the topic of business ethics. We want the user of this book to have the reality of these dilemmas and conflicts always in mind. Accordingly, we have drawn the following cases partly from published accounts of the experiences of business practitioners.

The chapters are presented sequentially according to the level of moral reasoning depicted in the case examples. Each chapter is also prefaced by discussions of the specific value issues that arise in the cases and by the application of some of the major theories of ethics related to these issues. In addition, the chapters include analyses of some of the "middle-range concepts" (such as exploitation and custom) that we find helpful in clarifying the issues involved. Our goal in these chapters is to provide the conceptual *tools* to help prevent the discussions of the cases from degenerating into mere "bull sessions." We believe that disciplined and clearheaded reflection on these issues is possible —and necessary.

Ethics and the Causes of Human Conflict

Conflict is relevant to ethics in at least two ways. First, ethical issues frequently present conflicts (for example, where one person believes an action to be morally right and another person disagrees). And, second, conflicts between persons lead to the need for ethics in the first place because people and businesses compete for scarce resources (for instance, as when two competitors each try to win a valuable contract). The cases in this book illustrate both types of conflict.

Writers on ethics have long recognized that conflict between persons gives rise to the need for standards of ethics. This insight goes back at least as far as Socrates and Plato in ancient Greece. Without some kind of ethical and/or legal limitations on human behavior, the inevitable conflicts between people would lead to neither the efficiency nor effectiveness that marks a successful business operation.

What causes such conflict? Traditionally, two basic causes have been mentioned: human selfishness and scarcity of many things that people want. Human selfishness—or at least "limited altruism"—stems from the fact that few persons are as concerned with the interests of others as they are with their own. We need not take sides in the ancient debate about the extent to which it is natural for humans to be selfish. We need only observe ourselves and our neighbors to recognize that there are limits to what most of us will do to help others when their needs conflict with our own. Add to this fact the recognition that humans compete for limited resources such as land, possessions, positions, and status, and you can see the virtual inevitability of frequent conflict in human groups. This, at least, is the traditional analysis.

Some more recent writers (Philip Slater, for example)[5] have questioned the so-called "scarcity assumption," in part because it seems to overemphasize the desire for the limited physical goods such as land. After all, there are many things that humans need or want that are not necessarily limited. The famous "hierarchy of needs" formulated by the psychologist Abraham Maslow[6] begins with physiological and safety needs, for example, but goes on to include the needs for love, esteem, and self-actualization. Obviously not all of these needs involve competition for a limited supply of goods. Hence, harmony rather than conflict may be more likely to occur in some situations than in others. Still, however, harmony is frequently an elusive goal in ethical deliberations. Just why this is so should become more apparent to you as you progress through the following chapters.

The order of the first six chapters is important. We developed these in the light of the theories of cognitive and sociomoral development worked out over the past several decades by a variety of philosophers and social scientists. Each chapter presents a method for resolving ethical conflicts that arise in a business environment. Some of these methods will already be familiar to you: for example, trying to eliminate conflict by silencing the opposition ("Don't complain or you are fired") or by bargaining of some kind ("If you'll go along with me on this, I'll return the favor when you need something"). But some of these ways of resolving conflicts may leave you dissatisfied, given your particular moral state or level of moral reasoning. So an initial sketch of the current work in the field of moral development may help provide you with some initial orientation. We take this approach in light of a statement of the contemporary philosopher, G. E. M. Anscombe, who commented that moral philosophy "should be laid aside until we have an adequate philosophy of psychology."[7]

Theories of Moral Development

For over thirty years, first at the University of Chicago and then at Harvard, the late Lawrence Kohlberg and his associates have researched the moral development of large numbers of individuals. Basing his work on the general approach to human development presented by the psychologists Jean Piaget and William McDougall, Kohlberg postulated six states of moral development that he believed form "an invariant and universal sequence in individual development."[8] Each of us goes through the same stages in the same order, although some of us may get "stuck" at one stage of moral development and never progress to the next. Passage through these stages is related to age to some extent—although, again, passage is not simply a function of age.

Kohlberg's work aroused much interest among both social scientists and philosophers, many of whom have proposed additions and revisions to his original theory. For example, the extent to which the stages are "invariant and universal" has been questioned by several recent researchers. James Rest, for instance, has found that while people evolve in their moral development, they keep vestiges of their earlier stages with them, and thus the behavior and reasoning marking those earlier stages sometimes reappear.[9]

Some recent writers have argued that Kohlberg's stress on *cognitive* factors such as the reasoning involved in moral decisions provides too little attention to the *motivation* behind moral actions. They believe that emotion as well as reason has an important motivating role. These writers also question whether persons living in different cultures and under different social conditions really go through the same sociomoral development, especially in what Kohlberg described as the later stages.

Finally, as will be discussed below, there has been some discussion of a possible "seventh stage" beyond the six originally identified by Kohlberg.

Yet even with modifications such as these, Kohlberg's format provides a useful tool for examining the ways in which business people attempt to resolve conflicts from their own moral vantage points. Since the first six chapters of *Practical Business Ethics* will make use of Kohlberg's theory of "stages," we will now briefly describe each stage.

Kohlberg's Six Stages

Stage One may be referred to as the "obedience and punishment" stage. The sole criterion of right for the person at this stage of moral development is obedience to the will of those in authority—or more precisely, to those persons who have the power to punish. The primary motivation for doing what is right is to avoid punishment. According to Kohlberg, we all begin our lives as moral agents at this stage.

Stage Two may be referred to as the "individualism and reciprocity" stage. Here the criterion of what is right is that of the greatest good for the individual making the decision. This stress on the individual's own needs or interests, however, includes the recognition that to advance one's own good one sometimes must enter into agreements or "deals" with others. What is right is relative to the interests or good of each individual, although certain concrete exchanges ("reciprocity") may be thought of as "fair." Self-interest, however, is always the motive for entering into and maintaining such agreements.

Stage Three is called by Kohlberg the "interpersonal conformity" stage, but might also be labeled the "good boy/nice girl" stage. The idea here is that what is right will be determined by what is expected of you by people close to you or by people generally. Within a certain social group or business organization, there are relatively clear ideas about what makes someone a "good member of the team" or a "good employee." The person at this stage of moral development tests his or her attitudes and behavior by such expectations. The person at this stage does not think in terms of having a "system of ethics," but may often reflect on a moral situation by trying to imagine being in the other person's shoes—since thinking in that way is part of what is usually expected of people who are "good."

Stage Four may be labeled the "social system" or the "law-and-order" stage. Morality is seen by persons at this stage as a matter of playing one's part in the social system, of doing one's duty, of obeying the rules. Generally there is a fixed set of duties and rules that one must honor. Kohlberg's view is that most American adults are fixated at this stage. A major motive for persons at this stage of development would be to keep society as a whole—or some institution of society—going.

Stage Five is sometimes referred to as the "social contract" stage. This stage presupposes a kind of philosophical reflection on morality and a growing independence from the actual or concrete rules or duties recognized in a particular society. Some basic values, such as life or liberty, may be appealed to even if they are not built into the laws or rules of one's own group. An appeal to the "greatest good for the greatest number" is seen to be a test of right and wrong that would be freely agreed to by rational persons generally. (The "greatest good for the greatest number" test follows the same theme as that followed by the moral utilitarians' aim for "the greatest balance of good over evil.") This hypothetical social contract is taken as the basis for moral decisions by persons at this stage. According to persons at this level, there are moral values or rights that are independent of or that occur prior to the actual laws that might be adopted by society. Thus the basic perspective taken is that of the rational individual who asks the following questions: "What is best for everyone on the whole?" and "What could all of us in principle agree to?" Some, but not all, adults reach this stage, according to Kohlberg.

Stage Six, the highest of Kohlberg's proposed stages, is called the stage of "universal ethical principles." At this stage, moral decisions are not based simply on what is best for everybody. They are based instead on principles that are chosen freely by the agent, but that the agent would be willing for everyone to live by as well. Such principles as the equality of human rights and respect for the intrinsic dignity of all human beings would be plausible examples of these. Even if the greatest good for the greatest number could be obtained in some situation by violating these principles, the person at Stage Six would not approve of their violation. There are higher ethical laws beyond simple utilitarianism. People are to be treated as ends in themselves, not just as means to one's ends or even to the ends of a whole group or society. According to Kohlberg, very few persons in our society reach this stage of moral development.

A Seventh Stage

Over the years since Kohlberg's views on moral development began to be widely discussed, several writers have proposed revisions to his theory of the six stages. One such revision postulated a *seventh* stage. At one point, Kohlberg himself postulated a seventh stage, a religious one, beyond Stage Six. This level was said to be the stage of moral development reached by such religious figures as Jesus or the Buddha. But Kohlberg later revised this view in order to admit a separate path of religious development alongside that of moral development.[10] Also, at one time Jürgen Habermas,[11] a leading German social theorist, proposed a seventh stage in Kohlberg's system. This seventh stage, in Habermas's view, would be a stage involving a deeper kind of social or political freedom than that which is found in stages five or six. A still further version of a Stage Seven was proposed by James Gilligan, who argued for a stage of moral development based on love.[12]

Kohlberg's theory has been criticized for other reasons as well. Carol Gilligan, for example, has argued that the theory applies to masculine moral development but not to feminine moral development (which is characterized by what she calls "caring").[13]

In the case studies for each chapter, you will see examples of each of the six (or seven) stages of moral reasoning. One of your goals in studying these cases should be to evaluate the merits and feasibility of the actions exemplifying those stages. These cases were chosen for inclusion in this textbook precisely because they *are* controversial; they represent different personal values and different stages of moral reasoning.

By the time you start Chapter 7 and focus your attention on conflict resolution, we hope that you will have come a long way toward realizing the first four goals that we mentioned in the beginning of this introduction. We invite you to pay particular attention to Goal 3, that is, the formation of a personal position on ethics that you can test on the cases in the last four chapters.

Some Definitions

To reduce the chance of basic misunderstanding, several rather common terms need to be defined. These terms and others are included in a glossary at the end of this textbook.

Consider the word *values*, for example. When used as a noun in this way, the term usually refers to what is desired or thought to be worthwhile by a particular person or group. This is the sense intended when persons speak of the "values of today's society," for example. This sense of values is what might be called a "descriptive" one, since the desires or beliefs of an individual or group are simply being reported.

There is another sense of the term that is relevant to this book, however. In this sense, *values* refers to those principles or goals that actually are worthwhile, good, or desirable, as distinguished from those that are merely thought to be so. In other words, to label something a *value* in this second sense is to claim that it is (somehow) objectively correct or praiseworthy. This second sense might be called a "prescriptive" one, since the values referred to are being recommended to or prescribed for others. *Values* will be used in both these senses in this text since both senses are essential to understanding our subject.

Several other terms are crucial as well. *Morality* is one of these. Morality refers to the human institution or practice of guiding our behavior by rules or goals that are in some way related to human welfare. In this respect, morality resembles the institutions of law and etiquette. Among the ways in which morality differs from law are that it typically lacks set punishments (such as fines or imprisonment) and lacks set procedures for determining moral rules and settling moral disputes (such as are found in legislatures and courts). Morality differs from etiquette, on the other hand, by being concerned with more important aspects of human behavior, aspects that may lead to major benefits or harm, rather than with the more aesthetic concerns of manners. One twentieth-century philosopher sums all of this up by saying that morality is humanity's "endeavor to harmonize conflicting interests."[14]

The word *ethics* traditionally refers to systematic or philosophical thinking about morality. In other words, ethics in this sense is one of the branches of philosophy. Writers on ethics usually distinguish between two branches of the subject: normative ethics and meta-ethics. Normative ethics is the systematic attempt to formulate and defend theories about what is right, good, or obligatory. Meta-ethics, on the other hand, is concerned with the philosophical analysis of the meaning and justification of the concepts and principles put forward by normative ethics. For example, while a typical theory of normative ethics might be that "it is right to seek the greatest good for the greatest number of persons," a typical question in meta-ethics might be "What is the meaning of words like 'right'?" or "How, if at all, can we be sure that our theories of normative ethics are correct?" Normative ethics and meta-ethics together make up the general field of ethics, or moral philosophy, one of the traditional academic disciplines.

There is still another sense in which the word *ethics* is sometimes used, however. The social sciences might be said to be concerned with ethics in a descriptive sense when these disciplines provide accounts of the moral beliefs and theories held by a particular group of people. Historians and psychologists may also work in the field of ethics in this descriptive sense. So a third branch of ethics, more disinterested than the first two branches, might be called *descriptive ethics.*

It should be noted that some writers distinguish between ethics and morals. In this book, however, we use these terms interchangeably in the present descriptive or social-scientific sense. The major difference between the words *ethics* and *morals* is that the first is derived from a Greek word, the second from a Latin one. Both words originally referred to the customs or habits of a society or an individual. In other words, the original sense of both words seems to have been descriptive.

The introductory pages in each of the ten chapters of *Practical Business Ethics* will concentrate on applying some of the concepts of normative ethics (rather than meta-ethics or descriptive ethics) to the business situations presented in the case studies. The focusing of normative ethics on cases in this way is sometimes referred to as *applied* ethics, or, as in the title of this book, *practical* ethics. Our goal as authors is to provide you with just enough theory to help you make good, practical decisions about ethical situations in business. Toward this end we will rely on the following definition of ethics in the text:

Ethics consists of a set of normative guidelines directed toward resolving conflicts of interest, so as to enhance societal well-being.

This definition follows from Kurt Baier's proposition that a meaningful treatment of ethics must focus on conflict resolution.[15] Conflict resolution is also the crux of Ralph Barton Perry's approach to morality.[16] The cold fact behind this focus is that after several thousand years of discussion no one view of morality has been so enticing or self-evidently correct as to gain universal acceptance. Thus, our focus is on guidelines to resolve conflicts. Still, to be meaningful in a business context, that set of normative guidelines must suggest how the obligations as well as the benefits of a cooperative undertaking are to be distributed.[17]

Readers who have studied ethical theories in a traditional philosophy course will already be familiar with the technical labels often used to classify the major schools of ethical thinking. Although *Practical Business Ethics* downplays this technical vocabulary, our stress on moral development is quite compatible with these standard philosophical approaches to the subject.

Some Standard Theories of Ethics

Most contemporary philosophers of ethics divide the various theories about what makes something morally right (or wrong) into two groups: *teleological* and *deontological* theories. Teleological theories of ethics claim that whether or not an action is morally right or wrong depends completely on the consequences or results of that action (or, in some cases, the consequences of having a rule or policy requiring one to act in that way). Deontological theories, in contrast, claim that consequences are not the only factor in rightness or wrongness. Some deontologists hold that consequences should be recognized as only one factor, along with others, in determining rightness or wrongness. Such deontologists are sometimes called "mixed" deontologists. Other deontologists argue that consequences have no legitimate role at all to play in determining what is right or wrong. Holders of this view are sometimes called "pure" deontologists.

Varieties of Teleological, or Consequentialist, Theories

Both the consequential and the deontological views need to be divided into still more specific theories before they will be useful in analyzing the moral dilemmas that arise in business situations. Consequentialists, for example, can be further divided according to the answer they would give to the questions "What sort of consequences are relevant to determining right and wrong?" and "Consequences for whom?" Let's look at this latter question first. Suppose for the moment that we have agreed that the sort of consequences to be aimed at in deciding about an ethical issue can be summed up in the word *happiness*. Then the question becomes "Whose happiness is it that determines whether something is morally right or wrong?" Two basically different kinds of answers may be given to this question by consequentialists. One of these answers has already been referred to—the answer given by the utilitarian. The utilitarian, who might be called a "universal" consequentialist, would hold that everyone's happiness is relevant to such decisions. In contrast to this, the other kind of consequentialist might be called a "restricted" consequentialist.

The holder of a "restricted" view would maintain that it is not everyone's happiness that needs to be taken into account but only that of some limited or restricted group, one's family or friends, for example. The most extreme version of the restricted consequentialist view is the theory of ethical egoism, the view that it is the consequences for oneself alone that are relevant to whether something is morally right or wrong. These restricted theories could obviously be placed on a continuum depending on the size of the group that is taken into consideration. The view that one's own family is all that counts is broader than the view of egoism. The view that only the consequences for one's family and one's friends are important would be even broader. Still broader would be restricting concern to the citizens of one's state, region, or country. In the business context, one obvious example of a restricted theory would claim that the only factor relevant to determining whether something was morally right or wrong was the consequences for one's company.

Apart from a few extreme laissez-faire capitalists, restricted theories of the sort described above are rarely defended publicly. This reluctance to be publicly identified with such theories is somewhat understandable—given the widespread negative feelings about selfishness and chauvinism in our society. A rational holder of one of these theories would want to protect himself or herself from the scorn that might be shown by others. None of this means, however, that one of these restricted consequentialist theories might not in fact be a plausible theory of ethics. In any case, such theories are widely held in practice even if they are not often publicly confessed. We shall examine them in some detail in connection with the cases in *Practical Business Ethics*.

Varieties of Deontologism

The distinction between pure and mixed deontological theories was explained earlier. But just as one could not apply a restricted consequentialist theory to a moral dilemma without having more details about the theory, so too it will not be very helpful in practical situations merely to know that one's theory is a pure deontological one. Such a designation would simply tell us that the consideration of consequences is being completely excluded as something relevant to moral judgment. One would still not know what the moral judgment in question was to be based on. So it will be important for our purposes to provide several developed examples of pure and of mixed deontological theories. Only in this way can we see how theories of this type might be applied to business situations.

One strongly held view is that moral right and wrong depend completely on the commandments or laws of God. For any of the ordinary interpretations, this view would be an example of a pure deontological theory. It does not matter what the consequences might be or who might be affected. If God has commanded (or forbidden) a certain type of action, then the action is morally right (or wrong). Consequences or results have nothing at all to do with the matter. With this view one would find out whether something is right or wrong by attempting to determine the will of God, whether through scriptural study, prayer and meditation, or consulting spiritual authorities.

Another type of pure deontological theory that is sometimes held is what might be called the "authentic choice" theory. Some persons have believed that the only factor relevant to whether an action or type of action is right or wrong is whether it is freely or "authentically" chosen by the person acting. The phrases declaring "Do your own thing" and "Be true to yourself" suggest this sort of view. If these phrases were interpreted as meaning that one should do that which will bring about the best consequences for oneself, then we would have an example not of deontology but of the restricted teleological theory of egoism. But if they mean that one's own free and independent decision, quite apart from whatever the consequences might be, is the very criterion of something being morally right, then we have another example of a pure deontological view. This general view is characteristic of some versions of the type of philosophy known as existentialism, so we will refer to theories of this sort as existentialist theories when they are discussed in connection with our cases.

Since the criterion for a mixed deontological theory is simply that consequences are claimed to be one factor but not the only factor in determining the rightness or wrongness of something, there can obviously be several different types of mixed deontological theories depending on the different additional factors that are cited by the theory. For example, one would be a mixed deontologist if one held that the greatest good for the greatest number of persons determined what was right, except that there are certain types of actions that could never be justified even if they clearly would lead to the greatest general good. These exceptions include human slavery or torture, for instance.

One famous mixed deontological theory of right and wrong was put forward by the British philosopher W. D. Ross in the 1920s.[18] Ross held that there were seven different factors to take into account in deciding whether an action was right or wrong. He called these factors "*prima facie* duties" since he argued that each was a duty "at first glance" in the absence of mitigating factors. When these separate duties came into conflict with each other, the one that was most important would be seen to be the actual duty in a given situation. Ross's list of prima facie duties included fidelity (especially to promises made), reparation (for previous wrongs of one's own), gratitude, justice, beneficence (or bringing about good consequences for others), self-improvement (or bringing about good consequences for oneself), and nonmaleficence (or not bringing about bad consequences for others). Ross thought of the first four of these factors as independent of consequences and the last three as necessarily involving consequences. Thus his deontological theory was a mixed one.

The standard ethical theories presented thus far may be seen more clearly in the following diagram:

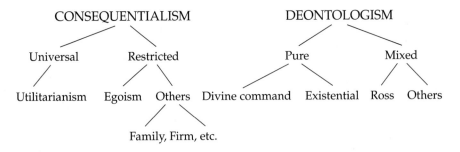

These theories and the six stages of moral development provide complementary ways to analyze the approaches to business values adopted by the individuals within the case studies. As shown in Table I-1, the elements upon which moral stages are judged can be cross-classified using the traditional ethical categorization titles.

Table I-1 Decision Elements Upon Which Moral Development Is Gauged

Deontologism	Consequentialism
Obedience	Reputation
Blame–approval	Reward–punishment
Retribution–exoneration	Individual consequence
Rights	Group consequences
Duties	Character upheld
Balance of perspective	Self-respect upheld
Positive desert	Social ideal served
Equity maintenance	Human dignity served
Social contract maintenance	

Adapted from Ann Colby et al., *The Measurement of Moral Judgment.*, Cambridge, Mass., Harvard University Center for Moral Education, 1980.

Valuable insights into an analysis of behavior may be obtained if we classify each of the individuals faced with value conflicts within the cases presented in this book according to (1) the varieties of deontologism and consequentialism, and (2) the six stages of moral development. Such a classification, combined with the approach to conflict resolution suggested in the final four chapters of the text, may provide the tools needed to help realize the fifth and sixth goals mentioned at the beginning of this introduction—integrating moral competence into management and eliciting a sense of moral responsibility.

Why Bother?

In general, the value issues on which *Practical Business Ethics* focuses are usually called "moral" or "ethical." But many persons these days are suspicious that discussions of such issues are too vague, hypocritical, or biased to be of much worth. For example, one contemporary philosopher begins a book on ethics as follows:

> Moral talk is often rather repugnant. Leveling moral accusations, expressing moral indignation, passing moral judgment, allotting the blame, administering moral reproof, justifying oneself, and, above all, moralizing—who can enjoy such talk? And who can like and trust those addicted to it? The most outspoken critics of their neighbors' morals are usually men (or women) who wish to ensure that nobody should enjoy the good things in life which they themselves have missed. . . . When challenged, they can substantiate their charges only by fine phrases. Yet there can be no doubt that the very best reasons are required, for it is an outstanding characteristic of morality that it demands substantial sacrifices.[19]

What should we make of such a view of "moral talk"? Are we stuck with analyzing the cases in this book in a way that will be "rather repugnant"? We do not think so, for two reasons. First, the goal in discussing the cases will not be to moralize. The point is not to support or condemn the persons whose actions are described. The point will be to analyze the issues and the conflicts involved, and then to ask ourselves what we believe we should have done had we been placed under those same circumstances. Second, our conclusions about what should have been done must always be supported by what we consider to be good reasons. Just what constitute good reasons in the process of making ethical decisions is, of course, a controversial issue in itself. Our hope is that the experience of carefully analyzing the actual situations described in this casebook—and of discussing them in a class or group setting—will enable the reader to develop greater sensitivity to what constitutes a good reason in today's business world.

Notes to the Introduction

[1]Charles W. Powers and David Vogel, *Ethics in the Education of Business Managers* (Hastings-on-Hudson, NY: The Hastings Center, 1980).

[2]*The Teaching of Ethics in Higher Education* (Hastings-on-Hudson, NY: The Hastings Center, 1980).

[3]Ibid., p. 48.

[4]Powers and Vogel, pp. 47–53.

[5]Philip Slater, *The Pursuit of Loneliness: American Culture at the Breaking Point* (Boston: Beacon Press, 1970). See especially Chapters 4 and 6.

[6]Abraham Maslow, *Motivation and Personality* (New York: Harper and Row, 1970). See also Abraham Maslow, *The Farther Reaches of Human Nature* (New York: Van Nostrand Reinhold, 1968).

[7]G. E. M. Anscombe, "Modern Moral Philosophy," in W. D. Hudson (ed.), *The Is–Ought Question* (London: Macmillan and Co. Ltd., 1969), p. 175.

[8]Ann Colby et al., *The Measurement of Moral Judgment* (Cambridge, MA: Harvard University Center for Moral Education, 1980), p. 9.

[9]James Rest, *Development in Judging Moral Issues* (Minneapolis: University of Minnesota Press, 1979).

[10]Guido Kung, "The Postconventional Level of Moral Development: Psychology or Philosophy?" in Marvin W. Berkowitz and Fritz Oser (eds.), *Moral Education: Theory and Application* (Hillsdale, NJ: Lawrence Erlbaum Associates, Publishers, 1985).

[11]Jürgen Habermas, *Communication and the Evolution of Society,* trans. by Thomas McCarthy (Boston: Beacon Press, 1979).

[12]James Gilligan, "Beyond Morality: Psychoanalytic Reflections on Shame, Guilt, and Love," in Thomas Likona (ed.), *Moral Development and Behavior* (New York: Holt, Rinehart and Winston, 1976).

[13]Carol Gilligan, *In A Different Voice: Psychological Theory and Women's Development* (Cambridge, MA: Harvard University Press, 1982).

[14]Ralph Barton Perry, *Realms of Value* (Cambridge, MA: Harvard University Press, 1954), p. 90.

[15]Kurt Baier, *The Moral Point of View* (New York: Random House, 1965). See especially Chapter 6, "The Social Factor in Morality."

[16]Perry, p. 135, and *The Humanity of Man* (New York: George Braziller, Inc., 1956), p. 18.

[17]James Rest et al., "An Overview of the Psychology of Morality," in James Rest, *Moral Development: Advances in Research and Theory* (New York: Praeger Publishers, 1986).

[18]W. D. Ross, *The Right and the Good* (Oxford: The Clarendon Press, 1930).

[19]Baier, p. 3.

Part One

MORAL
REASONING

Chapter 1

POWER

People in business sometimes do good things for bad reasons and bad things for good reasons. This statement reflects an opinion that we share, and our viewpoint dates back to medieval times.[1] We also think that a constructive approach to developing practical business ethics is not to list a series of do's and don't's. As mentioned in the Introduction, we view ethics as *a set of normative guidelines directed towards resolving conflicts of interest so as to enhance societal well-being*. Rather than condemn acts that we are sure are "plain, flat-out wrong," we can start to resolve ethical conflicts by analyzing the motives behind questionable actions. What better place to start than with our most basic or primitive motivation—fear. Specifically, we mean fear of punishment by a more powerful force. Experience shows that there are competitors, suppliers, clients, and bosses who, on occasion, will attempt to instill fear in those with whom they deal.

We begin, therefore, with a notion central to much of our thinking about the role of fear in business: the concept of *power*. Power is almost a dirty word in some circles. It brings with it images of one party treating the other unfairly, being indifferent to basic human needs. Power sometimes suggests brute force used in a selfish and insensitive way.

In other contexts, however, the word *power* has a more appealing connotation. It may be associated with competence, strength, and perhaps authority.

What accounts for these two so different senses of the same word?

Power and Moral Development

Much of the current writing about power, whether by political scientists, philosophers, or persons in business, is concerned with the *definition* of "power" and with distinguishing between its types.

Power refers to a capacity. It stems from the Latin word *potere*, which means "to be able." Put in very practical terms, power is the ability to get someone to do something that he or she otherwise would not do.[2] Its operationalization rests on the interaction of two factors—dependence and goals.[3] Within the bounds of this model of the power relationship, several types of power may be distinguished. In a classic paper on this subject, John French and Bertram Raven contrasted different types of power: Coercive Power, Reward Power, Referent Power, and Legitimate Power.[4] Interestingly, these four categories appear to be causal factors underlying the typical behavior and reasoning in the first four stages of moral development that Kohlberg studied (see the Introduction). For the purposes of the present chapter, however, we focus most of our attention on coercive power—and on its connections to Kohlberg's Stage One of moral reasoning.

Coercive Power

The type of power that French and Raven call coercive is based on a relationship between persons in which one individual has the ability to hurt or punish the other. Such punishment is assumed to interfere with the satisfaction, need, or desire of the person punished. Obviously, one consequence of coercive power is that it can sometimes cause the person over whom the power is being exercised to leave the field of the other's influence, whether by being absent, transferring, or quitting.

A currently much-discussed and very insidious form of coercive power emerges in cases of sexual harassment. Fortunately, businesses today have become more sensitive to the basic wrongness of using coercion of any kind to obtain sex. Coercive power in the form of sexual harassment has existed for a variety of reasons in business situations. Both fellow employees and supervisors sometimes use harassment to attempt to get rid of workers whom they perceive are not performing well. Harassment may also be based on a fear of the victim's potential for advancement and the envy this fear generates. Sometimes harassment results simply because some factor threatens the comfort level of the harasser, as in cases where members of one sex begin to work in roles that traditionally have been the exclusive domain of the other. And, finally, some harassment occurs solely because an employee wants to dominate others, a not-unknown human trait found in the diverse fields of business, government, education, medicine, and so on.

Coercive power is based on fear of punishment, and its purpose is to have one party meekly give in to the other. This, of course, is just what characterizes

Kohlberg's Stage One, the *obedience and punishment* stage. According to Kohlberg, all of us start life using this level of moral reasoning, though most of us progress to "higher" stages. The fact remains, however, that coercive power is most likely to be accepted by persons who are at Stage One of moral development since they consider themselves to be ethical when they obey a more powerful force. In effect, Stage One adherents narrowly interpret the third component of our definition of ethics—societal well-being—to mean only their own personal well-being.

The coercive power that is typically found in Stage One of moral reasoning often combines selfish interest with some types of primitive rules based on fear. In truth, the wrath of those in authority is a strong motivating force. Although we might be inclined to scoff at this view, such a theory would be feasible and understandable under certain circumstances. For example, there are situations in which the conditions of life are very simple and when the knowledge or power (or both) of the person over whom the power is exercised is very limited. In other words, there are times when a kind of rudimentary fear of punishment and a blind obedience to authority may be quite effective. Early childhood is one such time—hence the appropriateness of assigning Kohlberg's Stage One to that period of life. The self-centeredness of those adopting Stage One reasoning, as well as the reasoning used at Stage Two, has been labeled "preconventional." *Preconventional* means that the welfare of people not directly affected by an act is left out of the judgmental process. In effect, at this level the social conventions are given limited consideration.

Reactions to Coercive Power

Another relevant aspect of morality has been stressed by many writers on ethics.[5] When we speak of a "moral" choice or decision, we imply that the choice is (at least in some important sense) free or autonomous. But obviously when we are being subjected to coercive power our choices may be less than fully free. (*Free choice*, in the morally relevant sense, is often taken to mean just "uncoerced choice.") Equally obvious, however, is that the kind and degree of coercion make a difference. Financial rewards and punishments are frequent kinds of coercion in business, as has already been noted. In extreme situations, the threat of direct bodily harm may even be present (as happens when business is undertaken with persons who might be described as "gangsters"). And then there are mild forms of coercive power, such as the simple raised eyebrow or some other expression of social disapproval. One question that you might want to ask yourself is just when does coercive power begin to undermine the freedom or autonomy that is a precondition for moral choice? Can you still act freely when your life is being threatened? What about the lives of family members? Are you acting freely when you sense that your fellow workers disapprove of something you are doing? And just when is "giving in" under coercive pressure morally justified? In your view, is there any way to answer the question of "where do we draw the line?" in the face of coercive power? These are questions to keep in mind as you read the cases in this chapter.

The eighteenth-century philosopher Jeremy Bentham saw little benefit from punishment but admitted that it might be used if "it promises to exclude some greater evil."[6] Could you envision certain business situations and businesspersons for which or whom coercive power and Stage One moral thinking may be the only feasible approaches? Consider, for example, a firm close to bankruptcy. A strong leader demands staff cuts, restructuring, and more work for reduced pay. Those who do not accept these new job conditions know that they will be terminated. Will those employees submit to coercive power? How far will they go to keep their jobs? An *Industry Week* survey found that two-thirds of those requested by a supervisor to act against societal norms did so. These employees justified their actions by saying that they had to follow orders or risked losing their jobs.[7]

The problem with the simple use of coercive power, however, is that reliance on punishment and blind obedience will not continue to work when we become more sophisticated and more conscious of our situations. When we realize that those in authority over us—whether they be parents, political leaders, or employers—do not always "know best," we tend to move beyond this very simplified approach to life.

Use of Coercive Power

Many of the individuals who rely on Stage One reasoning can be identified by the defensive nature of their statements. They are not so much interested in resolving conflicts as in presenting their perception of the facts and principles underlying their positions. Their approach to an ethical discussion would be at the base level of communication that the social philosopher Jürgen Habermas has outlined in the steps toward reaching consensus in conflict resolution.[8] Ethical scholars currently examining Habermas's steps have labeled such defensive justifications as "Ordinary Communicative Action."[9] Ordinary Communication is self- or ego-centered rather than focused on the listener or the listener's position. Users of Ordinary Communicative Action really do not try to understand the other person's point of view. This failure to comprehend all the ethical ramifications of a conflict led James Rest to document the obvious conclusion. After analyzing the results of a series of empirical studies, Rest concluded that the lower a person's comprehension of ethical issues, the more selfish and less societal will be his or her frame of reference when making moral decisions.[10]

Threats and coercive power are tempting to use when the other party does not have many options available and when future negotiations with that party are not important to our business.[11] What we have to remember is that in corporate climates many business relations, dependent on multilevel authorizations, take on an impersonal air. And, as Stanley Milgram's benchmark study of people's behavior has shown, the more impersonal our involvement with another party, the easier it is for us to use coercive power to harm that party.[12] When explaining the results of his electric shock experiments, Milgram concluded that his subjects put conscience and moral judgment aside in favor of obedience to hierarchical authority.

It needs to be remembered, of course, that power of some sort (though not necessarily coercive power) is essential for coordination in any social group. The ethical imperative here, then, seems to be the judicious, prudent, or moral use of power rather than its total rejection.

The seventeenth-century philosopher Thomas Hobbes wrote that absence of moral or legal restraints on coercive power would lead to human life being "solitary, poor, nasty, brutish, and short."[13] He also warned that the weak can destroy the strong. Those who are the objects of coercive power can even sabotage your efforts by feigning stupidity—in effect, by acting out the stereotyped role that you have attributed to them. The question is, when is the use of coercive power likely to be dysfunctional? Two Swiss moral philosophers, Oser and Schäfli, doubt that ethical conflicts can really be resolved unless there is empathy for the other person's position as well as equal participation of both parties in the effort toward resolution.[14] These two conditions are noticeably lacking when coercive power is used.

Not the Golden Rule

Carl Sagan casts a scientist's eye on human behavior and finds that we follow rules of behavior other than the Golden Rule which states "Do unto others as you would have them do unto you." In the Pacific Lumber case in Chapter 10, one of the parties says, "He who has the gold, rules!" Sagan labels this admonition the *Iron Rule*.[15] It embodies the concept of coercive power.

A variation of his Iron Rule is what he calls the *Tin Rule*. It may depict the operating philosophy of some people whom you have met in business. Briefly stated, the Tin Rule says, "Suck up to those above you, and intimidate those below." But will following this rule—a rule that might explain the behavior of animals in the wild—bring about a lasting resolution to moral conflicts?

Views of Power over Time

Plato, in ancient Greece, taught that one has power when one does what one wills. He assumed, however, that one naturally would will to do good. He also anticipated the later notion of a benevolent dictator or monarch through his concept of rule by the so-called "philosopher kings."[16] Aristotle, on the other hand, redirected Plato's emphasis and presented a perspective of power more pertinent to today's business environment. He viewed the focus of power as the means used to attain a goal, and he separated power from Plato's assumption that the wielder of power would naturally seek to do good.[17]

A more extreme, but not atypical view, was provided in the nineteenth century by the controversial philosopher Friedrich Nietzsche.[18] Nietzsche's view was that power is in fact the chief good in human life, but that one's attitude toward it is determined by whether one identifies with the "masters" or the "slaves." Nietzsche used the expressions *master* and *slave* in a broader sense than the literal one. What he had in mind was any relationship in which one person dominates or controls another to a substantial degree. He was also thinking of power over oneself, or what might be called "self-mastery."

Contemporary Views of Power

There are attitudes towards power other than those found in ancient Greece or Nietzsche's Europe. Most of us in this country have difficulty giving *power* a fair hearing. It is almost synonymous with *oppression* or *abuse*. Those involved in international business, however, are aware that in some societies there exists a de facto caste system in which people are born into a social role with very limited mobility. By custom, many people in those societies have become objects of coercive power. Roger Burton, in fact, has noted that throughout the world, punishment inflicted by those in power is used more frequently than rewards to shape people's behavior.[19] We should withhold judgment on this mode of operation for awhile, however, since one of our goals is to develop a degree of tolerance for those who hold opposing points of view on moral issues.

Aristotle's description of power as the means to attain goals is embodied in evolutionary trends within our society. Power in the form of the Colt revolver was relied on to settle the American West, and, with some reluctance, we condoned its use. As our country evolved, power in the form of the dollar became the most potent motivating force in business. Dollars withheld can be just as effective in producing results as is using that money for a reward.

Aside from our fear of lost income, there is another fear present in our business environment. It is the fear of being embarrassed by our ignorance. Intimidation by facts and data presented by another party is quietly becoming the most difficult mode of coercive power to stand up against as we approach the twenty-first century. This ties in with research by James Gilligan that points out how shame stemming from loss of face (often caused by ignorance) is actually more relevant than guilt is for most people.[20]

With our ethical focus on conflict resolution, one potential approach to consider is the power of intimidation through verbal coercion. At the heart of such coercion is the strategic use of communication to repudiate the other person's point of view. Repudiation through verbal coercion may even be directed toward capturing the emotions of a third party who will evaluate opposing points of view. Power in the form of verbal coercion can actually win over groups of people.

Examples of Coercive Power

While laws and federal agencies set guidelines for coercion, such guidelines are rarely unchallengeable. Exceptions generally are allowed. Since most guidelines are restrictive and negative, a society that promotes constructive economic growth almost by nature allows for exceptions to rules. The use of coercive power by a business can, on occasion, produce positive economic results. For instance, should local zoning authorities reconsider their ordinances when a local manufacturer wishes to expand operations if zoning variances are allowed? What if the manufacturer threatens to move unless the authorities change the zoning? Is this an example of a bad act (subverting a community standard with a coercive threat) for what is perceived to be a good reason (creating and sustaining employment)?

Another example of the use of coercive power in the business world concerns the activities of Political Action Committees, or so-called "PACs." Such groups are usually industry-wide (representing, say, the tobacco industry rather than a particular tobacco company), and they attempt to influence public opinion as well as legislative actions. Because of the large amount of money that PACs typically have available, PACs can exert a great deal of power. Such power seems to fit under our heading of coercive power. The voices of individuals advocating a position seem to have less influence than that of a well-funded PAC. The questions are, then, as follows: Do Political Action Committees represent a kind of unfair coercive power in the relations between business and government? Or is using a PAC, so long as it acts within the bounds of what is legal, simply a way in which businesses can "play by the rules" in a manner that is likely to be to their own advantage? Regardless of your particular answer to these questions, note that they raise the possibility at least of coercive power being unfair even when it is not illegal.

Ethical Limitations to Power

In this book we will not advocate any one particular school of ethics. We will, however, explain and advocate certain criteria that we believe are necessary for any viable ethical position. These criteria are means rather than ends; that is, they are guidelines to help resolve conflicts of interest in the moral domain. The necessity for such guidelines is emphasized by James Rest, who has stated the following: "The function of morality is to provide basic guidelines for determining how conflicts in human interest are to be settled. . . ."[21] If these guidelines are to be effective, they should provide reasons for action as well as suggestions for actions. The title of this text is *Practical Business Ethics,* and the word *practical* suggests the first of our guidelines: *feasibility.* When coercive power is used in a heavy-handed, imprudent way, for example, it will frequently not produce the results intended by the person exercising it. Persons who feel themselves abused by coercive power can often find ways to sabotage the efforts of the powerful. This is both a lesson of history and a lesson most of us learn simply through experience. For a business to attain its goals, not only those goals but also the methods used to attain them must be feasible. What is feasible, of course, will depend on the situation. A question to ask, therefore, is whether a particular use of power is an appropriate response to the situation or merely a comfortable habit. Feasibility as a normative criterion or guideline has a long philosophical tradition behind it—despite the popular stereotype of philosophers as impractical and unrealistic.

Feasible Use of Power

One way in which the feasibility criterion has been expressed in the past is in the saying "Ought implies Can."[22] This motto simply means that it makes little or no sense to claim that a person "ought" to do something that in fact he or she cannot do. However, our present criterion of feasibility is just a bit different from this "ought implies can" doctrine. We are instead maintaining that it makes little sense to suggest that a person "ought" to do something that he or she "cannot reasonably do under the given circumstances." Considering feasibility, then, requires us to consider carefully the circumstances of each case rather than laying down some pre-decided rule.

One current ethical concern to which the feasibility criterion may be applied is with the issue sometimes referred to as *employment at will.* The "will" referred to in this phrase is the will of the individual employer, not the employee. In brief, is the will or desire of the employer the prime determinant in deciding who should be hired or terminated? For example, changes in the law may make it difficult to require that an employee retire at a certain age. Imagine, for instance, that an employee who has served your firm successfully over many years has reached the age of 65 and is eligible to retire with excellent benefits. The employee, however, says, "I enjoy my job and I am going to work until I drop." This employee does an acceptable job, but no longer shows the inclination to innovate or become more effective. You feel that a new MBA could be hired at a lower salary to perform the same job adequately. And the younger employee will most likely have more energy and be more flexible in the job. From a purely economic standpoint, it seems that the older worker should be forced to retire so that a younger (and less expensive) worker can be hired. But—apart from any law that might prevent forcing such retirements—how feasible would this action be in terms of the firm's reputation? The potential ill will of the older employee (and this employee's family and friends) might make the action just not feasible overall. On the other hand, circumstances might be such that it is feasible to replace such employees. The survival of the firm might, for example, require drastic cutbacks in salaries. So although feasibility is an important guideline, it will depend on the circumstances of the case.

Power is a business tool, and like any tool it can be misused. Its effective use demands a continual assessment of both people and conditions. Power must rely on reason rather than habit or emotion. As you draw conclusions about the use of power in the cases at the end of this chapter, estimate how feasible the use of that power is in sustaining a productive economic system.

Power and Consequentialism

Where does power fit into the traditional taxonomy of ethical theories that we sketched in the Introduction? We divided ethical theories into teleological and deontological categories. The consequentialist (or teleologist) bases his or her ethical reasoning on consequences, results, or goals (*telos*, in Greek). The deontologist bases his or her ethical reasoning on duties or obligations (*deontos*, in Greek). In the case of those using Stage One reasoning, rules are followed not because of acknowledged obligations but because of the fear of punishment for breaking those rules. This suggests that a certain type of ethical egoism is typical of those who reason at Stage One, an ethical egoism that is primarily concerned with avoiding harm to the self rather than gaining benefits for the self. This would be a particularly simple type of ethical egoism. (Remember that ethical egoism is the doctrine that maintains we should seek only our own interest.)

Those who factor consequences into their ethical judgments must consider the results of someone's threatened use of coercive power when making decisions. The two questions to answer are these: What would be the results if power were used? And what would be the results if power were *not* used?

Conditions Under Which Coercive Power Is Used

We have a strong suspicion that reliance on coercive power is more common in crisis situations. In times of economic growth when even inefficiently run firms can make money, it is easy to play by genteel rules of the game. Conversely, in tight economic times, when the survival of the firm is at stake, are we tempted to sidestep rules of "etiquette" and accomplish our goals however we can? And do we not sometimes begin to think that the basic principles of morality are "merely questions of etiquette"? Some of these questions will be addressed in the following chapters. In this chapter, we are more interested in pursuing the first of the goals that we mentioned in the introduction to the text—*stimulating your moral imagination*. Specifically, we want you to realize that your thoughts about morality may be different from someone else's perspective.

That different perspective may come from those persons who remain at Stage One of moral development. These people reason primarily in terms of fear of punishment. This fact raises the distinction between "freedom from" and "freedom to." All of us are concerned with having freedom from certain kinds of things, such as threats of pain, whether that pain is from punishment, illness, or natural disaster. The most pertinent "freedom-from" issue in a typical business situation might be a worker's fear of the loss of his or her job.

As individuals and groups move on to more advanced stages of moral development, the so-called "freedom to" becomes more pertinent. For example, a worker's attention may turn from his or her fears in the face of various real or imagined threats to his or her hopes or desires, say for better working conditions, including such features as more autonomy in the workplace. The coercive power discussed in this chapter is characteristic of the "freedom-from" type of thinking. Chapter 2 is concerned with another kind of power, reward power, characteristic of the "freedom-to" type of thinking.

Conclusions

As a final note in this chapter, taking power as the benchmark for moral action seems to isolate the various dimensions of ethics quite quickly. The self-centered nature of Stage One thinking means that those who abide by this stage usually are easy to classify. Such persons would be: (1) more motivated by personal goals than by societal obligation, (2) more motivated by situational actions and consequences than by universal principles, and (3) more motivated by instinct (especially fear) than by a reasoning process that looks at the long-term consequences of their behavior. While there are exceptions to this classification, judgments based on coercive power tend to reflect a reliance on short-term expediency. A typical thought pattern grounded on the use of raw power is captured by the command, "Get it done, now!"—with an implied "or else. . . !" The motto of those succumbing to coercive power is captured by the simple acronym "CYA."

Resolving conflict with people who demonstrate Stage One fear of punishment reasoning calls for a subtle approach. Trying to dispel their fears may not prove as fruitful as desired. Rather, a more successful approach may be to replace their current fears with a different one. If their behavior is not congruent with the purpose of ethics, which is "to enhance societal well-being," the possible negative reactions to their behavior can be emphasized. The social disdain occurring from their behavior, should that behavior be made public, might constitute an effective punishment for them.

In the following cases, some general questions should be addressed concerning the use of power:

1. What would be the business consequences if an effort to use power were rejected on ethical grounds?

2. Is there an ethical hierarchy that you would apply to the types of power being applied? Are some of the types of power "better" than others for ethical reasons?

3. Does the use of power appear to be consistent with the moral statements of the parties involved in conflict within the cases? Will conflicts of interest be resolved so as to enhance societal well-being (which is our definition of ethics)?

❖   Case Study 1–1   ❖

J. P. STEVENS

The Southern Textile firm J. P. Stevens had its origins in Massachusetts. It started as a woolen factory in the early 1800s, but it moved south to escape the high cost of labor in the north. The escape proved temporary. Before the firm was bought by a syndicate led by West Point-Pepperell, it had experienced a series of conflicts with organized labor. These conflicts were acrimonious and entailed the use of coercive power by both sides. Whether a feasible resolution to the conflict was reached is open to question.

From the time of the Great Depression up until 1980, the textile industry in the South had been holding off the efforts to unionize its workers. The challenge was sometimes bitter. Sporadic court actions and National Labor Relations Board (NLRB) rulings marked the conflict. J. P. Stevens, the second largest producer in the industry, had experienced especially difficult times with the textile workers union. Communications with the union forces were often adversarial. The NLRB had ruled on a number of occasions that Stevens had improperly coerced workers not to join the union. Its history of active resistance to unionization made Stevens the prime target of the union. The union conceded that its task would be difficult since textile firms in the South often exert both political and social control over the communities in which they are located.

The American Clothing and Textile Workers Union (ACTWU) labeled J. P. Stevens as the number one corporate lawbreaker. This claim was based on the count of NLRB rulings against Stevens. Stevens chairman James Finley was angered by the label. He did admit that there were times when the NLRB disagreed with Stevens's interpretation of labor laws. His statements indicated that the firm had made mistakes in the past, and that human error would probably cause the company to make mistakes in the future. But he also claimed that the company neither approved of nor condoned the actions of any of its management personnel who broke the law.

Despite Finley's claims, the ACTWU pressed on with its efforts against Stevens. The firm had high visibility. If it could be unionized, then other textile firms would surely follow.

Two shop floor incidents embodied the hostility between both sides. Joseph Williams was accused by his supervisor of neglecting his work at Stevens to pass out union literature. His supervisor told him to perform his duties and not interrupt the work of others. He ignored this admonition and was sent home. He was later reinstated but then fired. The company claims that he was fired because he refused to clean the spindles on his loom. Williams did not deny that charge. His counter claim was that although spindle cleaning was his job, the task unfairly increased his workload.

The second incident involved Crystal Lee Jordan. Jordan was employed in a Stevens fabricating plant. In her efforts to organize a union she tried to copy an anti-union letter written by management that was posted on a bulletin board within her plant. For this action plus a phone call to her union representative she was called to the supervisor's office. Feeling that she was being picked on for her union activities, she at first refused to go. Later, when she did go to the office, she refused to talk to the supervisor. She was fired.

The union's plan to prevail against Stevens was not to concentrate on shop floor activities. Rather, it was to embarrass J. P. Stevens in public. A national boycott of Stevens's products was called for. A group made of ACTWU members and clergy created cards listing all of Stevens's trade names of products. The public was encouraged during rallies in several cities to refrain from buying those products. There was also the consideration of industrial boycotts. Almost half of Stevens's sales were to clothing manufacturers. Those manufacturers who employed union personnel might be persuaded from purchasing fabric from Stevens.

To lead its battle against Stevens, the ACTWU chose strategist Ray Rogers. Rogers's tactic was to isolate J. P. Stevens from the business community. James Finley was removed from the board of directors of Manufacturer's Hanover Bank when unions threatened to remove pension funds from the bank. Threats of boycotts caused Finley to be removed from the boards of directors of Sperry Rand and Borden. In turn, members of Stevens's board were pressured to resign by Rogers's tactics. Executives from Avon, New York Life, and Goldman, Sachs resigned from the board. Only Virgil Conway of Seamans's Bank did not give in to Rogers's pressure. One firm was threatened with a proxy fight if it did not act in the union's interest with respect to Stevens supporters on its board. That firm's chairman considered the $6-million dollar proxy balloting costs and then abided by Rogers's wishes.

It appears that Rogers's tactics worked. J. P. Stevens finally gave in and signed a contract with the ACTWU to cover the workers at its Roanoke Rapids plant. Nine other Stevens plants followed. Officials of the union believed that the contract accomplished its purpose. They pointed out that Stevens's executives began to involve top union officials in discussions about investments and forecasts. Subsequently, when Stevens closed five plants no unionized plants were affected.

The battle, though, was not over. The textile industry would lose 300,000 jobs during the decade, and it attributed a good part of that loss to labor costs. Unionization was still to be opposed. James Finley resigned as chairman at J. P. Stevens and was replaced by Whitney Stevens. Whitney Stevens publicly stated that he would continue to fight unionism in those plants that the ACTWU had not organized. Ray Rogers, in turn, resigned from the union. The rumor was that Stevens signed its agreement with the union only on the condition that Rogers would no longer play an active part with the union.

Ray Rogers then formed a private labor consulting firm called Corporate Campaigns, Inc. He described himself as a social activist with limited aspirations about income. His success against J. P. Stevens led other unions to employ him in subsequent campaigns against Campbell Soup, American Airlines, Hormel, and International Paper. Rogers defended his tactics, saying that corporations only respond to pressure. His strategy was "to break power down into much smaller, more manageable units, that you can challenge and divide and conquer." A labor leader, in stating his admiration for Rogers, said "I kind of like Corporate Campaign's tactics. . .they go for the jugular."

Questions

1. Which, if any, of the people mentioned in the case appeared to demonstrate Stage One reasoning?
2. Could J. P. Stevens have used another type of power to resolve this conflict?
3. Did Ray Rogers's tactics lead to enhancing societal well-being?

Sources

"An uneasy peace reigns at J. P. Stevens," *Business Week* (February 22, 1982), 116.

Walter Guzzardi, Jr., "How the union got the upper hand on J. P. Stevens," *Fortune* 97 (June 19, 1978), 86–87.

David Benjamin Jay, "Labor's boardroom guerilla," *Time* (June 20, 1988), 50.

"New weapon for bashing bosses," *Time* (July 23, 1979), 71.

Rudolph A. Pyatt, Jr., "For J. P. Stevens, 175th anniversary now requiem," *The Washington Post* (July 3, 1988), H1–H3.

Jane Slaughter, "Ray Rogers: Workers don't have to keep losing," *The Progressive* 52 (June 1988), 28.

"Stevens–union confrontation fiery, tumultuous, theatrical," *Textile World* 127 (March 1977), 23–24.

"The all-out campaign against J. P. Stevens," *Business Week* (June 14, 1976), 28–29.

"The 70 cent solution," *The Wall Street Journal* (September 2, 1986), 26.

"Who won the marathon," *Forbes* 127 (May 25, 1981), 12.

❖   Case Study 1–2   ❖

CALIFORNIA PROPOSITIONS

For years, cigarette manufacturers have been the target of legislative action designed to restrict marketing activities for tobacco products. The primary purpose of Proposition 5 was to protect nonsmokers from the effects of smoking by making separate smoking and nonsmoking sections mandatory in enclosed public places, offices, restaurants, hospitals, and school buildings. Violations would carry a fine of $50.

The proposal was created by a coalition of consumer and professional groups called Californians for Clean Indoor Air (CCIA). Members of the coalition included the California Group Against Smoking, the American Cancer Association, the California Lung Association, the California Parent Teacher Association, the California Medical Association, and the Sierra Club. These groups were joined by a large contingent of citizens; over 600,000 California residents signed the Clean Air Initiative that introduced the proposition onto the ballot.

On the other side of the issue was the American Tobacco Institute, supported by the four major cigarette manufacturers—Philip Morris, Inc., R. J. Reynolds Tobacco Company, Brown & Williamson Tobacco Company, and Lorillard.

Proponents of the Clean Air Initiative contended that nonsmokers' rights took precedence over smokers' rights in any and all conflict situations. There seemed little doubt that second-hand or "sidestream" smoke—the smoke from a burning cigarette, cigar, or pipe breathed by people other than the smoker—could be harmful. Sidestream smoke had been shown to contain nearly 50 times the amount of nitrosamines (proven cancer-causing chemicals) as mainstream smoke as well as twice the amount of tar and nicotine; three times the amount of nezopyrene (another carcinogen); and five times the amount of carbon monoxide. At a particular risk were young children, people exposed to second-hand smoke over extended periods, and people with heart or lung disease.

Proponents of the proposition also pointed to a secondary issue: potential cost savings. According to a University of California study, Proposition 5 would save the state nearly $1 billion per year by reducing the medical costs, extra sick leave and lost work hours, and fire damages caused by cigarette smoking.

According to the tobacco industry campaign, "Proposition 5 would cost taxpayers at least $43 million!"—$20 million to implement the law by putting up signs in state and local government buildings and offices, and another

$23 million to enforce it. In addition, "Proposition 5 would cost California businesses $260 million"—to erect walls, establish smoking and non-smoking lounges, and provide smoke breaks for employees and customers who could no longer smoke on the job.

There were other costs as well—to personal freedom from a "'Big Brother' government" applying "another restrictive law regulating conduct that is best governed by common sense," and to public safety as a result of the "unnecessary burden" imposed on law enforcement agencies who "should spend their energies fighting serious crime instead of arresting smokers." Proof for these claims came from incidents in Chicago in which women had been forced to spend the night in jail because they could not post bond for anti-smoking violations and from testimonials of police officials who claimed that such laws would be difficult, if not impossible, to enforce.

Of additional concern was the proposition's potential cost to the tobacco industry. A University of California study predicted that by making it more inconvenient to smoke, Proposition 5 could create a drop in cigarette sales of as much as 15 to 20 percent. Smokers in California accounted for nearly 10 percent of total U.S. cigarette purchases, and a drop in consumption there would have a significant effect at the company level. As the R. J. Reynolds Company described it, "If the current efforts of anti-smoking groups to restrict smoking in public places were to result in non-smoking laws which caused every smoker to smoke one less cigarette per day, the company stood to lose $92 million in sales every year."

Cost was not an issue when it came to funding the campaign against Proposition 5, however. The program to support the bill had generated just over $500,000. The effort to oppose it raised $5.6 million, 97 percent of which had come from four major tobacco companies. In August, polls showed a majority of voters (53 percent) in favor of the bill. By the time the tobacco industry's media blitz was over, the odds had changed. Polls taken in late October showed 56 percent of the voters against the proposition. In November, in spite of the fact that 63 percent of California's electorate were nonsmokers, Proposition 5 was defeated.

Anti-smoking groups also initiated Proposition 99, a state-wide anti-smoking program. The bill had a new form—a 25¢ per pack tax on cigarettes: and a new appeal—money. Opponents of the proposition still focused on costs and claimed that the new bill represented a regressive tax that would hit Hispanics and other poor communities the hardest. Proponents of the proposition had taken a different approach. While Proposition 5 had offered the state savings, Proposition 99 promised to generate revenues that could in turn be used for education about, treatment of, and research into tobacco-related diseases. Proposition 99 passed and in early 1990 California health officials started a $28 million anti-smoking campaign. Kenneth Kizer, the director of the health department in California, asked the universities in

California to divest their $500 million portfolio of tobacco company stocks. Of the Proposition 99-funded advertising campaign he said: "We want the public to understand that they have been sold a bill of goods, that they have been duped by the cigarette companies." An official of the Tobacco Institute questioned whether the ads were in line with the goal of educating people about the health effects of smoking. The official declared that the ads "seek to make the tobacco companies appear to be heartless, uncaring and even racist."

Questions

1. What types of power were used by both sides in this conflict?
2. Were the positions of each side based on principles, consequences, or a combination of both?
3. What is your personal view about the ethical justification for political action committees such as the American Tobacco Institute?

Sources

"Arrests, Fines, and Jail—Return to Prohibition?" (Los Angeles: Californians for Common Sense), 1978.

Philip Hager, "Tobacco firms' donations set L.A. campaign record," *Los Angeles Times* (November 4, 1983), 3.

"Let's Clean the Air" (Berkeley: Campaign for Clean Indoor Air, 1978).

Paul Loveday, "California's Proposition 5 on clean indoor air," *American Lung Association Bulletin* (October 1978), 2.

Sonia L. Nazario, "California ads attack cigarettes," *The Wall Street Journal* (April 11, 1990), B1 and B5.

Sonia L. Nazario, "California widens attacks on cigarettes," *The Wall Street Journal* (June 30, 1991), B1.

Harry Nelson, "Smokers' threat to nonsmokers studied," *Los Angeles Times* (October 13, 1978), 1, 2, 29.

W. B. Road, "Proposition 5 battle sets state campaign spending mark," *Los Angeles Times* (November 1, 1978), 3.

Mark A. Stein, "Both sides in cigarettes tax fight target minorities," *Los Angeles Times* (October 19, 1988), 3, 25.

"Why Californians Are Voting No on Proposition 5" (Los Angeles: Californians for Common Sense, 1978).

"Why tobacco fears the California voter, *Business Week* (September 11, 1978), 54.

Leo Wolinsky, "Tobacco lobby's unlikely foe," *Los Angeles Times* (February 9, 1988), 3.

❖   Case Study 1–3   ❖

A. L. WILLIAMS

Art Williams was a dedicated high school football coach. To supplement his coaching income he sold insurance as a sideline. Williams became so successful in his part-time job that he left coaching to sell insurance full time, working first for ITT Financial Services and then for Waddell & Reed. Williams's aggressive tactics brought him both financial success and attention. However, his marketing tactics did not quite fit Waddell & Reed's corporate image, so he left the company to form his own insurance marketing organization.

That organization, A. L. Williams and Associates, started selling policies for the Massachusetts Indemnity and Life Insurance Company. Within ten years, the Williams group became the leading firm of its type in the industry. Its part-time sales force of almost 200,000 people sold 900,000 policies which had a face value of close to $100 billion. The market to which Williams appealed, while broad, was decidedly not upscale.

The Williams sales organization sold term rather than cash value policies. Williams called cash value policies a rip-off. His claim was that a cash value policy, which provided death benefits and served as a savings plan, earned an interest rate of only 1.25 percent per year. He believed that insurance companies concentrated on selling cash value policies because they reaped the most profit. The payout of death benefits is usually much more from term insurance than from cash value policies. A consumer group, the National Insurance Consumer Organization, agreed with Williams's assessment.

The Williams team used football terminology in its sales training. Competitors were the enemy and the goal was to beat them. Competitors complained that the information that the Williams sales force used was somewhat misleading. One example was the quoting of a government brochure that seemed to dismiss the worth of cash value insurance. What was omitted from the quote was the fact that the brochure was seventy-five years old. In his football terminology, Williams called the use of dated information an acceptable "late hit."

Each client to whom the Williams organization sold term insurance was perceived as a future Williams salesperson. Williams claimed that obtaining a license to sell insurance was a relatively easy task. Each salesperson received a commission on the sales of his or her recruits and the sales of the recruits' recruits. A recruitment brochure expounded on the lure of making $1000 or more a month engaging in part-time sales. Critics in the industry claimed that this was akin to pyramid selling whereby there are more rewards for recruiting than for selling.

The National Association of Life Underwriters (NALU) challenged Williams's practices. The president of NALU noted that Williams was not a conventional insurer since both claims and commissions were paid from cash flow rather than from reserves. This practice is risky especially because at the beginning of the 1990s the number of policies sold by the Williams organization was about the same as the number of policies that had lapsed. One trade publication proclaimed that "A. L. Williams sales tactics threaten industry survival."

Certainly the Williams team had referred to competitors' cash value policies as trash value rip-offs. What was not disclosed was that there were much better term insurance policies available from competitors. Williams's term policies may have been more expensive because a great part of the first year's premium payment from the client went to pay salesperson commissions. Williams also had stated that some competitors acted like "low-life scum." Williams, using his experience as a coach, saw himself as a motivator whose role it was to fire up the sales force. Some of his agents may have gone overboard in their interpretation of the rules, Williams admitted. His reaction? "In the real world. . . sometimes you have to hit after the whistle."

Williams also admitted that he was almost fanatical in his desire to win. He demanded that same intensity from his sales team, as well as unquestioned loyalty. Those who succeeded could become wealthy. Those whom he felt let the team down would be chastised during his Monday morning in-house television broadcast. Said one of his former salespeople: "When you question Art, you're dead." One sales executive who crossed Williams was Randy Stelk. When Stelk left to form his own company he became the object of Williams's wrath. Williams considered Stelk as an enemy who had to be beaten. There is evidence that one of Williams's more dedicated subordinates even created a plan to infiltrate Stelk's new insurance company for the purpose of undermining its effectiveness.

Another target of Williams's attacks was Robert Michael, a regional sales director for the organization. Michael commented about Williams: "You saw emotional outbursts. . .and you really began to see how he could manipulate people." A vice president at Williams responded that Art Williams did not try to intimidate anyone. She added that the sales group accepted Williams's guidance "because he's such a tremendous leader." A salesperson agreed, saying: "I believed everything he said." Another commented: "This guy is a god."

The fervor of the salespeople led some critics to claim that the Williams sales organization was like a religious cult. Williams's response: "A cult is one of the nicest things they have to say about me." He said he enjoyed being derided by traditional insurance firms. He reverted again to his football background, with his quotes showing his attitude toward his critics: "You don't play football on the field to play nice," and "no one can beat us. . .the scoreboard tells the story."

Questions

1. From the material on the six stages of moral reasoning described in the introduction to the text, classify A. L. Williams.
2. In your view of what a sales organization is really like, is there anything wrong with the way Williams does business, given the words of the last sentence in the case?
3. Is "societal well-being," the last phrase in the definition of ethics, affected by the way Williams manages his firm? If so, how?

Sources

Ed Bean, "Fervent pitchman," *The Wall Street Journal* (March 4, 1987), 1.

Chuck Hawkins and Jon Friedman, "Did Art Williams take a walk on the wild side?" *Business Week* (August 6, 1990), 31.

Bill Husted, "250 jobs at A. L. Williams companies being eliminated amid restructuring," *The Atlanta Journal* (August 29, 1990), B1.

Robert G. Knowles, "ALW suffers setbacks in suits with former agents," *National Underwriter* (July 20, 1992), 1, 20.

Robert G. Knowles," Press, continuing the crusade, see ALW's 'day of reckoning,'" *National Underwriter* (May 21, 1990), 3.

James R. Norman and Dean Foust, "Meet Art Williams, the P. T. Barnum of life insurance," *Business Week* (February 15, 1988), 65–71.

Mercedes M. Perez, "Across the kitchen table," *Best's Review* 89 (January 1989), 14, 15, 16, 18, 19, 20, 105, 106, 107.

"Renegades; harassed & scorned, they did it their way—and won, "Strategist," *Success* 37 (January/February 1990), 37.

Howard Rudnitsky, "Tiger by the tail," *Forbes* 144 (August 7, 1989), 40.

Gene Stone, "In the money: Ex-football coach Art Williams runs winning insurance firm, but some people are crying foul," *People Weekly* (November 20, 1989), 161.

Steven Sullivan, "The rise and fall of A. L. Williams," *Life Association News* 87 (December 1992), 42–58.

Notes to Chapter 1

[1]Thomas Aquinas, *Summa Theologica,* trans. by Thomas Gilby (New York: McGraw Hill, 1967), Question 19.

[2]The political philosopher Stanley Benn has proposed a "power paradigm" which groups together a range of features that power relationships may have. Borrowing from the philosopher Ludwig Wittgenstein, Benn suggests that the various aspects of what we call "power" have a family resemblance to each other rather than some core of similarity. See Stanley Benn, "Power," in Paul Edwards, ed., *The Encyclopedia of Philosophy* (New York: The Free Press, 1967), vol. 6, pp. 424–427.

[3]Richard M. Emerson, "Power-dependence relations," *American Sociological Review* 27 (February 1962), 31–41.

[4]John R. P. French and Bertram Raven, *Studies in Social Power* (Ann Arbor: Institute for Social Research, 1959).

[5]R. M. Hare is one example of a contemporary philosopher who takes this position. In Hare's view, morality just *is* "the endeavor of a free agent to find for himself principles which he can accept as binding on all alike." R. M. Hare, *Essays on Philosophical Method* (London: The Macmillan Press, 1971).

[6]Jeremy Bentham, *An Introduction to Principles of Morals and Legislation* (London: Athalone Press, 1970). Reprint of 1789 edition, edited by J. H. Burns and H. L. A. Hart.

[7]Stanley Modic, "Forget Ethics—and Succeed?" *Industry Week* (October 19, 1987), 17 and 18.

[8]Jürgen Habermas, *Communication and the Evolution of Society,* trans. by Thomas McCarthy (Boston: Beacon Press, 1979).

[9]William M. Kurtines, "Sociomoral Behavior and Development from a Rule-Governed Perspective: Psychosocial Theory as a Nomotic Science," in William M. Kurtines and Jacob L. Gewirtz (eds.), *Moral Development Through Social Interaction* (New York: John Wiley & Sons, 1987).

[10]James Rest, *Development in Judging Moral Issues* (Minneapolis: University of Minnesota Press, 1979).

[11]James A. Wall, *Negotiation: Theory and Practice* (Glenview, IL: Scott, Foresman and Co., 1985), Chapter 5.

[12]Stanley Milgram, "Behavioral study of obedience," *Journal of Abnormal and Social Psychology* 67(4), (1963), pp. 371–378.

[13]Thomas Hobbes, *Leviathan* (London: Collier Books, 1969), p. 100. (This book was first published in 1651.)

[14]Fritz Oser and Andre Schäfli, "But It Does Move: The Difficulty of Gradual Change in Moral Development," in Marvin W. Berkowitz and Fritz Oser (eds.), *Moral Education: Theory and Application* (Hillsdale, NJ: Lawrence Erlbaum Associates, 1985).

[15]Carl Sagan, "A new way to think about rules to live by," *Parade Magazine* (November 28. 1993), 12–14.

[16]Plato, *The Republic,* trans. by G. M. A. Grube (Indianapolis: Hackett Publishing Company, 1974), p. 133.

[17]Aristotle, *Politics,* trans. by William Ellis (New York: E.P. Dutton & Co., 1923), p. 77.

[18]Friedrich Nietzsche, *The Will to Power,* trans. by Walter Kaufmann and R. J. Hollingdale (New York: Random House, 1967). See also Walter Kaufmann (ed. and trans.), *The Portable Nietzsche* (New York: Viking Press, 1954).

[19]Roger Burton, "Honesty and Dishonesty," in Thomas Lickona (ed.), *Moral Development and Behavior: Theory, Research, and Social Issues* (New York: Holt, Rinehart and Winston, 1976).

[20]James Gilligan, "Beyond Morality: Psychoanalytic Reflections on Shame, Guilt, and Love," in Thomas Lickona (ed.), *Moral Development and Behavior: Theory, Research, and Social Issues* (New York: Holt, Rinehart and Winston, 1976).

[21]James Rest, Muriel Bebeau, and Joseph Volker, "An Overview of the Psychology of Morality," in James Rest (ed.), *Moral Development: Advances in Research and Theory* (New York: Praeger Publishers, 1986), p. 1.

[22]William K. Frankena, *Ethics,* 2nd ed. (Englewood Cliffs, NJ: Prentice-Hall, Inc., 1973), p. 21.

Chapter 2

EXPLOITATION

In the previous chapter, we associated coercive power with the first stage of moral development—a stage based on fear of punishment. The second stage of moral development is also linked to power, but power of a different type. The title of this chapter, *Exploitation,* goes hand in hand with *reward power,* a motivating force used by many of us to resolve conflict.

Exploitation takes on a distinctly moral meaning when we use it in the sense of having to deal with conflicts associated with societal or personal well-being (and not in the common-usage sense of being "morally praiseworthy"). *Exploitation* could involve "taking advantage of another person or situation for personal reward" in a conflict situation. Typically, this "another" is a person; sometimes, however, as we shall see in Chapter 10 (Stewardship of the Environment), the "other" is not human. Exploitation can also entail enticing another person to do something which that person would otherwise not do by promising a reward.

Note that this moral sense of exploitation relates to the first of the goals we mentioned in the Introduction: the goal of *stimulating our moral imagination.* When you read the cases included here, for example, keep in mind that the persons whose behavior will be described may well view themselves as simply making creative use of an opportunity that has presented itself. They may be "exploiting" a situation without any consciousness of being unfair to (taking advantage of) anyone. One of your tasks will be to judge whether this is so.

Rewards accrue from more than just exploitative relationships between persons. Consider the differences between exploitation, reciprocity, and mutuality in relationships.[1] With *exploitation,* only one person uses another. With *reciprocity,* however, two persons are each using the others. With *mutuality,* the two parties are not simply using each other and not simply sharing favors; instead, they are treating each other not as means but as ends in themselves, by taking an active interest in the goals that the other has.

This interest in the other's ends or goals seems to lead naturally to the conclusion that of the three relationships discussed, mutuality is superior to reciprocity, which is superior to exploitation. This conclusion is a possibility to keep in mind when you read Chapters 2–4 and an issue that will be considered further in Chapter 5. For our present purposes, however, we will focus on exploitation and reciprocity, but not mutuality. Both exploitation and reciprocity involve people "using" each other to resolve conflict and gain rewards. Societal well-being, in the eyes of those directly involved, is gauged strictly by the benefits that the transacting parties receive.

Self-Centered Moral Reasoning

Lawrence Kohlberg's Stage Two of moral development, which was briefly discussed in the Introduction, is particularly relevant here. This is the stage in which the individual moves beyond fear of punishment and begins to recognize the value of rewards and even reciprocity. Even though Stage Two is defined as ego-centered rather than society-directed, the result does not mean that other people are ignored. Realistically, the rewards motivating Stage Two behavior are often obtained through other people who accept the rationale for Stage Two arguments and tolerate Stage Two behavior. Particularly note the use of different levels of rewards as motivators in the John Forist case at the end of the chapter.

Like those who use Stage One reasoning, those who rely on Stage Two reasoning can be identified by the nature of their statements. Whereas Stage One people are generally defensive, Stage Two advocates may be defensive too but are more likely to take the offensive. When using Ordinary Communicative Action, the speaker at Stage Two might try to use degrees of clarification to get a point across. More likely, though, is the person's reliance on what Jürgen Habermas calls "Strategic Action."[2] While Ordinary Communicative Action is directed at bringing about an understanding of one's own position, communications of Strategic Action in their base form are bluntly directed toward obtaining an agreement, even if there is no consensus. The stronger their stake in an issue, the greater the tendency for the Stage Two people to use Strategic Communication. Persuasive tactics are given free rein.

Adversarial Communication

Berkowitz has listed under Strategic Action six separate verbal methods geared to overwhelming the opposition.[3] His categories are as follows:

1. Paraphrasing the listener's position in a negative way.
2. Noting logical inconsistencies in the listener's position.

3. Attacking the listener's type of reasoning.
4. Extending the listener's reasoning to implausible extremes.
5. Introducing an example that cannot be incorporated into the listener's position.
6. Representing the listener's position as incompatible with the speaker's well-reasoned position.

While the power of rewards may be the prime motivator of Stage Two reasoning, people at this level are not above using verbal coercion to elicit Stage One compliance in order to get those rewards. Manipulation and occasional deception are also tactics that may be employed to attain the sought-for rewards.

Self-Interest and Ethics

Some cynics might claim that Stage Two ego-centered behavior characterizes most actions in business, and data exist showing that personal ambition and financial gain are the most frequently mentioned reasons for violating social norms in business.[4] No one can deny that self-interest is a major motivating factor in business behavior. The question is, just how major is this factor indeed? Is self-interest, for example, the only factor that people use (or should use) in making their choices? And if not, what other factors limit our pursuit of our own interest? A typical ethics class taught in a philosophy department might include the discussion of such questions in connection with a distinction between the claims of psychological egoism and those of ethical egoism.

Psychological Egoism

Psychological egoism is a theory about human nature that claims that all human behavior is ultimately motivated by self-interest alone. Psychological egoists believe that all actions stem from a person's desire to benefit himself or herself; that is, actions stem from self-interest. Psychological egoism, in other words, is a psychological theory or a theory about human behavior. It claims to describe how people in fact (always) behave, or to be more precise, how they always try to behave. Psychological egoists admit that people sometimes fail to achieve what is in their best interest—and sometimes do not even know what *is* actually in their own interest. Psychological egoism is a theory that attempts to describe human motivation or to explain human behavior by reference to this one basic motive.

Many people believe that the theory of psychological egoism is true. Underneath even our apparently altruistic behavior lie self-interested motives, they claim. But while it is possible that such psychological egoists are correct in these beliefs, the doctrine of psychological egoism has still not been proven. The usual arguments in favor of psychological egoism strike most contemporary philosophers and psychologists as "begging the question." For example, the psychological egoist has to argue that a person (say, Mother Teresa) who devotes his or her life to helping the needy is motivated solely by self-interest, just as much as a person whose sole concern is building up a private business. The psychological egoist appears to be arguing that since all of our voluntary actions are our own (since who else's could they be?), their goal must necessarily be some benefit for oneself. However, the critic of psychological egoism would object, pointing to the concept of mutuality mentioned earlier in this chapter. Some persons have concern for others as one of their motives, along with self-interest. If this concern for others is also viewed as self-interest, then self-interest is so broadly defined as to be irrelevant.[5]

Ethical Egoism

Ethical egoism, on the other hand, is a theory about how people *ought* to act. Its premise is that the only correct test for moral behavior is whether or not one acts in one's own interest. Ethical egoism, in other words, is an ethical theory. Specifically, it is a part of that variety of consequentialism that claims that the morally right thing to do is whatever produces the greatest balance of good over evil consequences for the actor or agent. One of its few proponents was the nineteenth-century German philosopher Johann Schmidt. He proclaimed, "Let us therefore not aspire to community but to *onesidedness*. Let us not seek the most comprehensive commune, 'human society,' but let us seek in others only means and organs which we may use as our property."[6]

If Schmidt's reflections are correct, should businesspeople show concern for anyone's welfare but their own? Perhaps our role model should then be the wolverine, one of the few animals that gathers more than it needs.[7] Apart from pious moral commentary, maybe we should face the fact that greed does motivate some people's behavior.[8] Or would this be confusing what *is* with what *ought* to be (the naturalistic fallacy)? In contemporary terms, the naturalistic fallacy would be embodied in the phrases, "That's just the way business operates. The market regulates itself through the 'invisible hand' of capitalism."

Still, one advantage of ethical egoism is that it is a very simple theory; many would say it is indeed too simple. The idea of pursuing self-interest, however, appeals to many of us, and ethical egoism appears to justify this pursuit. Note, however, that the "self-interest" that is endorsed by ethical egoists is understood in a rather "everyday" way, pertaining to those things that would benefit the individual and fulfill his or her needs or desires. Ethical egoists typically do not construe self-interest as "that which is in the interest of what philosophers call the 'true self' or the 'authentic self'"—where these latter terms are thought of as going beyond short-term selfish interest.

Ethical egoism is a view that has been much discussed by philosophers. You should be critically evaluating this category as you read the cases in this chapter. The doctrine could be interpreted as involving a broad sense of self-interest. For example, a rational ethical egoist might conceivably realize that blatantly "selfish" behavior is not likely to be in his or her own long-term self-interest. However, this realization would be based not on genuine concern for others but on the feeling that other persons may become hostile as a result of the egoist's obviously selfish behavior.[9] In brief, both the psychological egoist and the ethical egoist recognize exploitation and reciprocity as means one uses and/or ought to use to promote self-interest.

Although it is clear that obviously selfish behavior, or exploitation, will not necessarily advance the egoist's interest, it is easy to imagine situations in which exploitation could actually be in the egoist's interest. The egoist might, for example, hold such power that no type of revenge could be taken against him or her. Or the party treated unfairly might not realize what is happening or who is doing the exploiting. In more typical cases, however, exploitation is unlikely to lead to the best results for the exploiter. The social cooperation necessary for business transactions to succeed and a preoccupation with personal reward above all else are two factors that just do not work well together.[10] Quite apart from possible pangs of conscience, exploiters tend to be noticed, disapproved of, and frequently shunned or attacked. If your behavior is directed totally toward your own interest at the expense of others, the resulting isolation may be less than pleasant.

Examples of Self-Interest

Two business-related issues that may generate charges of selfish interests are the rights of shareholders and executive salaries. Let us think about each in turn.

In a publicly held corporation, the shareholders own the firm. Understandably, they expect the managers to make money for them. They are willing to take risks, of course—but the risks must be reasonable. The shareholders express their opinions through their votes at annual meetings and through their degree of support for the firm's board of directors, rather than through more direct involvement in the running of the company. Boards of directors, and managers generally, have the responsibility to work for the shareholders. If the management of a firm tries to exploit a situation in ways that run counter to the interests (or to the perceived interests) of the shareholders, this management risks some type of rebellion on the part of the shareholders. While many shareholders are passive for a time, eventually an active, vocal group of shareholders may be expected to speak out for their own interests. A question to ponder is whether shareholders' rights to expect a level of managerial performance are partially contingent on their responsibility to monitor that performance. Or are there guidelines for reasonable performance that exist apart from shareholder monitoring? Were any such guidelines enforced or adhered to by the Savings and Loan executives whose investment decisions lead to insolvencies in the late 1980s, or was the operating guideline shortsighted ethical egoism? These S&L officers invested heavily in high-risk junk bonds that paid high interest rates before they defaulted.

Another relevant business-related issue concerns the salaries earned by top executives. At what point are these salaries unjustified? Do high salaries constitute exploitation of the stockholders? What should the benchmark be for adequate executive salaries? Should it be the salaries of comparable executives in the same industry, or of top executives in other industries? Should the profitability of the firm be the main (or sole) consideration in setting salaries? If so, then stock options and bonuses become viable alternatives to high salaries. Obviously, opinions and practices differ widely here. In an extreme example, one particular firm limits the highest executive salary to ten times the salary of the lowest-paid full-time employee in the company. Reflect on this last issue for a moment. Then take the position of a shareholder who will vote on the salary levels for top management. To what reciprocal conditions would you tie their compensation?

Reciprocity and Ethics

No one likes being exploited—and nearly everyone finds a direct or indirect response when exploitation occurs. This statement essentially reflects the views of Thomas Hobbes, who observed how easy it is for the weaker to harm the stronger.[11] Such statements are what lead the typical egoist to advance to the second level of moral development: the level of reciprocity. Inherent in reciprocity are a stability and balance that are absent from exploitation. Each party is being "used" in a sense, but each party also gains something of value. "You scratch my back and I'll scratch yours" involves a trade-off that often may be a *fair* one. Once egoists recognize this elementary fact, they tend to adopt reciprocity—at least publicly and for the most part.

In our view, reciprocity seems to have real, practical advantages over exploitation. The "give and take" that characterizes reciprocity less often leads to the anger and desire for revenge that typically result from exploitation. Reciprocity, in our definition, is not based on altruism but on rewards. Reciprocity is satisfactory to the parties involved when the rewards are mutually agreeable and when the parties' behavior is consistent with attaining those rewards.

Reciprocity, then, is a viable option in personal relations, a type of behavior with real advantages over exploitation. For this reason, it is what might be considered the norm for business situations. In fact, one contemporary philosopher states that reciprocity and justice should be considered the two major ethical standards for society.[12] Although both parties in a simple transaction are aware that temptations to slip into exploitation, unfairness, cheating, and the like are always present, the parties are likely to consider their transaction ethical if each receives something from the other that is worth at least as much as each has given in return.

The question to be asked, of course, is whether there is really anything wrong with people always simply pursuing their own interests and using each other for their own ends. The psychological egoist holds that this is the way in which everyone always and inevitably behaves in reality. A typical ethical egoist uses this psychological claim to support the theory that self-interest is the very criterion of what makes an action morally right. The crux of the belief is that "What is good for me is ethical." In turn, the ethical egoist, when defining societal well-being, would look no farther than to himself or herself and, to a lesser extent, to the persons with whom he or she has interdependent, reciprocal relations.

Decision Criteria and Goals

In the first chapter, we discussed the test of feasibility to gauge the acceptability of an ethical conclusion. In this chapter, we add a second test: *consistency*. In using the term *consistency*, we mean two things: first, that the various beliefs and principles a person holds should not contradict each other, and, second, that a person's beliefs be in harmony with subsequent behavior. This first aspect of consistency is a simple requirement of logic. After all, if a person's thinking is self-contradictory, what hope is there that his or her conclusions will be acceptable? The second aspect of consistency, however, raises an important moral issue.

Why, exactly, should our beliefs be consistent with our behavior? The basic answer, in our view, is that ethical thinking, beliefs, attitudes, and other *mental* activities are undertaken primarily to guide us in our behavior. What would be the point of thinking about moral questions at all if we did not at least intend to act on the conclusions we reach through our thinking? Of course, humans do not always act consistently with their beliefs. We are frequently tempted to do things that we do not really believe in—and we sometimes give in to these temptations. Mordecai Nissan, in fact, believes that many of us set up a personal compensatory moral balance system to rationalize our behavior. Under this system, we judge ourselves to be at or above the moral line in most of our behavior. In so doing, we build up what we think are moral credits. A credit surplus allows us to feel that we can dip below acceptable norms of behavior at times and still judge ourselves to be generally good.[13] This normative guideline for conflict resolution—consistency—is at odds with the temptation to rationalize. Our reputation in business is built on consistency—especially on doing what we say we will do. We should strive for this regardless of our particular moral theory or beliefs. It is a minimal condition for our ethics to make sense.

However, we must admit that human behavior often appears to be inconsistent. Sometimes, it should be noted, this inconsistency is only an illusion. Sometimes we may need to resolve a conflict of interest, for example, in a way that may leave some witnesses with a false impression that we are being inconsistent. At times, however, our behavior is both realistic and consistent in the deeper sense because we *change* a particular habit or pattern of behavior in the service of some higher goal. Ralph Waldo Emerson wrote, "A foolish consistency is the hobgoblin of little minds."[14]

Some Examples

Nonetheless, human beings are sometimes inconsistent in reality as well as in appearance. Even when consistency is difficult, however, it is still a valuable guideline. Its practical value is that it provides a reasonable basis for defending our actions. It is also a fact of business life that the more consistency we demonstrate, the more trust we will be granted by others. Reflect on a business issue that we discussed at the beginning of this chapter. Suppose a Savings and Loan executive had released a public statement claiming that the investments he had approved were reasonably safe, in accordance with the norms of the entire banking industry, and in the shareholders' best interests. Suppose further that these investments subsequently led the institution to bankruptcy. Our claim is that the investment official's bad business decisions, by virtue of the inconsistency between his statement and performance, merit ethical as well as business criticism.

Now that we have presented the concept of consistency, we have come up with a partial set of "good reasons" that we suggest as a minimal test for any ethical behavior to be acceptable behavior. To be ethically or morally acceptable, behavior must be at least:

- *feasible*, that is, viable or capable of being done or sustained.
- *consistent*, that is, the actor's acts, words, and thinking must not contradict each other.

These factors, then, act as limits or constraints on behavior that apply to all ethical situations, not just to those that arise in business.

Our normative guidelines might, at first glance, appear to fall into the same category as traditional philosophical virtues such as prudence. Virtues, however, are usually defined as the traits or predispositions that we seek to incorporate into our general demeanor. Our normative guidelines, in contrast, should be viewed as tests for our arguments and positions. These guidelines function as filters for judging the acceptance of verbal claims and/or behavior that has caused conflict. More importantly, they also serve to identify common ground for building a consensus position that resolves conflict. The appropriateness of these guidelines will be more apparent in the last four chapters of this text—chapters that deal with the actual process of conflict resolution.

For now, we need to consider another ethical issue currently facing business. Reciprocity is often expressed by more than just the verbal agreements between the transacting parties. At times, gifts are offered and accepted by one or both of the parties. To move from generalities to specifics, what would you do if a contractor offered you an expensive, fleece-lined suede coat after he had successfully completed a job for your division? This experience actually happened to the brother of one of the authors. In his case, the firm had an ironclad rule about gifts: no tangible gifts of any value could be accepted. Other firms forbid personnel to accept gifts valued at more than $25.

Should there be a dollar limit on gifts, or should acceptance be determined by circumstances and expectations? Do the policies also apply to gifts between personnel within the same firm? Using the normative guideline of consistency, formulate a short corporate policy to resolve potential ethical problem about accepting gifts. To make this exercise more thought provoking, do not include dollar limits or total prohibitions. Now, why do you think that the policy that you have formulated is feasible, given contemporary business practices?

Moral Reasoning and Business Objectives

We believe that at least three aims or objectives direct business behavior and thus are integrally related to ethical dilemmas. We also believe that these objectives, although nonmoral in nature, have moral overtones because of the ways in which they are pursued. As final objectives, then, reasonable ethical choices seem to be related to three factors: survival, rewards, and acceptance:

1. Survival of the firm in business situations—or of the individual in personal situations. Even though it may be possible to describe cases (usually called "hard cases") in which the only morally acceptable choice appears to require the firm to go out of business, or the individual to sacrifice his or her life, for all practical purposes *survival* may be postulated as the first of the final objectives to bear in mind. Survival, however, need not necessarily suggest the exploitation of others. Synergy—the fact that things often work together better than they work separately—is a feature of many business situations and deserves always to be kept in mind. My survival typically enhances rather than hinders the chances of your survival.

2. Rewards of many kinds, whether for the firm or for the individual, are also important objectives in virtually all situations. Financial rewards may be the most visible or most often discussed, but personal rewards such as recognition or the satisfaction of doing good work are vitally important for most people. In our view—a view shared by most philosophers, theologians, and moralists—we hold that there is nothing immoral about wanting to be rewarded for what one has done. Charges of immorality typically arise when these rewards are sought at all costs and regardless of the consequences for others.

3. Acceptance of the firm or of the individual by society or by other individuals is the final objective. In a way, acceptance is connected to both survival and rewards. Social acceptance is almost a necessary condition for the *survival* of a firm or of an individual; without such acceptance, a firm is unlikely to show a profit, and an individual will at least have a harder time making his or her way through life. Social acceptance might also be seen as one of the nonmonetary *rewards* toward which we aim. We list *acceptance* separately as a final objective, however, because it is so important and so that it will not be overlooked. As with the other aims, it is possible to describe cases in which acceptance is neither an acknowledged objective nor an appropriate one. An entrepreneur, for example, may set up a firm specifically to exploit a unique situation where the repeat business which most firms require is not a

possibility. Our point here, however, is that this is not typical of business ethics cases.

Note that survival is of major concern in Stage One moral reasoning, that rewards are of major concern in Stage Two, and that acceptance is the major concern in Stage Three (see Chapter 3). The different approaches complement each other.

Although we believe that these final objectives should always be kept in mind, there are certain immediate, practical ("working") objectives that may guide our daily behavior and choices. We call attention to two of these: individual physical effort and individual mental effort. As individuals, we must put forth adequate effort, both physically and mentally, toward realizing the final objectives for our firms and for ourselves. This, of course, is part of what has long been referred to in this country as the work ethic. Still, it is worth noting that work *is* an essential means towards our final objectives.

Work or effort, however, can be focused along at least two very different paths. We can try to do only those things that will benefit us as individuals (or perhaps benefit our individual firms), or, on the other hand, we can attend to the broader social consequences of what we do. Since synergy (as referred to in our discussion of survival) does exist in many business situations, this second path will ordinarily be preferable.

Conclusions

Any behavioral guidelines we offer will fall on deaf ears if we deny the existence of actions motivated by self-interest. Our goal, instead, is to direct the moral reasoning process toward resolving those conflicts of interest that are bound to arise in business situations. Behavior that results from reasoned, long-term self-interest is not always, by nature, unethical. Our belief is that appropriate ethical decisions can be made in line with the general goals of business. For this to occur, however, moral reasoning must take into account the constraints we have suggested—that business actions with ethical implications be feasible and consistent. In future chapters, we will add two additional constraints: that business actions be based on reason rather than emotion and that they be universalizable (that is, be actions that the actor would be willing for everyone else in a similar situation to perform).

When you read the cases at the end of this chapter, consider the second of our goals mentioned in the Introduction. That goal is to *identify* issues that have moral overtones. As you evaluate the actions of the people described in the cases, try to distinguish between issues related to coercion, exploitation, and reciprocity. Do those actions fulfill part of the definition of ethics—resolving conflicts of interest so as to enhance societal well-being?

When you form your evaluation, remember that the self-centered nature of Stage Two, like that of Stage One, makes those who follow this stage easy to classify. People at Stage Two would be: (1) more motivated by personal

goals than by societal obligation; (2) more motivated by situational consequences than by universal, deontological principles; and (3) more motivated
by immediate, hedonistic gains than by a reasoning process that looks at long-
term consequences of their behavior. A typical thought pattern grounded on
reward power is captured by the phrase, "What's in it for me?"

Because people using Stage Two moral reasoning both understand and use
Strategic Action communication, this type of approach can prove useful when
we attempt to resolve conflicts with people at that stage. Societal well-being
in itself is not much of a motivating force. Rather, people at Stage Two should
be taught that enhancement of reputation can be realized in the foreseeable
future through a specific act, even if they do not receive tangible rewards.
Only then will they give consideration to personally rewarding behavior that
also happens to enhance the well-being of society in general.

We invite you to reflect on three questions when you read the following
cases:

1. Is exploitation or reciprocity the approach taken by the parties involved?

2. Is there an apparent consistency of both beliefs and behavior, especially
in the last two cases of the chapter?

3. To what degree is each of the goals mentioned above realized by the
individuals cited in the cases?

❖   Case Study 2–1   ❖

JOHN FORIST

Conflicts of conscience have marked my career. As the Assistant Manager
of our West coast distribution center my duties involved the control of all
inbound and outbound traffic. Nearly 75 percent of our finished goods
were received by rail from our manufacturing plants on the East coast. The
freight was usually travel weary by the time it reached us. We experienced
more than our fair share of damages. During my first week on the job I
noticed how badly our people would handle the merchandise while
unloading. They would double the amount of damaged cases by the time
they were through emptying a car. My predecessor would place all the bro-
ken cases in one corner of the warehouse and then file a freight claim with
the railroad for the total amount.

I quickly learned that the freight agent for the railroad would come by and
make his "Inspection of Damaged Goods" report agree with my predecessor's report. The damaged material was always marked as "junk." Actually,
the freight agent would take the damaged goods in his pickup truck and

sell them at a weekend "flea market." When I took over the job there was an accumulation of damaged goods and freight claims that had to be resolved.

Meanwhile, traffic agents kept beating down the doors for business. The novelty of free lunches had worn off, so much so that I would go only once per week and only with the members of the half dozen or so firms with which we dealt. The first Christmas on the job proved to be a windfall. I received a dozen fifths and quarts of liquor from the many trucking companies we used. It was at my first Christmas banquet that I found out that many of the other managers received much more than liquor as gifts. Weekend trips to Lake Tahoe or San Francisco were almost expected by the managers of larger firms.

It wasn't very long after the holidays that I was offered a $600 color TV set by an old business acquaintance. Joe had been a part owner of an intrastate carrier that had gone bankrupt. Now he was working for a large interstate carrier. He was on a 90-day trial with them to see how many new accounts he could deliver. He wanted part of the business that our number one carrier was handling to the Northwest. All I had to do was to give him a couple of truckloads over the next month, just enough to demonstrate new business to his boss and the set was mine. If Joe's firm were used, the customer would have received his goods a few days late because of handling problems.

Carriers were usually willing to go a long way to promote goodwill. One instance that comes to mind was my plan for a deep-sea fishing expedition. Some of the fellows from the firm were also interested in going so I contacted one of our freight handlers about using the cabin cruiser they had on charter. They not only lent us the boat but also stocked it with beer.

Part of the services handled by our distribution center involved the delivery of goods to firms in many of the surrounding communities. This was done by renting a truck and driver and setting up a daily local delivery run. The trucking company we used wanted to handle other large deliveries on an exclusive contract basis. The general manager of the firm invited the distribution center manager, myself, and our wives to spend the day in San Francisco to discuss this business venture.

We made arrangements to meet him on a Saturday in the city. When we arrived he took us to lunch, then sightseeing, then dinner, and finally, nightclubbing. This whirlwind courtship ended in his apartment in the wee hours of the morning at which time he presented us with a contract ready for signature which would have made him a contract carrier for a period of three years. He also made it clear that what we had done that day was just the tip of the iceberg compared to what we could expect in the future. His firm owned a resort cabin in Lake Tahoe that would be available for our use and that we also could expect season tickets to a sports event of our choosing. He also suggested that a car leasing arrangement could be worked out through his company for a nominal fee. After examining the contract we found some very beneficial rate structures being established for us if we would change the classification of our freight to a less expensive category. He had found loopholes in the tariffs that he thought could benefit both of us.

Soon thereafter I was promoted to manager of our distribution center on the East coast. This center handled all the packaging and exporting of merchandise for our international division. The first lesson I learned was "Love thy freight forwarder." Without his assistance, nothing would ever get on board a ship intact.

I'll always remember a particular dock strike. We had just completed packing and loading three truckloads of goods bound for Europe. When the forwarder arrived at the docks the dockworkers had gone into a "slowdown" in anticipation of the strike. They were only handling goods that came with "special" reward. The forwarder phoned and advised me that if we wanted those orders to get shipped before the strike we would have to move quickly. I just needed to bring cash and meet him on the waterfront.

I grabbed $1,000 out of petty cash and before I knew it I was giving Larry the money and listening very carefully to his instructions. We drove to the pier where two cargo ships were docked. It wasn't long before the dock boss arrived and the three of us went for a walk. Larry explained the urgency of getting our goods loaded most expeditiously because some of the goods were earmarked for the military. The boss listened unsympathetically until $400 had made its way into his jacket. Then quickly he motioned for the gates to be opened and by nightfall the mission was accomplished. The amount was billed by the freight forwarder as "special handling charges" as part of his overall freight bill. After three years as manager of the center, I was assigned the special project of finding a new location for doing business. We had outgrown our present facility and now had finished goods located in three public warehouses plus our own. We investigated over fifty sites and finally narrowed the field to three. Two of the sites were in established industrial parks with rail service, while the other site was in a newly formed industrial park with rail right-of-way negotiated, but with no service established.

The president of the firm developing the new industrial park was anxious to get a large company to build in his park so he could use the deal to attract smaller companies. His package was very attractive because his building cost was a few cents less per square foot than the other two, but he did not provide city water or sewage and the floor would have to be built on pilings to overcome the porous conditions of the soil. During one of our lunches he asked how this move was going to affect me and my family. I told him that we were presently renting but that we hoped to buy a house near the new location of the distribution center. He then told me that if I could persuade my company to go with his firm, he would arrange a deal through his real estate branch to get a house at no cost to me.

Questions

1. Under what conditions would you have paid to get your merchandise on the ship described in this case?
2. What criterion would you set for yourself to decide whether it was ethical to accept a gift from a supplier?
3. Evaluate the following comment: "To get ahead in business you have to look out for number one." Does this mean that only ethical egoists will be successful?

Sources

The data for this case came from the recollections of John R. M. Forist.

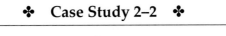

❖   Case Study 2–2   ❖

ALLEGHENY INTERNATIONAL

Robert Buckley was admired as a visionary willing to commit his firm to high-risk ventures. As chairman of Allegheny International, he had tripled sales in his first seven years of stewardship. His career path was the fast track to success. Armed with a law degree from Cornell, he had first made his mark at General Electric. His promotions were rapid during his tenure with that company. His services were in demand. Later, after running Standard Steel and Ingersoll Milling, Buckley moved to Allegheny Ludlum. Within three years, he took charge of the firm and decided that a bold change was needed. He spun off the core steel business and steered the firm into consumer products. Acquisition of Wilkinson Sword and the Sunbeam Corporation were keys to his strategy. Revenues at the renamed firm, Allegheny International, grew to $2.6 billion.

His success and his personality led him to become a forceful chief executive. Buckley decided to make some risky investments in areas other than consumer products. Those investments were in oil, gas, and real estate. The real estate ventures are especially worthy of note. Allegheny obtained controlling interest in a Florida condominium in which Buckley owned a unit. Buckley was unhappy with the previous management's unwillingness to make repairs and threatened to do something about it. He did. This acquisition was made despite a negative recommendation issued by Allegheny's real estate unit. The unit head saw neither the return on investment nor the internal rate of return potential from that investment.

Allegheny also acquired two properties in the Pittsburgh area. One was a Tudor home for entertaining clients and directors. The rationale for its purchase was that the Pittsburgh hotels were inadequate. The other property was a condominium next to an exclusive golf course. It too was designated as a place to entertain clients of Allegheny. Buckley liked the place so much that he used it for family vacations. These purchases totaling more than $1 million attracted interest because of the financial reverses that Allegheny was beginning to experience.

The financial reverses had put a crimp in the company's plans for a new headquarters building. The 32-story building was to have been Allegheny's visual statement that it was a force to be reckoned with. It had arranged financing through a lease-back arrangement. When income sagged, the company was forced to sublease part of the building to Consolidated National Gas. Not only did Consolidated negotiate to pay a lower rent than Allegheny paid, but it also had the honor of having the building named the CNG Tower rather than the AI Tower. To make matters worse, Allegheny also had to take a $40 million write-off on another office tower that it was building in Houston.

Perhaps the real estate purchase that attracted the most attention was the Dover Hotel in Manhattan. The hotel was purchased for $5.7 million. It could not be turned into a time-sharing venture as had originally been planned. Allegheny then renovated the building for use as a hotel. The cost of renovating the penthouse area alone was more than $1 million. The manager hired for the Dover was Buckley's son Christopher. This choice raised eyebrows since Christopher had little experience in hotel management. Christopher also became the renovated penthouse's resident.

First-rate treatment funded by Allegheny was not enjoyed by Buckley's family alone. Personal loans totaling more than $30 million were granted to Allegheny executives at a 2 percent interest rate. Approximately two-thirds of this money allowed the executives to acquire Allegheny stock. Other perks included a fleet of five corporate jets. Travel was not alien to Allegheny executives. Up to 100 executives and their spouses were flown to annual management meetings in resort areas. The cost of such meetings could run to over $100,000 in places such as the Bahamas. Weekend vacations to London at company expense were also allowed.

This corporate lifestyle led to a high corporate overhead. One disgruntled Allegheny stockholder claimed that the rate was twice that spent by similar companies. More than one stockholder was disgruntled. Another, a former dean at a graduate school of management, wrote to Allegheny's board of directors. He criticized the board's lack of control over both management and assets. Could this board really be controlled by management? Among its members were Anthony O'Reilly, CEO of Heinz, and former Secretary of State Alexander Haig.

Questions were raised about the dependence of some directors on Allegheny. Three outside directors earned money from Allegheny apart from their directors' salaries. Another received a rather high fee for special services provided to the company. While Allegheny's financial fortunes were declining, Buckley's salary still earned respect. A comparison study of other companies in the Pittsburgh area showed that Buckley earned more than his counterparts at Westinghouse and USX.

Allegheny's fortunes continued to decline, and Buckley started to restructure the company. But net income turned from positive to negative, and the price of Allegheny's stock fell. Capital was needed and needed quickly. A sell-off of its share of a European kitchen-appliance maker brought less than the expected revenues. Nor would oil and gas investments reverse the firm's fortunes; a $32 million loss forced it to abandon further efforts in that industry. Allegheny seemed to have few options available. It filed for bankruptcy.

Questions

1. Is there a criterion you would use to decide if a reward accruing to a corporate position is appropriate?
2. How would you decide if nepotism within a publicly held corporation is unethical?
3. How do you preclude potential conflicts of interest (i.e., assure objective decisions) by members of your board of directors?

Sources

"Allegheny International faces a Chapter 11 delay," *The Wall Street Journal* (August 16, 1990), A4.

Clark Ansberry, "Allegheny International's Buckley quits post amid charges of corporate waste," *The Wall Street Journal* (August 11, 1986), 4.

Clark Ansberry, "Allegheny International gives details of acts leading to ex-chairman's ouster," *The Wall Street Journal* (June 10, 1987), 37.

Dean Forist et al., "Al Haig: Embattled in the boardroom," *Business Week* (June 17, 1991), 108, 109.

Michael Schroeder, "Allegheny's battle to come back from the abyss," *Business Week* (June 26, 1989), 130, 134.

William C. Symonds, "Big Trouble at Allegheny," *Business Week* (August 11, 1986), 56–61.

William C. Symonds and Pete Engardio, "How a leaky roof may cost Allegheny dearly," *Business Week* (August 11, 1986), 60–61.

William C. Symonds, "Why something's got to give at Allegheny International," *Business Week* (May 19, 1986) 120, 122.

❖   Case Study 2–3   ❖

RELIANCE

Saul Steinberg is an astute financier. As founder and head of Leasco, he sought to take over an undervalued insurance firm that had an asset value of almost three times the amount of his company. His firm, though, traded at 40 times earnings; the insurance firm, Reliance, sold at less than 12 times earnings. Leasco offered $72 per share for Reliance. But the management at Reliance opposed the takeover.

Steinberg sought out Richard Carroon and Edward MacArthur, who controlled over 13 percent of Reliance's stock. He offered them risk-free Leasco stock for which he had arranged a subsequent cash sale to a group of financial institutions. Steinberg had guaranteed to buy back Carroon's and MacArthur's Leasco stock from the financial institutions at $72 per share plus a generous carrying cost. Other Reliance stockholders received no such guarantees; they received only Leasco stock and warrants for their Reliance shares. With Carroon's and MacArthur's stock in hand, Steinberg's takeover attempt proved successful.

His next takeover was a disappointment. He invested $24 million in Pergamon Press, based on that firm's audited financial condition. A second audit by another accounting firm showed that the profit was only 7 percent of the original estimate. Steinberg took a huge write-off. The Leasco computer-leasing business was also going badly. Obsolete hardware and other problems caused the company losses. In its short history Leasco, not counting its profits from Reliance's insurance business, had lost more money than it had made.

Steinberg, now head of Reliance, spun off the Leasco division. The majority of the shares of the newly independent Leasco company were bought by him. He then leveraged his new Leasco stock to buy more of Reliance. Reliance, under Steinberg, went private.

Reliance's insurance business provided the financial backing for other takeover ventures. Threatening to take over a firm is often more profitable than is succeeding with the takeover. The target firm often seeks outside support to thwart the takeover. The hostile aggressor, such as Reliance, is offered a higher price than what it paid for the target firm's stock. This is called "greenmail" as opposed to blackmail. The greenmail buyout is usually made on the condition that the takeover firm agrees not to renew its takeover efforts at a later date.

Steinberg's takeover ventures received greenmail payments from Walt Disney Company, Green Tree Acceptance, and Lomas & Nettleton Financial. An executive at Disney, in defending the $325 million greenmail payment to buy out Reliance's 11 percent share of Disney, said that he didn't want Steinberg "to come back and rape the company again." Steinberg agreed to refrain from future purchases of Disney stock. One of the Disney family questioned the motive behind the proposed takeover and commented that takeover firms are "motivated only by greed."

Steinberg sensed an opportunity to reap further gains by taking Reliance public again. He was correct in his assumption. While he still kept control of 60 percent of the stock, the public offering proved successful. The value of his stock, in fact, rose 400 percent over what its worth had been when he took the firm private. The firm, though, remained highly leveraged. "Highly leveraged" is perhaps a mild description since its $10.5 billion of assets rested on a $350 million equity base.

Investors bought Reliance for Steinberg's financial expertise, not for the company's insurance business or its junk bond portfolio. Admittedly, all of his ventures have not panned out. An investment in a Spanish-language television network recently resulted in a $94 million write-off. But Steinberg's worth can be seen in the salary that Reliance paid him. With an annual salary and bonus of $6 million, he continued to make the list of the country's highest-paid executives. This compensation was awarded despite Reliance's lackluster performance in insurance and Moody's downgrading of Reliance's financial strength rating.

As the property and casualty business got worse, Reliance's debt registered a ratio greater than 2+ times its equity. Sell-offs of its General Casualty unit and its Frank B. Hall unit helped a bit. Steinberg didn't seem too concerned. His strategy was simple: "We can always sell more assets and then refinance the debt." With a personal worth estimated at $300 million, accumulated through exploiting market opportunities, perhaps his vision should not be doubted.

Questions

1. What stage of moral reasoning seems to reflect Saul Steinberg's actions?
2. Do you have any ethical qualms about the buyout terms offered to the financial parties represented by Richard Carroon and Edward MacArthur?
3. Create an ethical justification for Saul Steinberg's compensation package, given Reliance's poor financial performance.

Sources

"Bid up, Mr. Maxwell," *The Economist* 237 (November 21, 1970), 96, 98.

Betsy Bauer, "N.Y. financier starts Disney raid," *USA Today* (March 30, 1984), 2B.

Abraham Briloff, "$200 million question," *Barron's* (December 18, 1972), 5, 12–16.

Abraham Briloff, *Unaccountable Accounting* (New York: Harper & Row, 1972), pp. 77–79.

Al Delagoch, "Former Disney executive rips Saul Steinberg," *Los Angeles Times* (June 30, 1989), 4.

"Double Standard?" *Forbes* 106 (July 15, 1970), 30, 31.

Daniel Hertzberg, "Saul Steinberg, Wall Street's brash outsider, may gain much from taking affairs private," *The Wall Street Journal* (July 29, 1981), 25.

"How's that again?" *Forbes* 107 (January 15, 1971), 14, 15.

Steve Kichen and Eric S. Hardy, "Putting it in perspective," *Forbes* (May 25, 1992), 174–176.

Larry Light, "Saul Steinberg's honey pot named Reliance," *Business Week* (July 12, 1993), 129, 130.

Larry Light, "Still preaching faith in Reliance," *Business Week* (August 10, 1992), 24.

"Pergamon," *The Economist* 236 (November 21, 1970), 96, 98.

Hilary Rosenberg, "Saul Steinberg," *Institutional Investor* 21 (June 1987), 43–45.

Hilary Rosenberg, "Saul Steinberg's insurance blues," *Institutional Investor* 21 (April 1987), 171–176.

Linda Sandler, "Saul Steinberg, edging away from market, sells some holdings," *The Wall Street Journal* (December 22, 1988), C1, C2.

Linda Sandler, "Saul Steinberg's Reliance deal eases squeeze," *The Wall Street Journal* (March 20, 1990), C1, C2.

"What Saul Steinberg is buying into now," *Business Week* (March 16, 1981), 144, 146, 150.

Notes to Chapter 2

[1]Aristotle, for example, distinguishes between types of friendship in a way similar to this in Book Nine of his *Nicomachean Ethics*.

[2]Jürgen Habermas, *Communication and the Evolution of Society*, trans. by Thomas McCarthy (Boston: Beacon Press, 1979).

[3]Marvin W. Berkowitz, "The Role of Discussion in Moral Education," in Marvin W. Berkowitz and Fritz Oser (eds.), *Moral Education: Theory and Application* (Hillsdale, NJ: Lawrence Erlbaum Associates, 1985).

[4]Stanley Moder, "Forget ethics—and succeed?" *Industry Week* (October 19, 1987), 17–18.

[5]William K. Frankena, *Ethics*, 2nd ed. (Englewood Cliffs, NJ: Prentice-Hall, 1973), pp. 20–23, presents the case against psychological egoism in a relatively clear way.

[6]Johann C. Schmidt, *Max Stirner: The Ego and His Own*, edited by John Carroll (New York: Harper & Row Publishers, 1971). Reprint of 1845 text, p. 214.

[7]Thomas F. Graham, *Anatomy of Avarice* (Canton, OH: Beacon-Bell Books, 1968).

[8]Matthijs Poppe and Lisbeth Utens, "Effects of greed and fear of being gypped in a social dilemma situation with changing pool size," *Journal of Economic Psychology* 7 (1986), 61–73.

[9]For further discussion of these distinctions, see Frankena's *Ethics*, cited above, and also Tom L. Beauchamp, *Philosophical Ethics* (New York: McGraw-Hill Book Co., 1982), especially pages 57–61.

[10]J. Jan Bruins, Wim B. G. Liebrand, and Henk A. M. Wilke, "About the saliency of fear and greed in social dilemmas," *European Journal of Social Psychology* 19 (1989), 155–161.

[11]Thomas Hobbes, *Leviathan* (London: Collier Books, 1969). First published in 1651. See especially Chapter 13.

[12]Lawrence C. Becker, *Reciprocity* (London: Routledge & Kegan Paul, 1986).

[13]Mordecai Nissan, "The Moral Balance Model: Theory and Research Extending Our Understanding of Moral Choice and Deviation," in William M. Kurtines and Jacob Gewirtz (eds.), *Handbook of Moral Behavior and Development* (Hillsdale, NJ: Lawrence Erlbaum Associates, Publishers, 1991), vol. 3.

[14]Ralph Waldo Emerson, "Self Reliance" in *The Collected Works of Ralph Waldo Emerson, Essays: First Series* (Cambridge, MA: The Belknap Press, 1979), vol. 2., p. 33.

Chapter 3

CUSTOM, CONVENTION, AND COURTESY

A s was the case in the first two chapters, a particular type of power is associated with the stage of moral development discussed in this third chapter. The type of power most applicable to the third stage of moral reasoning is called *referent power*. Based on respect for knowledge or values, referent power may be possessed by an individual, but the form most pertinent here is held by a group. Conventional wisdom strongly recommends that we follow the values imbued by corporate culture if we want to advance in a firm. As individuals, we acknowledge group referent power when we align or constrain our personal behavior in order to benefit the firm that employs us.

Group values, then, serve as the benchmarks by which we judge the ethics of our acts. But if we attempt to resolve conflicts by enhancing the well-being of the firm, have we, in our minds, enhanced the well-being of society?

Origins of Ethics

The word *ethics* is derived from the Greek word *ethos*, which means custom or habit. Similarly, the word *morality* is based on the Latin root *mora*, also meaning custom. These facts about our language suggest that the subject of this chapter is not as far removed from the heart of business ethics as might at first appear.

Words change, of course. The origin of a word does not dictate its present meaning in a simple and straightforward way. In the case of ethics and morality, for example, there is obviously more to being ethical or moral today than simply following custom. Still, the way in which all of us first encounter moral considerations as we grow up is through the customs, habits, traditions, and practices of those with whom we live. In truth, we normally tend to give little thought to moral issues that do not have much impact on our lives. We tend to evaluate those issues in terms of the conventions set up by customary morality. John Dewey recognized these points and then drew a distinction between *customary morality* and *reflective morality*. Customary morality obtains its legitimacy from what Dewey calls "ancestral habit." [1] Reflective morality, in contrast, "appeals to conscience, reason, or to some principle which includes thought." [2] The real significance of this distinction, however, is that reflective morality attempts to provide a standpoint from which customs themselves can be morally evaluated.

Some cultures draw less of a distinction between social and moral regulations than is found in our country. In those cultures, custom and social convention are more appropriate focal points of ethical behavior than is the notion of justice. [3] But, once reflective reason has entered in, can simple appeals to custom, habit, or tradition any longer be the last word in morality? Payoffs to expedite imports into developing countries, for instance, may be socially accepted and customary in some parts of the world. Yet, this practice may also be subject to moral criticism in countries like ours, where lengthy deliberations and hearings led to laws such as the Foreign Corrupt Practices Act.

Normative Guidelines

In Dewey's view, reflective morality does not hold that morality has a certain content. It is more a matter of arriving at one's ethical beliefs and actions through certain guidelines or criteria—criteria like those we have earlier called "good reasons." Feasibility and consistency are examples of such criteria. Although we do not advocate a particular ethical theory, we do endorse or recommend what Dewey calls reflective morality as a third normative guideline to resolve conflicts with ethical implications.

Socrates held that an ethical person is a reasoning person. We endorse that view. If the focus of ethics is on resolving conflicts of interest, such resolution is more likely to occur through careful reasoning than through reliance on either tradition or mere emotion. Our credibility in an argument with others increases when we ground our positions in empirical evidence that is related to underlying principles. In brief, we believe that the criteria to resolve conflicts of interest must include reasoned as well as feasible and consistent behavior.

Our belief, according to the third goal that we set out in the Introduction, is that you, the reader, should *develop your competence to make moral evaluations.* Relying on reasoning power should help in that process. In your business career, you will face situations for which custom has no precedent. In such situations, you will find it easier to justify your reasoning process publicly than to explain decisions based on "gut feeling."

Reason, in fact, has been incorporated to some extent into the legal customs of our country. You probably have heard of the "reasonable man" test employed by the courts. Under that test, a jury is asked to ask what people using reflective reason would have done if they were the parties in the case that had been brought to trial. This test has been taken one step further in British Commonwealth law by the test of "reasonable foreseeability." This other test holds a person responsible if the consequences of an act are reasonably foreseeable (that is, if a reasonable person, placed in that situation, would have predicted the outcome as likely).

The conditions of our social lives are changing more rapidly today than ever before. This phenomenon means that our morality needs to be constantly applied and adapted to new situations. Custom, however, changes slowly and is unlikely to keep up with the changes in our lives. For this reason, a morality (whatever its particular teachings) based on reason and reflection rather than on custom is likely to be far more helpful and relevant in a business world marked by rapid technological change. This basic approach, with its stress on morality, is the orientation that we hope the discussion of the cases in *Practical Business Ethics* will foster.

Etiquette

Most of the cases in this book focus on developed and relatively affluent societies. In this current chapter and in Chapter 8, however, we ask you to think briefly about the effects that living in a different type of society might have on our ethical choices. (In Chapter 8, we discuss international business situations in more detail.) *Custom, convention, and courtesy* may seem at first to be more important factors in affluent societies than in those societies that operate at a subsistence level. The topics we consider in this chapter may seem to be mere "social niceties" to persons who have to struggle daily for their basic survival. As one anonymous cynic has stated, "Ethical principles have no force when people are hungry."

Admittedly, custom, convention, and courtesy are related to business etiquette as much as to business ethics—and some would think that questions of etiquette are less important in a poor society than in a wealthy one. The practical difference between etiquette and morality reflects a difference in their impact on cooperative activity within the community. Morality is significantly more important than etiquette in fostering the mutuality needed for community life.[4] Of course, poor societies may place as much emphasis on form and custom as well-to-do societies. Tribal cultures, for example, have elaborate rituals. The "dress code" for participants in commerce in a tribal society will differ from the "dress for success" expectations in our own society—but it may be the case that these matters are equally important to the two cultures. Still, what differentiates this etiquette from what we call *ethics* is the degree to which the physical, financial, intellectual, and not just the social well-being of society are actually harmed.

Our focus on customs in this chapter may help to remind us that social *action guides* (as such practices may be called) change to some extent over time. Everyone knows, for example, that the customs of Victorian England were different from those of today. This point is relevant to business ethics in the following way: the codes of ethics and the ethical practices and expectations in the business community also change and evolve over time. This is true even though some people believe that ethics is a matter of "eternal truths." Some general principles of ethics are unchanging—a principle like "Don't do unnecessary harm," for example. Such a general principle applies in a particular way to a particular culture and situation. Ways of application would constitute the codes of ethics that we apply in a given business context at a particular point in history.

Application

One interesting change in business custom over the past few decades has to do with *corporate due process*. This concept refers to the growing expectation that employees have certain rights if an employer is considering termination or discipline. Historically, hiring and firing of employees was the prerogative of the "boss"—and the boss could do as he or she pleased. As a result of the increasing size and complexity of business firms, and as a result of both legislation and litigation, companies today are generally expected to: (1) have a clear and publicly available set of guidelines for what is required of a particular employee; (2) have a clear and publicly understood set of penalties for violations of these guidelines; (3) allow an employee charged with violating a guideline to offer an explanation for the questioned violation; and (4) document the facts that company policy and procedures are consistently and fairly applied. These expectations are closely related to the three normative guidelines that we have offered in these first three chapters. Those guidelines—feasibility, consistency, and reasoning—act as touchstones in our efforts to resolve conflicts of interest where societal well-being is at stake. Interestingly, corporate due process typically applies more often to personnel in nonmanagerial positions than to managerial personnel. This is especially so for managerial personnel at the higher levels. Perhaps it is implicitly assumed that managers are inherently more able than workers are to look out for their own interests. Or perhaps it is just that managers have brought fewer lawsuits against their companies than have workers (and their unions). Another feature to note about corporate due process is that while it is very widespread in large companies, it is far less universal in small firms. However, it seems likely to continue to spread in the decades ahead.

Universal Virtues Versus Cultural Values

We expect the practice of corporate due process to spread from large companies to smaller firms. This issue leads us to ask whether we may also expect such practices and the values upon which corporate policies are based to spread from American businesses to business communities in other parts of the world. After all, it seems quite obvious that values and practices differ considerably from one culture to another. Some writers, however, urge that we look beyond merely cultural values—that is, those values that clearly differ from one culture to another—toward some set of universal values that underlie profit-driven businesses.

Of course, we do not require anthropological studies to know that moral prohibitions of murder and of incest are virtually universal. But are business values universal? Many twentieth-century philosophers have held that the way people actually behave does not answer the question about how they *should* behave. Again, just because something *is* does not mean it ought to be. Furthermore, several traditions in twentieth-century intellectual life hold that value judgments of all kinds are essentially arbitrary, subjective, or relative. In sharp contrast to such skeptical or relativistic thinking, a few recent philosophers have attempted to articulate a way of thinking about ethics that emphasizes the concept of virtue. Their approach holds that certain universal features of human life give rise to what might be considered universal virtues.

The most influential of these recent philosophers is Alasdair MacIntyre. In his books *After Virtue* [5] and *Whose Justice? Which Reality?* [6] MacIntyre defends his view that certain virtues—that is, certain moral attitudes, habits and practices—are universally required for satisfactory human living. However, even such basic virtues as *justice,* Kohlberg would counter, seem to take on cultural twists. The details of this renewed stress on the virtues are still being worked out by philosophers. In Chapter 8, we will give further attention to the notion that common virtues or common values possibly underlie all human societies.

Ethical Conventions Set by the Firm

Our reflections on custom, convention, and courtesy provide an appropriate point at which to consider further Lawrence Kohlberg's Stage Three of moral development. Stage Three is the first stage of what Kohlberg calls the "conventional level" of moral thought (in contrast to the earlier "preconventional level"). This is the stage characterized by "mutual interpersonal expectations, relationships, and interpersonal conformity." [7] The person at this stage is motivated to follow the rules and expectations of his or her social or business group.

The classic stereotype associated with this stage is that of the "Organization Man." Loyalty to the firm more than any other characteristic marks this person's behavior. Stage Three people seek acceptance and respect from others and do not mind giving up personal autonomy in the interest of mirroring the group's image. Hence, the connections with *custom* and *convention* should be obvious.

The group-directed values of those in Stage Three, as contrasted with the self-centered nature of people in the first two stages, stem from a different motivating force. *Shame,* rather than punishment or deprivation of personal rewards, is the perceived penalty that results from behavior that does not live up to the ethics of this "Organization Man" mentality.

In a business setting, the divisions and specializations of labor demand coordination among people within a firm. Firm members not only must cooperate with each other, but they must also have at least a minimal degree of trust that other members of the firm will live up to their responsibilities. The force that keeps the operation running smoothly is made up in part by commonly held goals and in part by a corporate culture or set of expectations about behavior. Group norms of behavior provide a degree of comfort to employees. These norms furnish a more concrete and soundly defensible set of standards to draw on than do perceived ego-centered motives.

One aspect of corporate culture that is not company specific is the expectation of sound financial management. This would start, of course, with the usual business expectation that the firm is seeking to make a profit. But it would also include assumptions about the use of standard accounting practices and recordkeeping. (Some assumptions that are widely held in American corporate culture are not held in all countries of the world—as those who begin to do business overseas sometimes discover in unfortunate ways.)

Cash management is one aspect that has caused ethical concerns. Witness the disclosures about the investments of now defunct airlines such as Eastern. For example, Eastern's transfer of valued assets at a nominal price to sister firm Continental was highly questionable. Sound cash management seems to require that investment in capital goods be in line with the firm's stated goals and that the investment of surplus funds be in line with those same goals. This might require, for example, that if high-risk investments are made, candid disclosure should be made both to the board of directors and to the stockholders. And, according to the normative guideline presented in the last chapter, we would raise ethical questions if the manager's actions were not consistent with his or her statements.

Sound cash management also entails investing for the firm's benefit rather than for personal benefit or comfort. Our prevailing business culture dictates receiving personal rewards only as a result of meeting performance standards. We do not give our business leaders a license to dip into their companies' resources for their personal benefit. One reason for the crisis in the savings and loan industry in the late 1980s was that the reasonable expectations of cash management were widely violated. And one reason why some persons are cynical about government leadership is that they imagine that such violations are also too common there. Even the suspicion of such abuses is enough to erode public confidence in its leaders. This is one reason why high personal standards—as well as a good public relations department—are essential to preclude appearances of conflict of interest.

Social Appearance

The *courtesy* aspect of our chapter title is related to Kohlberg's statement that at this stage "'Being good'. . .also means keeping mutual relationships, maintaining trust, loyalty, respect, and gratitude."[8] Loyalty to the firm is the hallmark of an "Organization Man." While the temptation exists to criticize loyalty as a sacrifice of autonomy, there is still another point of view. Howard Kaminsky fears that if we repudiate loyalty, we are to some extent repudiating the organization that views loyalty as integral to its viability as an operating system.[9]

Persons at Kohlberg's third stage of moral reasoning want most of all to "fit in," and a major way they attempt to do so is by emphasizing courtesy in their relations to others. While such behavior makes people less than fully autonomous, it does represent the earliest form of conventional moral development. It achieves this moral development because behavior and motivation of this kind contribute to genuine moral progress away from the Hobbesian "state of nature" that finds a "war of every man against every man."[10] It is, therefore, important not to underestimate the usefulness of this stage nor to devalue it completely. Customary morality, to put this same point another way, is not reflective morality, but it is nevertheless superior to relying merely on instinct or on an egocentric point of view.

In our society, customary morality is often embodied in the moral teaching of mainstream churches and other religious institutions. When a business violates one of these institutionalized customs, it may threaten the social harmony in a particular community—which would, in itself, be one reason to rethink a business decision. (Issues such as whether or not retail stores should open on Sunday, or if and when alcoholic beverages should be sold, are examples of areas in which tension has existed in the past.) However, cultural institutions evolve slowly—often very slowly—and sometimes do not take extenuating circumstances into account.

These factors suggest that a thinking person must be prepared to consider whether there might be a reasoned justification for violating some religious guideline in a particular situation. For example, there may be situations in which the general well-being of a community is at odds with the moral views of a particular religious denomination. Or there may be situations in which a particular business decision is opposed by the leaders of a church but nevertheless is compatible with the underlying or essential principles of that particular faith. For example, Swiss Calvinist church leaders may have frowned on firms trading with South Africa's past racist regime, but the profit realized was in line with church values. Sometimes, though not always of course, intelligent business leaders are as morally sensitive and informed as the leaders of the traditional moral and religious establishments. Dialogue—and even tension—between different groups in society can serve as a useful system of checks and balances when decisions are made.

The expectations that businesses have of their employees may differ from firm to firm, but are often rooted in the assumption of Stage Three morality. These expectations are based not only on the firm's goals but also on the approved means to be used and the image to be portrayed in attaining these goals. As a result, firms and trade associations establish guidelines for the behavior of employees or members. Such guidelines usually include what we call *ethical standards*, but they may prescribe other types of behavior as well: for example, an expected way of dressing while at work. These guidelines exist quite apart from the legal statutes of the country. In a few firms, as you will see in several of the cases in this book, the ethical custom can be summed up in one informal rule—"The end justifies the means," signifying that the end justifies *any* means. In other instances—IBM provides a good example—a strict protocol of behavior covers many details of business life and may not be violated.

Since there is a natural tendency in the business community to think in terms of results—and since results for the firm are understandably important—a very common justification for business customs is what we call *firmism*. Firmism is a restricted consequentialist theory of right and wrong. It holds that the results for the firm are the sole factors determining whether an action or practice is morally acceptable. Adopting firmism, people will admit to sometimes doing bad things, but they claim to do so for the best of unselfish reasons: to enhance the well-being of the firm. This thinking process is different from the logic used by traditional moral philosophers who attempt to explain questionable acts for good reasons. *Their* good reasons are more likely to be grounded on universal principles than on the situational consequences used by firmists to justify behavior. Still, in many businesses, firmism is the form that customary morality has taken. As much as the pressure to adopt firmism exists in the United States, the pressures are even greater in other areas of the world, especially in the Orient.

Intercultural Lessons on Corporate Customs

In recent years, the American business community has claimed to have learned a number of lessons from business experiences in Japan. One of these is relevant here. Because business transactions take place in a competitive environment, there will inevitably be intense pressure to find efficiencies of various kinds. Striving for these efficiencies will in turn produce conflicts of interest between, for example, workers and their supervisors, or between producers and distributors. Understandably, these conflicts tend to interfere with the efficiencies being sought. The effects of such conflicts can be minimized if both parties to the conflict pursue a common goal or have a common interest. All parties must recognize that their common interest will often require mutual compromise and sacrifice.

Such is the stereotype of business ethics in Japan, where personal compromise and sacrifice may be directed by the interest in the firm that interacting parties have in common. And this type of cooperation works best when the custom, convention, and courtesy of the society or firm expect and support it. The fact that contemporary Japanese society and business firms have customs, conventions, and courtesies in common is a large element in their success and a part of what makes them so intriguing to American businesspersons. In a sense, the Japanese experience is a validation of the much-maligned maxim, "What's good for General Motors is good for the country." Here, however, the relationship appears to go both ways: what's good for Japanese business is good for the country, and what's good for Japan is good for its businesses.

Because a society's customs are so closely related to its morality, one could also ask whether business provides significant leadership in the moral change that takes place in society or whether business simply follows. We believe the answer in many cases is that business does not simply mirror the customs of a society. Competing effectively in today's business environment often requires changes in business practices. With the stress on results that is typical of most businesses, competitive pressures can cause reevaluation of company practices that have moral implications. There is a strong temptation to adopt a Stage Three morality, trusting the company to provide the means to attain a desired lifestyle. This would seem to require that personal behavior conform to company goals.

Yet, those accepting the legitimacy of firmist morality are likely, when solving conflicts, to use the same methods of argumentation as those used by Stage Two proponents. That type of communication is part of Strategic Communicative Action. The objective of Strategic Communication Action is to win over the party who has views conflicting with the company's position. The emphasis is on the end, rather than on the means, as long as the means do not embarrass the firm.

More Than Profit?

Business transactions, and the business climate in general, have enormous power to affect various publics. The result of this power is that the moral customs of a society may gradually (or even suddenly) be changed as a result of business decisions. Obvious examples range from the commercialization of gene splicing techniques (products dealing with life) to deciding which nations shall be allowed to purchase nuclear reactors. We invite the reader to think of other examples that illustrate the impact of business on moral customs.

One issue of concern to business today is how to react to social issues raised by religious groups. While a number of issues come to mind, let us consider a particular one. The World Council of Churches has taken an activist role in promoting individual rights throughout the world. What would be your reaction if the World Council of Churches asked your firm to cease doing business with a certain developing country? Suppose, too, that such business is approved by your government. That developing country is ruled by a tyrannical dictator who stifles internal criticism with brutal force. Your business there accounts for one-fourth of your total sales and profit. Unfortunately, there are no other markets immediately apparent for your products. Formulate an answer for the World Council of Churches. Then explain whether your answer, in addition to being well reasoned, is feasible and consistent with your personal morality. In your resolution to this conflict, whose well-being is enhanced?

The question raised by this issue is how responsible business leaders should feel for the possible moral changes that come about as a result of their actions. If one took the view that the only concern of business should be to make the maximum profit, it would be actually wrong for businesspersons to pay attention to such social or moral implications. At the other extreme would be the view that business, because of its great power, should be the moral guardian of the entire society. As is usual in such cases, the truth is probably somewhere in the middle. But where, exactly?

One type of answer to this question is proposed by the philosopher William Frankena in his book *Ethics*.[11] Frankena argues that the two most basic principles in an adequate system of ethics are *beneficence* and *justice*. By *beneficence*, he means that we should always take into consideration whether our behavior causes harm or benefit to persons, the (unreachable?) ideal being to do no harm and do only good. By *justice*, Frankena means that, ideally, we should treat all persons equally, not showing special favor to one person or group without special justification. If we were to take these two factors into account in all of our decisions, Frankena claims, our actions would be more in harmony with the highest or most reflective level of moral development. Exactly what these two principles might dictate in business practice is an issue to be considered in reading the following cases.

Conclusions

Here are some general questions to keep in mind when reading the cases that follow this chapter:

Questions

1. What differences can you isolate between customary morality and reflective morality in this case?

2. Does the nature of this particular business bring pressure to bear to adopt a given ethical approach?

3. Is the difference between ethics and courtesy simply dependent on the social consequences of an act?

An individual at Stage Three will have a specific approach to these questions, but the approach will be geared to a constrained definition of ethics. The constraint comes from the final phrase in the definition of ethics: "to enhance societal well-being." Societal well-being for the Stage Three person appears to go no further than his or her reference group.

To oversimplify somewhat, the individual at Stage Three is likely to be (1) more motivated by group acceptance and complimented for team play than motivated by selfish gain; (2) more motivated by consequences benefiting the reference group from which self-worth is derived rather than by consequences for society as a whole; and (3) more motivated by only those deontological norms that are held as sacred by the chosen reference group rather than by universal principles. Individuals may go far in the business world, at least as employees, by adopting a Stage Three profile of behavior. Their thought pattern can be captured by the phrase, "Be a team player."

That theme can be played on in negotiations with people at Stage Three. Our task is to show that the group benefits by the resolution to conflict that we have suggested. People reasoning at the third stage of moral development have to be shown that their firm comes out better if the well-being of the larger society is enhanced. Strategic Communicative Action might work with these people. But some semblance of a higher level of communication called *Discursive Communicative Action* might also be called for. This would entail refining and elaborating aspects of the conflicting party's position in order to reach a mutual understanding. The idea is to concentrate on those aspects of the opponent's position (not principles) that would enhance the well-being of society. What we seek is a modification rather than a complete change of their position. Approaches to this procedure are outlined in more detail in Chapter 7.

❖   Case Study 3–1   ❖

HOLLYWOOD ACCOUNTING

Art Buchwald obtained what appeared to be a large financial settlement from Paramount Pictures. The court ruled that the idea for the Eddie Murphy picture *Coming to America* had originated with Buchwald.

Estimates of the film's worldwide gross revenue ranged from $275 million to $325 million. Paramount gave credit to the film in its annual report for contributing to healthy corporate earnings. The question now is whether Buchwald and his partner Alain Bernheim will reap financial rewards from the picture. By the accounting convention used in the motion picture indus-try and by the film studio, *Coming to America* hasn't done too well.

Buchwald and his partner were awarded $250,000 plus 19 percent of the film's net profits. Now they are waiting for the film to show a net profit. The charges against revenues for the film *do* raise eyebrows. The costs paid out to Eddie Murphy's staff—bodyguards, valet, trainer, and so on—totaled $1 million. The cost of his office staff came to another $3.7 million. Even a portion of Murphy's signing bonus from Paramount appeared to be charged off to the film. Paramount took $40 million as a distribution fee and another $34 million to cover the costs of distribution. Those costs included advertising and making prints for distribution. Production cost another $58 million. If the film does show a profit, another $6 million is due Paramount to cover interest expense.

Buchwald's attorney is quoted as saying, "The net profit system in Hollywood is a scam." But that system has a long tradition behind it. Such movie hits as *Alien* and *Ghostbusters* are said to have never shown a net profit. Over a decade earlier, questions were raised and then shunted aside about the profit-allocation system in Hollywood.

At that time, television producers Aaron Spelling and Leonard Goldberg were questioned about having moved money from one of their shows, *Charlie's Angels,* to another of their shows, *Starsky and Hutch.* The producers owned a larger percentage of *Starsky and Hutch.* Los Angeles District Attorney John Van De Kamp then said that insufficient grounds existed to pursue the matter in the courts. What Van De Kamp did observe was a practice of "sloppy business practices and a kind of Alice-in-Wonderland bookkeeping."

Some investors in *Charlie's Angels,* specifically Robert Wagner and his wife Natalie Wood, were content with Van De Kamp's ruling. Wagner and his wife were to share profits of 43.7 percent. That share was awarded based in part on Wagner's and Wood's agreement to appear in subsequent Spelling–Goldberg productions. Other profit participants, including screen-writers Ben Roberts and Ivan Goff, were not pleased with the accounting practices. Roberts and Goff had written the script for the pilot, plus a half dozen episodes for the television series. Their share was to be 12.5 percent of net profits.

Wagner and Wood were informed that the series had lost $1 million for its first three seasons. Roberts and Goff had received a statement declaring a much larger loss. The difference was attributed to different definitions of profit rather than to deception. Profit participants and studios can negotiate the details of how profit is calculated. Sometimes profits are arbitrarily declared when revenues reach an agreed upon multiple of production costs. In the film business, top talent can usually negotiate a better deal. For example, Stanley Jaffe and Sherry Lansing, producers of *Fatal Attraction,* based their participation on gross rather than net profit. Their share of profit totaled about $20 million. Writers like Roberts and Goff usually are offered only percentages of net profit.

One industry insider stated that when faced with net profit participants, a film studio benefits by charging for expenses totaling more than the revenue it takes in. James Garner had questions about such expenses in *The Rockford Files* series. He was concerned about creative accounting practices that appeared to overstate cost. One Beverly Hills lawyer views these accounting practices as a matter of industry convention. His reasoning is that the film industry will "do what's necessary to protect their bottom line." Another lawyer has observed that the film industry is more creative than professional. The gist of his comment was that a certain degree of flexibility had to be allowed in calculating charges when making films. A film industry insider believes a savvy studio accountant can charge off the same expense to multiple productions. A more cynical producer, commenting on the convention of net profit participation, bluntly stated that "A net is for tennis, not for profits."

For those who have a high public profile—for example, Jane Fonda suing for her share of profits from the film *On Golden Pond*—an out-of-court settlement can be negotiated. For those with less of a public presence—for instance, screenwriters—conflict resolution may be less satisfactory. Commented one screenwriter: "As soon as you take a share in a film, you know your goose is cooked."

Questions

1. Are there any reasoned grounds for criticizing the traditional means for calculating expenses and net profit according to customs within the film industry?
2. Do all the profit participants in a film have to be treated identically to have an ethical business situation?
3. What ethical responsibilities would you attribute not only to film producers but also to the profit participants if claims of unethical behavior are to be precluded?

Sources

Andrew Baird, "The accounting is creative too," *Fortune* (November 17, 1980), 47.

Gerald Clarke and Martha Smilgis, "A bombshell case goes phfft!" *Time* (December 15, 1980), 72–73.

Jeff Garth, "ABC under inquiry on alleged irregularities in fees," *The New York Times* (August 17, 1980), 1, 30.

Ronald Grover, "Curtains for Tinseltown accounting?" *Business Week* (January 14, 1991), 35.

Dennis McDougal, "Paramount's net profit central to Buchwald suit," *Los Angeles Times* (March 23, 1990), F4, F23, F34.

David Robb, "Par to Buchwald: We're $18-Mil in hole," *Variety* (March 28, 1990), 5, 10.

Roy Rowan, "ABC covers itself," *Fortune* 102 (November 17, 1980), 45–48.

David Sheff, "Lawyer Jennifer Martin tilts the halos on 'Charlie's Angels' and gets fired for her effort," *People* (May 19, 1980), 115–116.

Robert W. Stevenson, "Movie's bottom-line challenged," *The Atlanta Journal—The Atlanta Constitution* (April 14, 1970), F1, F4.

Dana Wechsler, "Profits? What profits?" *Forbes* (February 19, 1990) 38–40.

❖   Case Study 3–2   ❖

FUNERALS

Man, unable to cure death,
hit upon the idea of not
thinking about it.

Does this opinion, attributed to the philosopher Blaise Pascal centuries ago, still hold? A funeral is the third most expensive purchase made by the average person. Americans spend $6 billion for funerals each year. Are the expenses associated with a funeral the result of what we would call a wise preplanned purchase? Arthur Angel of the Federal Trade Commission wonders how wise some of our decisions are when we make funeral arrangements. He notes that "The buyer of funeral services is emotionally upset." His fear is that some funeral directors use this emotionally vulnerable time to sell their most expensive packages.

An earlier critic of funeral industry, Jessica Mitford, had some harsh words for the business side of the industry. Her claim was that the licensing boards of some states tended to act in a way that restricted competition. Those boards, in most cases made up of undertakers, set requirements that inflated the prices for embalming, casket use, and cremation.

Mitford particularly questioned the need for embalming. Her research showed that few countries other than the United States routinely required embalming. Industry representatives, however, have felt that Mitford's view is biased. The executive director of the National Funeral Directors Association stated that embalming provided safety from infectious organisms for those who had to handle bodies. Mitford's response was that if embalming were an essential health measure, then why did other affluent countries not require it?

Another industry representative believes that embalming is part of grief therapy. Embalming gives the mourners a better-lasting impression of the departed loved one. To this claim, Mitford answers that grief therapy now means encouraging people to buy expensive caskets so that the mourners will not feel guilty. Grief therapy has become the explanation for many of the related services accompanying the burial. A sociology professor who consults for the industry believes that some of the related services are thera-peutic to the point of precluding subsequent emotional problems with the bereaved after the burial. At the San Francisco College of Mortuary Science, classes are now offered in marketing and psychology, as well as in tradi-tional subjects. As one funeral director stated: "We realized that to really serve a family, you must go beyond the funeral."

Part of the aftercare service involves support groups, memorial cards, and videos that highlight events of the person's life. With fewer customers choosing embalming and more favoring cremation, funeral directors are searching for services that will reverse declines in profits. "Tribute" videos have been especially popular, and annual sales have passed the million dol-lar mark. One mortuary in Minnesota reports that two-thirds of the families mourning the deceased have ordered videos from its funeral homes.

Even with these post-burial services, the public relations chairperson of the California Funeral Directors Association feared that people would still think of funeral directors as a gang of thieves. A strong part of that feeling comes from reactions to the price of a casket. A funeral director in Oklahoma believes that many families do not want to go the low price route. His best-selling casket had a mattress and box spring similar to a bed. His thought was that the family of the deceased did not think the simpler cotton founda-tions were appropriate. Arthur Angel disagrees, saying that "The casket selection room is the central theater for the funeral home rip-off."

Casket prices and the associated markups can be quite high. Al Thacker, owner of the Family Heritage Casket Gallery in Tennessee, sells his caskets at discount prices. He points out that his most expensive model costs half the price that is charged at nearby funeral homes. He states that his markup is 200 percent, while funeral homes earn at least double that amount. An industry representative states that such markups are necessary to cover the costs of items such as chapel and limousine use. A problem thus occurs when the funeral home uses a casket bought elsewhere. One solution to this problem has been to charge customers handling fees.

Casket stores are not appreciated by many funeral directors. Sheralee and Kyle Nyswonger found this out when they opened their Hillmark Casket Gallery. Sheralee Nyswonger said she tried to work within people's budgets, and that her prices were significantly lower than those charged by local funeral homes. Her goal was to make a living by helping families save money. But she stated that the owner of a nearby funeral home came into her shop and demanded to know the names of her suppliers. Later, one of these suppliers stopped selling to the Nyswongers. Sheralee Nyswonger said that the local funeral homes had stopped buying from her supplier because it was servicing her business. The publisher of *Mortuary Management* magazine negatively equated the discount casket shop to "wholesale butchers."

Sheralee Nyswonger now removes all the manufacturer identification from her caskets. Nor will she disclose the names of her suppliers. "I'm just so tired of getting beat up," were her words. "The customers like you. Everyone else wants to cut you to pieces." Are funeral homes making outrageous profits at the expense of the emotionally upset customers? The largest firm in the industry, Service Corporation International, is highly profitable. Conversely, many of the smaller funeral homes are not showing much profit.

Questions

1. Are the discount casket shops, with their emphasis on lower price, disrupting the cultural tradition of grief therapy—a tradition that serves to enhance the emotional well-being of the bereaved?
2. What stage of moral reasoning seems to mark Nyswonger's local competitors? What brought you to this conclusion?
3. Are your views on the conflicts over embalming and casket markups based on customary or reflective morality? Find one legitimate argument for an opposing point of view.

Sources

Charles P. Alexander and Christopher Redman, "A move to ease death's sting," *Time* (May 14, 1984), 53.

Ruth Darnstadter, "Blocking the death blow to funeral regulation," *Business and Society Review* (Winter 1983), 32–36.

John R. Emsheviller, "Rules may change in funeral industry," *The Wall Street Journal* (May 19, 1992), B1.

"Facts worth knowing about funeral costs," *Changing Times* 29 (February 1975), 51–52.

"Giving undertakers something to cry about," *Business Week* (October 6, 1975), 93, 94, 96.

Jerry Jakubovics, "R. L. Waltrip livens up a growing industry," *Management Review* 77 (September 1988), 15, 16.

Maria L. LaGanga, "Casket controversy," *Los Angeles Times* (August 16, 1989), IV 1, 5.

Joshua Levine, "Cash and bury," *Forbes* (May 11, 1992), 162–166.

Randall Pou, "The selling of mortality," *Across the Board* (March 1986), 34.

Doster Rand, "Five undertakers," *Esquire* 83 (February 1975), 102–107.

Carlee R. Scott and Carrie Dolan, "Funeral homes hope to attract business by offering services after the service," *The Wall Street Journal* (April 11, 1991), B1, B6.

"Should funeral homes be regulated?" *U.S. News And World Report* 80 (May 10, 1976), 45–46.

❖   Case Study 3–3   ❖

ATLANTA ADULT ENTERTAINMENT

In 1989, the Georgia Supreme Court ruled that "mere nudity" could be considered as constitutionally protected free speech. Thus, state laws and local ordinances were rendered unenforceable if they restricted clubs that had nude entertainers.

Reactions to the court ruling were not universally favorable. Said one metro Atlanta resident: "A strip dancing club is not a proper environment for our residential neighborhood." Another resident who lived near a new "topless" club wondered: "Why are they trying to spread it to where our children play and grow up?"

Club owners had a different perspective. "I'm supplying 100 jobs here," said Don Gravley, owner of the Platinum Plus club. "A lot of girls go to college and this pays for their tuition. Some women are divorced, or out of work, and this feeds their kids. It's like working for a bank or any other business." At the nearby Gold Club, the club's master of ceremonies was heard to announce to the crowd: "Gentlemen, those women are working for tips. If you see a lady on your table that you want to be naked, slip her a bill." The owner of the Gold Club praised the court ruling related to nude dancing and alcohol sale; at the same time, his attorney said: "We object to any neighborhood input. It's a matter between the police and the applicant."

Some club owners thought that their businesses were good for the community. Betty Jo Harrison at the She Club claimed: "We run a clean, decent, respectable club, and they're trying to say we don't." One employee at the Cheshire Cat stated: "We don't hurt anybody. I wish someone would tell me who we are bothering." A restaurant owner near the clubs expressed little concern over their proximity, saying: "It doesn't bother us. People gonna eat anyway."

There is no question that the clubs are popular with some members of the community. The Cheshire Cat's "businessman's special"—the choice of a lady, waterbed, whirlpool, and steambath—found a market demand. Amateur night at the She Club also drew crowds.

But the clubs have created local tension. "Sophisticated perversion" is a term heard to describe their entertainment. Local residents fear that the clubs will "drag the neighborhood down," and this fear was also voiced by the mayor. The City Solicitor claimed that the only weapon that the city had left was a statute against "lewd nudity," and even that definition depended on a very questionable interpretation of terms. Where was the solicitor supposed to draw the line between sin and nudity? The Solicitor was also worried about incidents of crime in the form of credit card rip-offs and prostitution that had been associated with similar clubs.

Some merchants with stores near the clubs did not care for their new neighbors. One pointed to the loitering and littering at his doorstep. Another said he was embarrassed to tell people where his store was located. Richard Ribble, pastor of a local church, feared that the affected area would deteriorate as the clubs drove established business away. Pastor Ribble believed that the clubs "play on the lower aspects of our nature." He said, "In the long run they are not conducive to the highest kind of morality that God called us to." Mack Close, a neighborhood resident, echoed these feelings: "Most people don't like strip joints because immoral things go on inside."

In addition to the "strip" clubs, bars catering to a gay and lesbian clientele also opened in the area. Deana's and the Sports Page were two of these establishments. The clientele at the two types of clubs did not always mix well. Said Nancy Forsyth, a bartender at Deana's: "Straight people can come in here as long as they don't harass anyone." But she didn't appreciate the attitude of the topless club's patrons when they came into Deana's: "Rednecks at a topless bar want the challenge of gay women. . . .They think that they can talk tough to get anyone they want."

The reaction to the gay and lesbian bars has been mixed. The owner of a nearby upholstering company said: "I saw two men carryin' on. . .I hate it." The manager of the neighborhood delicatessen disagreed, saying: "Customers are customers. Gay bars bring in people. You can't afford to be fussy about who your clients are."

Questions

1. To what extent should morality be legislated? Explain in detail.
2. Create ethical justifications for both sides to the dispute about "pleasure" establishment in the area.

3. Is societal well-being enhanced, impaired, or unaffected by the presence of the clubs?

Sources

Gary Abramson, "Gold club lifts a glass to high court," *The Atlanta Journal and Constitution* (December 6, 1989), B1, B10.

Scott Bowles, "Nude clubs aim to bare all in face of opposition," *The Atlanta Journal* (May 23, 1991) E1, E9.

Scott Brownstein, "Nude dancing draws men, not crime," *The Atlanta Journal and Constitution* (October 16, 1988), B4.

Actor Cordell, "Groups fight new nightclub on Piedmont," *The Atlanta Journal and Constitution* (June 5, 1987), B4.

Bill Dedman, "Witnesses assail 'sleaze' of new strip club," *The Atlanta Journal and Constitution* (June 27, 1987), B1.

Steven Holmes, "Club stripped of adult status," *The Atlanta Journal and Constitution* (August 5, 1978), 1A, 4A.

Dave Lieber and Ron Taylor, "Cheshire bridge clubs for sophisticates," *The Atlanta Journal and Constitution* (July 23, 1978), 1-B, 12-B.

Donna Lorenz, "North Fulton crowd opposes nude dancing near 2 schools," *The Atlanta Journal and Constitution* (September 6, 1990), D6.

Lyn Martin, "Protestors hope to strip away zoning from topless night club," *The Atlanta Journal and Constitution* (August 1, 1978), 1-C, 3-C.

Duane River, "City fails to block reopening of nude club," *The Atlanta Journal* (April 10, 1990), C1, C3.

Tyrone D. Terry and Lyn Martin, "City closes down last 2 bathhouses," *The Atlanta Journal and Constitution* (August 9, 1978), 1C & 2C.

Notes to Chapter 3

[1]John Dewey, *Theory of the Moral Life* (New York: Holt, Rinehart and Winston, Inc., 1960), p. 1.

[2]Ibid.

[3]William Demon, *The Moral Child: Nurturing Children's Moral Growth* (New York: The Free Press, 1988).

[4]James D. Wallace, *Moral Relevance and Moral Conflict* (Ithaca, NY: Cornell University Press, 1988).

[5]Alasdair MacIntyre, *After Virtue: A Study in Moral Theory,* 2nd ed. (Notre Dame, IN: University of Notre Dame Press, 1984).

[6]Alasdair MacIntyre, *Whose Justice? Which Rationality?* (Notre Dame, IN: University of Notre Dame Press, 1988).

[7]Ann Colby et al., *The Measurement of Moral Judgment* (Cambridge, MA: Center for Moral Education, Harvard University, 1980), vol. 1, part 1, p. 78.

[8]Ibid.

[9]Howard Kaminsky, "Moral Development in a Historical Perspective," in William M. Kurtines and Jacob Gewirtz (eds.), *Morality, Moral Behavior and Moral Development* (New York: John Wiley and Sons, 1984).

[10]Thomas Hobbes, *Leviathan* (London: Collier Books, 1969), Part 1, Chapter 13, p. 100. First published in 1651.

[11]William Frankena, *Ethics,* 2nd. ed. (Englewood Cliffs, NJ: Prentice-Hall, 1973).

Chapter 4

THE LETTER OF THE LAW VERSUS THE SPIRIT OF THE LAW

The three previous chapters contained brief descriptions of specific types of power depicting stages of moral reasoning. The Fourth Stage of moral development—law and order—is also associated with a type of power called *legitimate power*. Legitimate power is endowed in individuals because of their role in formal, interpersonal relations. Department heads, for example, are given legitimate power by the firm over those reporting to them within the firm. This power is distinct from any referent, reward, or coercive power that they might also possess. In this chapter, however, the type of legitimate power that concerns us is not found within a firm. Rather, it is created by the law as it relates to guiding the firm's actions.

One way to approach business ethics is from the standpoint of the law. The law provides an external reference point for resolving conflicts. That reference point is usually more unbiased than the individual and group perspectives that underlie the first three stages of moral reasoning. The law also draws a detailed boundary about what constitutes the society over whose well-being the business community must be concerned. But laws are not perfect; in many cases they show both an obsolescence and a vagueness that bring consternation to business decisionmakers. As Luigi Bagolini has warned:

> When there is a halt in the movement of a legal system—a halt in the necessary process by which a legal code, by being interpreted, is constantly adapted to the surrounding conditions of its applicability—then a conflict between law and morality becomes inevitable.[1]

This lack of adaptation gives rise to obsolescence and thus to possible dangers of following "the letter of the law."

In ethics or morality, however, an important distinction exists between the letter and spirit of the law. Saint Paul wrote: "The letter killeth, but the spirit giveth life."[2] The basic point of this commonplace contrast seems clear enough: virtually any law, rule, practice, or tradition can be interpreted in a literal, strict fashion. On the other hand, there is often a spirit or purpose that can be discerned behind the law.[3] Occasionally, the spirit of a given regulation might be respected even when actions violate a legalistic interpretation of the law. More common, however, are cases where the spirit of law seems to require us not only to conform to the literal interpretation, but even to go beyond it in some way. An example would be the obligation to deliver satisfaction with a product when the literal interpretation of the law simply requires a company not to create harmful goods.

Law and Morality

In the Introduction, we quoted a brief definition of the word *morality* as one of humanity's attempts to "harmonize conflicting interests." It should be clear that law is another such attempt. One medieval philosopher wrote that "Law is nothing less than an ordinance of reason for the common good, made and promulgated by him who has the care of the community."[4] Law formalizes the social contract under which the community limits the harm that members can do to the social fabric.[5] In spite of the occasionally expressed view that "what is legal is ethical and what is ethical is legal"—a phrase sometimes heard in discussions of business ethics—we believe that differences as well as similarities exist between law and morality.

As we see it, law resembles morality in that both are social institutions that aim to improve human life in various ways. Law, however, presents certain minimal standards of "civilized" conduct—standards that we as a society require our fellow citizens to live up to. Some laws aim at forcing us to bear the burdens of our life together in an equitable manner (tax laws are an example). Other laws prohibit us from giving in to temptations that would directly harm others (for example, laws against exposing employees to hazardous work conditions). Still other laws require us to help those who are dependent on us (providing nutrition information on food packages is one case). Although the goal of both law and morality is a "harmonious society," morality aims at this in a way differing from law, except perhaps in societies governed under religious law. As a case in point, obedience to Islamic law supersedes individual qualms of conscience among Moslems; secular law is secondary. In their societies, there is neither reason nor advantage to adopting moral standards other than those required by Islamic law.[6]

Apart from religious nations of this sort, the necessity for morality rests on at least two things: (1) the need for more than bare minimum standards of behavior if a society is to flourish, and (2) the need for a less rigid, cumbersome, and costly system of social control to supplement the social control exerted by the law itself. These needs, in our society and in most others, are met by what we usually call *morality*.

Both of these apparent shortcomings deserve further analysis. It is true, we believe, that all societies require certain minimal standards of behavior from their members if these societies are to survive. And, no doubt, even higher standards of behavior are required if these societies are to flourish. Could a system of laws be formulated that would embody these higher standards? Perhaps. But even if this could be done, it would still be difficult to get these "higher standards" embodied in actual laws. One reason is that there is more disagreement about higher standards than about minimal obligations. For instance, what sort of obligation do we have to help a customer? Does the simple fact that a customer is in need place us under an obligation to help that person? And if we do have some obligation to help a customer, how pressing is that obligation? (For example, how much inconvenience must we bear if we are to be justified in not giving the help required?) People frequently disagree about the answers to these questions. Because we differ so often when we discuss issues of higher standards of obligation (as opposed to minimal obligation), we typically lack the social consensus necessary to get such higher standards enacted into law.

Furthermore, even in cases where there exists the social consensus necessary to enact some particular moral obligation into law, this is frequently not done. Among the many reasons for such failures to embody particular moral beliefs in laws are (1) the recognition that although the great majority clearly supports a particular view, a conscientious minority opposes it, and (2) the recognition that the "costs" of enforcing certain laws would outweigh the benefits that the laws would provide. This latter consideration looms large in many discussions of the proper role of government regulation in the business world.

Balancing Rights

Most of us believe that all persons share some natural rights regardless of political or social situations. A right to self-preservation is an example of one such right. Other rights, like the right to own property, are acquired within and bestowed by the community. In the latter case, there seems to be a responsibility that goes along with every acquired right. For example, when we acknowledge a right to privacy, we also acknowledge that the person whose right is being protected has certain responsibilities. As an illustration, consider an employee's right to privacy and the employer's responsibility to respect that right. It seems reasonable to suggest that the employee has the corresponding responsibilities not to engage in behavior that will injure societal well-being and not to issue negative statements about the employer unless the information has been verified, is given in context, and is necessary to prevent or correct some serious harm. In turn, we expect the firm to respect the privacy of its employees unless there are strong mitigating circumstances. What would be a feasible justification for a firm to violate an employee's privacy? At the least, that violation would have to pass public scrutiny as an act that enhances societal well-being. The act should also be consistent with stated corporate policy if not with conventional business practice.

In most cases, a kind of weighing or balancing of rights and responsibilities seems to be required—as when the right of free speech conflicts with a responsibility not to deceive or harm another by abusing that right of free speech. Laws about slander are written to attempt to provide public standards for resolving such conflicts. Even so basic a right as the right to life or to one's own preservation does not bring with it the responsibility of others to help one preserve one's life under all conceivable circumstances—for example, if one begins to threaten the lives of others. Still, however, if one starts with a widely held concept such as the right to life, one may go on to argue for rights to those things that are necessary for life.

Applications

Product safety has been a significant issue in recent decades. Relatively few products are likely to do physical harm to users under normal circumstances. Some products, however, may cause physical harm under extreme or unusual circumstances. Recall the controversy over the placement of the fuel tank in the GM pickup truck in relation to broadside collisions. The interest of the users on the one hand and the manufacturers or distributors on the other may easily come into conflict in such situations. Of course, it is sometimes hard to draw the line between reasonable and unreasonable use, or between normal and extreme circumstances. Apart from this, however, is it *feasible* to expect infallible safety from a product? Are we not willing to accept some tradeoffs that would contribute to less than 100 percent safety? Pickup trucks, for example, would be much safer if they could only move slowly and were armored like tanks—but the various "costs" associated with such trucks would be unacceptable to most of us. The point is that product safety is another area where interests conflict and where behavior that ignores or minimizes the interests of others typically creates problems.

Workplace safety, too, can lead to several kinds of conflict. Workers in a pharmaceutical laboratory, for example, have a right to be protected from exposure to hazardous chemicals. Such workers have a right, one might say, to a work environment that meets high standards of safety. But is there a right to "total safety"? Probably there will always be some risks at work. Is there a right to "the safest workplace possible"? Recall that one of the guidelines we earlier suggested for resolving conflicts of interest was *feasibility*. Perhaps there are situations where the costs of improving safety conditions in a particular workplace from a "high level" to the "safest possible" level would be so great that the firm in question could not survive. Of course, there might be products so hazardous to produce that their manufacture cannot be justified at all.

The other guidelines of consistency and the use of reason or reflection (rather than emotion) are also relevant here. Would top management allow their children to work on the shop floor? Arguments for rights to jobs or to living wages might be analyzed and discussed in a way parallel to this consideration of the right to a safe workplace.

Sometimes the rights and responsibilities in conflict are not just those of individual parties. The case of contracts between a government and its suppliers provides a good example. The government, by definition, is responsible for articulating and enforcing the laws under which business takes place. At the same time, however, the government itself must enter into contracts with various suppliers and other business partners. This generates a potential conflict between the government in its role as one party to a contract and the government in its role as the ultimate enforcer of contracts in general. The government itself thus has the ultimate responsibility of regulating the very contracts that it uses to conduct its own business. It has the right to enter into contracts and to receive what it has contracted for, of course. But it also has the responsibility to monitor its own contracts to check for behavior that would be detrimental to the society it represents. Reflect on this for a moment. Can you formulate a short governmental policy (in less than twenty-five words) that can serve to resolve potential conflicts between government and its suppliers—and do so in a feasible, internally consistent manner? Would this policy statement hold if you crafted it from the perspective of a private firm, rather than that of the government?

"Legalistic" Versus "Moralistic"

Another way to consider the differences between law and morality is by noting the connotations of the words *legalistic* and *moralistic*—terms that suggest the essence of law and morality carried to the position of demands rather than guidelines. The very word *legalistic* suggests that laws can function in ways that are objectionably rigid, inflexible, and lifeless. Laws, because of the very ways in which they have become laws—namely, through an historical process that embodies the ideas of a slightly earlier group of persons—tend to be somewhat dated and unresponsive to the demands of a particular situation. That is only natural.

With morality, however, the situation is somewhat different. Morality is that set of social guidelines which we collectively regard as overriding in particular decisions. Thus, unless we are dealing with a morality that has itself become "legalistic," we might expect our moral judgment to involve itself with the details of the particular situations we are confronting at the time.

That is, it is possible for our moral principles to change and evolve as we are faced with new situations that require moral decisions. Thus, our moral decisions can, in principle, be timely and flexible in a way that our legal decisions cannot be.

This advantage of morality over law, however, carries with it a disadvantage: namely, that we may be tempted to change, revise, or "improve" our moral principles in the light of specific situations—but in ways that are actually short-sighted or self-serving. In some sense, we have the freedom to do this (because of the nature of morality), but this freedom carries with it the temptation to abuse it.

The word *moralistic* has a different, though related, connotation. It not only suggests a morality (or a moral agent) that has become legalistic in nature, but it also suggests that morality itself can be practiced in a way that leads to disharmony rather than harmony in a person or society. Morality can be interpreted in narrow and rigid ways (it is this feature of morality that gives rise to such comments as the one quoted in the Introduction: "Moral talk is often rather repugnant"). Since morality is admittedly one of the ways in which we try to influence each other's behavior, and since it differs from law in being "administered" informally rather than by empowered groups such as legislatures and courts, there is always the potential for a particular expression of morality to be short-sighted or even harmful. But this is just to say that not every viewpoint that adopts the name "moral" for itself is worth accepting. Reasons must be given for accepting or rejecting a particular moral viewpoint.

Our focus on the dangers of a legalistic or a moralistic view are in line with the fourth goal that we set out in the Introduction. That goal is *to tolerate moral disagreement and ambiguity.* Conflict is rarely resolved by mere quoting of our interpretation of a rule. Quoting rules is simply a form of called Ordinary Communication (see Chapter 1). Ordinary Communication rarely resolves ethical conflicts since it concentrates more on speaking to rather than listening to the other party. A higher form of communication, based on dialogue rather than the monologue of Ordinary Communication, may be called for to resolve conflicts. This would entail a reflective rather than a customary approach to morality. Such an approach means analyzing the spirit as well as the letter of the law. It also reinforces the point that we should look at the reasoning behind an act as well as the act itself when we make a moral evaluation of another person's behavior.

Ethical Versus Legal Analysis

One further point needs to be made about the issues of law and morality: the cases collected in this text are not intended to be examples of criminal behavior. That is, you are not asked to read these cases to search for instances in which the letter of the law has been violated. That might be an appropriate task in a casebook on business law or business crime,[7] but our concern here is with the moral or ethical choices that people in business are called upon to make. There are, of course, points of overlap between morality and law (such as their common rejection of murder). Our point is simply that we presuppose in this book that most of the persons whose behavior is described in the cases saw themselves as operating within the framework of the law.

To be sure, it is not always easy to determine whether a particular action is within the boundaries of what is legally permissible. The law is complex and borderline cases may be unclear even to legal experts. Again, these are not the sort of problems to which this text is addressed. Rather, we assume that the business behavior reported in each of the cases is legal.[8]

Since laws are written by human beings, there are frequently ambiguities or other imperfections in the way they are worded. Loopholes in laws or policies are sometimes intentional, sometimes accidental. At times, however, it is possible to determine the underlying purpose of the original author(s) of the law—the goal or spirit that gave rise to the law in the first place. It may well be possible to obey the law as it is literally written without acting in harmony at all with its underlying purpose: for example, one may claim lavish and unnecessary business entertainment as a tax deduction.

It might even be suggested that morality itself can be identified with the spirit of the law; that is, behind the formal, codified laws of a society lie the informal, moral values that the laws in some way attempt to express (as, for example, the spirit of "fair play" might underlie Act 250 described in the Pyramid case at the end of this chapter). We now need to turn to a further consideration of one of the basic approaches to morality itself—rule deontology.

Another Look at Deontologism

In the Introduction, we briefly defined the type of ethical theory known as *deontologism*. This type of theory claims that there are moral duties or obligations that somehow are basic and that cannot be simply reduced to an underlying obligation to bring about the best results or consequences. We also distinguished between *pure* deontologism (which holds the view that consequences have nothing to do with the morality of an action) and *mixed* deontologism (which holds the view that consequences are one factor but not the only one determining the morality of an action). It is now necessary to distinguish between *act* deontologism and *rule* deontologism—a distinction that can be made within either pure or mixed deontological theories. The basic issue raised by this new distinction is whether we are to regard rules as somehow fundamental in our moral decisionmaking (which is the view of the rule deontologist) or whether we are to make our moral decisions by focusing only on the nature of the act before us (as the act deontologist recommends).

Rule Deontologism

The rule deontologist urges us to formulate a basic moral rule (or set of rules) that is not simply based on bringing about the best possible consequences (which would be the approach of the consequentialist). As might be expected, different candidates have been proposed for this rule (or set of rules). Two popular ethical theories are good examples of rule deontology: the Divine Command Theory and the theory of W. D. Ross.

The Divine Command Theory consists of one basic rule: "Obey the will of God." Since it makes no overt reference to bringing about the best possible consequences for anyone, it is an example of a so-called *pure* rule deontologism. The important point for our purposes is that the Divine Command Theory provides a rule or principle that we may use in making moral decisions. Fundamentally, it provides just one such rule—although if God's will is expressed through some further rules (the Ten Commandments, for example), there will be a plurality of rules at another, less basic level. Deontological theories that are based on one fundamental rule are sometimes referred to as *monistic rule deontologies*. Other monistic rule deontologies are fairly common as well. Examples include an ethical principle based on the Golden Rule and the ethical theory of Immanuel Kant, the latter of which is based on the so-called "Categorical Imperative" (explained in Chapter 6). The crucial point is that systems of ethics exist that are based on one fundamental rule or principle; this rule need not simply tell us to "seek the greatest good for the greatest number."

The ethical theory of W. D. Ross exemplifies the type of view called *pluralistic rule deontologism*.[9] W. D. Ross held that all human beings have several prima facie duties (Ross's list of seven such duties was presented in the Introduction). Some of these duties are based on bringing about good consequences; some are independent of consequences. In other words, while some of the rules of duty that Ross holds are tempered by consequences, others are in the form of pure obligations or are deontological in nature. That is, Ross's version of a pluralistic rule deontologism is an example of *mixed* rather than *pure* deontologism.

But the real question is whether anything of importance for business situations follows from our suggested taxonomy of ethical theories. We have drawn several immediate conclusions: First, since there is a variety of competing theories of ethics, we need to examine several theories critically to trace their possible implications for business—rather than concentrate on only one such theory. Second, whether or not attention to consequences is essential to ethical decisionmaking is a question that must be faced in our thinking about ethics and values. Deontological theories that attempt to be "pure" run the risk of leaving out this critical factor in business decisions. Yet, most of us experienced some exposure to rule deontology in childhood as part of our formative training. Vestiges of that training and its component rules are likely to linger in our subconscious through at least the initial stages of our business careers. Thus, rule deontology should not be dismissed when we evaluate business decisions. Third, forms of rule deontology that employ only one rule face the problem of winning general acceptance for that particular rule. Fourth, on the surface at least, the pluralistic forms of rule deontology, such as Ross's, face the problem of internal conflict between the several rules proposed by the particular system. Each of these issues is relevant to cases throughout this book.

Act Deontologism

In contrast to proponents of rule deontologism, act deontologists deny that rules are fundamental in making moral decisions. Some act deontologists reject the use of rules altogether. The French existentialist Jean-Paul Sartre defended this position. Sartre denied that any general rules could be validly used in ethics. Instead, wrote Sartre, the only correct moral advice that can be given is the following: "You're free, choose, that is, invent [your own resolution for each conflict]."[10] Ethics is similar to art, Sartre thought, in that both depend on creativity rather than on the use of rules.

Other act deontologists, however, allow the use of some nonfundamental "guidelines" or "rules of thumb." One such act deontologist was the British philosopher E. F. Carritt. Carritt held that one's own intuitive judgment of a situation was fundamental in ethical decisionmaking. Although moral rules are not fundamental according to Carritt, they do have a (limited) role to play in ethics. The rules function as "ballast rather than compass."[11] In other words, forming some ethical generalizations or guidelines, based on our past judgments or intuitions, can steady the ship of our life amidst the storms of temptation. In a sense, such an act deontologist is urging us to focus on the spirit of the law rather than on the letter.

One may well wonder whether Sartre's advice to just "choose" would be of much practical help in business ethics. Note, however, that Sartre also reminded his followers that they were responsible for their choices. Carritt's metaphor of moral rules as "ballast," however, seems clearly applicable to business situations; formulating and remembering such rules may well have good practical consequences. What might be doubted about both of these versions of act deontology is whether they offer enough content for basing one's moral decisions. After all, neither makes any mention of the moral worth of benefiting oneself, one's group (or firm), or even humans generally. Perhaps such theories are too subjective to be completely satisfactory in the social world of business decisionmaking. Despite the occasionally helpful points made by the act deontologists, perhaps the rule deontologists have more to offer for our present purposes.

Law and Order

A general understanding of deontological theories might suggest that they simply provide certain moral "laws" that their holders blindly follow. This understanding would interpret such theories as examples of Lawrence Kohlberg's Fourth Stage of moral development. It seems likely that those who stress the importance of adhering to the letter of the law when conflicts involving business values arise—rather than considering the spirit, intentions, or purpose behind the law—are comfortable with Stage Four reasoning (the so-called *law and order* stage). At this stage, according to Kohlberg and his associates:

Right is doing one's duty in society, upholding the social order, and the welfare of society or the group. Hence one is obligated to fulfill the actual duties to which one has agreed. Laws are to be upheld except in extreme cases where they conflict with other fixed social duties. Right is also contributing to society, the group, or institutions. . . .The reasons for doing right are to keep the institution going as a whole ("what if everyone did it?"), or self-respect or conscience seen as meeting one's defined obligations.[12]

Conclusions

As is the case with those adopting a consequentialist Stage Two or Stage Three approach to morality, the adherents of deontological Stage Four reasoning engage in Strategic Communicative Action to try to resolve conflicts of interests. They are not hesitant to take an adversarial position in order to win arguments. They ground their position in the legitimate power of the law and in the need for the societal order that legal rules bring about. In the seventeenth century, Thomas Hobbes strongly advocated this approach to moral thinking. He viewed man as a selfish, social animal engaged in constant competition. Law, he argued, is the only means to bring about order in society.[13] However, the law can be abused by those who use their legitimate power for personal gains. Contemporary scholar Ding-Ho Wang cautions that in some societies (such as in China) having authority over others is the most important goal.[14]

Although Kohlberg holds that there is a natural tendency for persons to progress through the various moral stages as they develop, he also claims that moral development beyond this Fourth Stage is relatively rare in our society. If this is true, it would seem likely that most businesspersons would be operating at the conventional level of moral development (that is Stages Three or Four). It is also relevant to note that Kohlberg believes that it is difficult for a person whose moral reasoning is at one stage of development to be able to understand or appreciate the moral reasoning of a person at a higher stage. Thus, a person priding himself or herself on adherence to the letter of the law might fail to see the point of another person who is urging that the spirit of the law be taken into account. A stress on the spirit of the law would be characteristic of moral reasoning at Kohlberg's stages Five and Six.

Whether Kohlberg is correct in claiming that stages Five and Six are somehow objectively "higher" or "better" than Stage Four is a question to be considered throughout this text. It is, nonetheless, a question you might ask yourself in reading the present chapter.

Those who adopt a Stage Four approach to morality are likely to be: (1) more motivated by maintaining order within the society than by personal gain, (2) more motivated by rules established by the political community than by consequences for themselves or their reference group, and (3) more motivated by deontological norms in the form of concrete duties than by universal principles. Societal well-being, in their eyes, is restricted to the welfare of those residing in the same nation state. If their ethical creed could be condensed into a single sentence, it would be: "What is legal is ethical, and what is ethical is legal."

Resolving conflict with those who use Stage Four reasoning calls for a type of Discursive Communication. The goal of that communication is to find a common ground by examining each party's principles. Stage Four people seek order in society and respect law as a means for maintaining order. The task then is to mutually examine positions, other than the one held by the Stage Four person, to see if order is maintained or even improved by any of the alternatives.

In reading the cases in this chapter, you are invited to keep several other general questions in mind:

1. To what extent can you identify the spirit or purpose behind the relevant laws or moral principles in each case?

2. To what extent did the various participants actually follow this spirit or purpose?

3. How do you suggest that conflicts between the letter and spirit of the law be resolved?

❖   Case Study 4–1   ❖

SEABROOK

Eighteen years and $6 billion after it was first proposed as an alternative source of electrical power for the New England power grid, the Seabrook Station nuclear power plant in New Hampshire came on line. On hand for the opening were hundreds of angry protesters.

Local residents and environmental groups had fought against the project from the beginning. Seabrook residents had rejected the Public Service Company's proposal for a nuclear plant by a vote of 768 to 632. Governor Meldrim Thomson asked the New Hampshire Public Services Commission to override the vote, and construction began as scheduled. At that point, locals joined forces with anti-nuclear groups, calling themselves the Clamshell Alliance, to stage rallies outside the Seabrook site. One rally attracted 15,000 demonstrators.

Tempers flared, and accusations were leveled by both sides. On one side of the contest were representatives of the Public Service Company of New Hampshire, backed by government officials and union leaders. Businesses, angered by protests that they claimed cost them as much as one-half million dollars in lost sales, also sided with the utility. On the other side was a loose coalition of residents and environmental groups from all over New England.

According to Public Service Company officials, the proposed Seabrook plant was a natural outgrowth of the area's need for electrical power. The plant would offer benefits to the community's residents and businesses. New Hampshire law required that the proposed electric utility provide a steady supply of power in answer to the area's demands.

The law also required that power be provided at a reasonable cost. Nuclear power had been shown to have a decided cost advantage. According to a report on projected fuel costs for the area, nuclear power cost 1.34 cents less per kilowatt hour than coal, its closest competitor. This translated into savings of $100 per year for the average U.S. household.

The final requirement set out by New Hampshire law was that power be provided without undue adverse effects on the environment. The Public Service Company felt confident that Seabrook answered these concerns as well. Officials admitted that a break in the reactor coolant system could create a loss-of-coolant accident (LOCA) that would release radioactive material into the environment. However, they were quick to point out that the Seabrook plant was equipped with a number of different emergency cooling systems that could cool the reactor core in case of a LOCA. The plant also maintained emergency diesel generators in case of on-site power failures during an accident. Jim Casey of the Electrical Workers Local 490, which had 100 employees working at Seabrook, testified to the safety of the plant, stating: "The protesters can't relate one death to nuclear power in 15 years and that's a tough record to beat."

Environmental safety had also been taken into account. Although the company admitted that waste products from the nuclear process contained radioactive iodine, strontium, americium, radium, and plutonium, they pointed out that measures had been taken to eliminate the escape of these materials into the environment. All wastes were to be sealed in stainless steel cylinders and buried, keeping them safely contained for tens of thousands of years.

As an added benefit, Power Company officials pointed out that construction of the nuclear plant would lead to jobs and new industry at Seabrook. In spite of protests to halt production of the plant, workers and union leaders threw their support behind the project. As John Flynn, vice president of the International Brotherhood of Electrical Workers, said: "We've been accused of being selfish, of being only interested in jobs for New England. Well, I plead guilty, because what is a man without a useful job to perform? We need energy for industry and jobs and we favor nuclear energy because it's here and now."

While plant supporters claimed an abundant water supply for cooling the plant's condensers, protesters pointed to the near-critical water shortage in Seabrook created by the plant's construction demands of up to 300,000 gallons of water per day. As the plant siphoned off water at an alarming rate, residents were prohibited from watering their gardens or washing their cars.

Residents also disputed the Power Company's claim of reasonably priced power. The utility, unable to keep up with spiraling construction costs, had instituted a series of rate hikes that increased electricity prices from 17 to 29 percent. Then, the New Hampshire Public Services Commission tentatively granted seven years of 5.5 percent annual price rate hikes to help the company out. The company still experienced cost problems and had to file for protection from creditors under federal bankruptcy law.

While supporters of the project claimed that the plant could be operated safely and that they would have no objection to having a plant nearby, opponents argued that nuclear power poses the most critical threat to humans and the environment the world has ever faced. The disaster at Chernobyl offered clear proof that no system was ever really safe. The Attorney General of neighboring Massachusetts opposed the opening of the plant, believing that evacuation plans were inadequate if a nuclear accident were to occur.

In spite of the Power Company's claims that its method of storing radioactive wastes underground in steel cylinders eliminated the danger, protesters pointed out that leaks have been reported from such storage areas in quantities ranging from several gallons to several thousand gallons. Seepage into the ground water and the soil posed a threat not only to humans, but to plants and wildlife in the surrounding areas as well.

And radioactivity is not the only source of danger. The Clamshell Alliance argued that the process of cooling the plant's two reactors would dump more than a billion gallons of heated water per day into nearby lobster, clam, and other sea-life breeding grounds.

As a final argument, the Clamshell Alliance disputed the Power Company's claims that nuclear energy creates jobs. According to Harvey Wasserman, a spokesperson for the anti-nuclear movement, Seabrook would create only 200 permanent jobs, and even those were only secure for the 30 to 40 years of the plant's life.

Questions

1. Under what circumstances do you believe a governor can override a locality's vote? Should the grounds for such an override, if you think that there are grounds, be based on obligations or consequences?
2. Would those favoring the Seabrook plant's opening be ethically bound to support the opening of a nuclear power plant under similar environmental circumstances in their own towns?
3. Which of the arguments presented by both sides to the conflict most influenced the ethical dimension of your decision about Seabrook?

Sources

Bruce Beckley, "Nuclear Wastes: Questions and Answers" (Public Service Company of New Hampshire, 1972).

William M. Bulkeley, "New Hampshire agency prods utilities in other states to lift stake in Seabrook," *The Wall Street Journal* (January 13, 1983), 10.

Helen Caldicott, "Medical Implications of Nuclear Power" (Knoxville, TN: Volunteers for Clean Energy, 1978).

Doina Chiacu, "NRC grants Seabrook operating license," *Scottsdale Arizona Progress* (March 2, 1990), 11.

Herbert S. Dennenberg, "Nuclear power: uninsurable," *The Progressive* (January 1974), 2–3.

Richard Grossman and Gail Danckev, *Guide to Jobs and Energy* (Washington: Environmentalists for Full Employment, 1977).

Keith H. Hammonds, "A utility runs out of juice," *Business Week* (August 24, 1989), 26.

Lawrence Ingrassia and Cynthia S. Grisdela, "Seabrook plant gets NRC nod for full power," *The Wall Street Journal* (March 2, 1990), A4.

Lawrence Ingrassia and Barbara Rosewicz, "Seabrook plant clears last big hurdle as U.S. safety panel gives its blessing," *The Wall Street Journal* (November 14, 1989), A2.

Michael Kenney, "Jobs and energy are their concerns," *Boston Globe* (June 26, 1978), 21.

Tony Pearson, "Workers rally for Seabrook," *Boston Globe* (June 26, 1978), 21.

"P.S., New Hampshire proposal on rates is cleared by state," *The Wall Street Journal* (November 17, 1989), A9.

"Seabrook official fired after plant shutdown," *Atlanta Journal and Constitution* (July 1, 1989), A15.

Seabrook '78: A Handbook For the Occupation/Restoration (Portsmouth, NH: Clamshell Alliance, 1978).

"Seabrook utility faces bankruptcy after mass layoffs," *Atlanta Constitution* (April 20, 1984), 5-A.

Harvey Wasserman, "Nukes and jobs," *New Age* (1978), 32.

Yankee Ingenuity: Nuclear Energy in New England (Public Service Company of New Hampshire, 1987).

❖   Case Study 4–2   ❖

SARKIS SOGHNALIAN

Sarkis Soghnalian is a Lebanese citizen who resides in the Miami area. His is a business success story. He is married to an American, owns an expensive home, and has enjoyed an annual income in the millions. Soghnalian also had an office in Beirut, Lebanon from which he conducted part of his business. That office was manned by personnel who appeared equipped to deal with intruders. This security was necessary given the nature of Soghnalian's business. He is an arms dealer.

Soghnalian refers to himself as a purveyor of defense equipment. As the Middle East representative of Colt's firearms, he held an export license from the United States. The State Department worried, however, when Soghnalian attempted to export 2000 revolvers to Lebanon. The death rate caused by internal strife might be exacerbated by the delivery of the weapons. Soghnalian claimed that the fear was unjustified. He stated that Lebanese law prohibited the sale of weapons to any party other than the government.

At that time, Les Aspin, then a member of the Congressional Armed Services Committee, expressed reservations about the revolver deal. Soghnalian retorted that Mr. Aspin was not really aware of the situation in Lebanon and should direct his attention to more pressing problems within the United States.

Soghnalian admitted that he was not always objective when making arms deals, but that he would never sell his personal dignity. While he stated that he would not break Lebanese law, Soghnalian did admit that he would be flexible in his approach to it. Still, he claimed that to stay in business he could not afford to make an enemy of the Lebanese government.

His firm, United Industries, typically took a 20 percent commission on the arms deals that Soghnalian arranged. His deals involved far more than revolvers. Patrol boats, intelligence equipment, helicopters, and rocket launchers all came under his purview. His operating philosophy was simple. He tried to meet the needs of his clients.

He expressed contempt for the arms merchants who came to Lebanon expecting quick profits. Connections that were built up over time and patience were what it took to be a success. His stated belief was that "trust and reputation mean everything in this business." What he didn't like was the publicity that his business was attracting in the media. The publicity, he thought, would either harm his buyers or offend his buyers' enemies when they learned of the purchase. Publicity was bad for business.

What gained him international publicity were his arms deals with Iraq. Before the Gulf War that brought forth Operation Desert Storm, the United States covertly supported Iraq in its border dispute with Iran. Open support was difficult because of an embargo on arms sales to the warring countries.

One of his transactions involved two former members of Richard Nixon's administration. They were John Mitchell, former Attorney General, and John Brennan, a retired colonel who once had served as a military advisor to President Nixon. Mitchell and Brennan's company, Global Research International, was based in Washington, D.C. This company contracted to sell uniforms to Iraq through Soghnalian prior to the Gulf War.

Although the uniform deal went through, the relationship between Global Research and United Industries soured. Global Research claimed that Soghnalian used $7 million of the $8.7 million commission that Global Research was to receive to settle a past debt with Saddam Hussein. Soghnalian countered that he owed Global Research nothing. Reconciliation must have occurred since Global Research used Soghnalian two years later during the Reagan administration for another deal with Iraq.

This second transaction saw Global Research selling twenty-six helicopters through Soghnalian to Iraq. In the previous year, Soghnalian facilitated the sale of another forty-five helicopters to Iraq. The Reagan administration had approved that sale on the condition that the aircraft were to be used by Iraq's Agriculture Ministry. The helicopters were, however, large enough to carry troops.

The sale of the twenty-six helicopters again caused a misunderstanding about Global Research's commission for the deal. John Mitchell wrote to Soghnalian, requesting quick payment of the $500,000 commission. Soghnalian's attitude toward the principals of Global Research was not especially positive. Some disparaging comments about their motives came forward—words suggesting that they might sell their family members if a profit could be realized.

Later, during the Bush administration, a question arose concerning the use of weapons, supplied by Soghnalian, against the United States in Operation Desert Storm. Documents confirm Soghnalian's claim that he had worked on the behalf of U.S. intelligence agencies in his deals with Iraq. Those documents also confirm that the government knew about his military transactions with Iraq and approved of supplying Iraq with weapons.

When he was asked about his business with Iraq after the invasion of Kuwait, Soghnalian proclaimed his innocence. He stated that although Iraq had approached him about breaking the 1990 embargo, he refused. He said he would not act against U.S. policy: "I'm staying away 100 percent now because I don't want to supply them with nothing—no spare parts, or nothing, no vehicles, no shoes, no clothes, no nothing—because that will support the enemy of today. A friend of yesterday is an enemy of today."

Questions

1. Do you think it ethical to defy an international embargo in order to pursue our national interests?
2. Sarkis Soghnalian's comments about respecting U.S. and Lebanese law seem to represent a stage of moral reasoning. Are his actions consistent with his words?
3. Whose well-being is enhanced by the actions of Global Research International? What stage(s) of moral reasoning do you project onto the principals of that company?

Sources

"All the ex-president's men," *U.S. News and World Report* (June 4, 1990), 40.

"Desert conflict may favor Iraq's 'simple' weapons," *Atlanta Journal and Constitution* (January 25, 1991), A6.

Anita Evans, "The caution of a mideast arms dealer," *The Washington Post* (July 28, 1975), A20.

Antonio N. Fins, "'Sunny South Florida' Where the Guns Are," *Business Week* (September 3, 1990), 42, 44.

Stephen J. Hedges and David Lyons, "Miami arms dealer indicted," *Miami Herald* (December 3, 1987), E3.

Robert L. Jackson, "Arms supplier for Iraq sees prolonged war," *Los Angeles Times* (January 24, 1991), A10.

Steve Kroft, "The Man Who Armed Iraq," CBS News: *60 Minutes*, January 20, 1991.

"One-stop shopping," *U.S. News and World Report* (October 7, 1991), 19.

✤   Case Study 4–3   ✤

Pyramid Companies

Burlington, Vermont had received $15 million in federal government grants to restore its downtown area. The old port at the edge of Lake Champlain used its grant money wisely, by the look of the quaint boutiques in the restored shopping area. But Burlington's tranquility came under siege. One of the country's largest mall developers, Pyramid Companies, sought to build a shopping center in the suburbs of the city.

Pyramid, a New York-based firm, wished to build a 400,000-square-foot shopping center in neighboring Williston. Williston had 4400 residents while the population of Burlington totaled 38,000. The 72-store mall would have more shopping space than existed in all of downtown Burlington. Preliminary estimates indicated that Burlington would lose 40 percent of its retail sales to the mall. Tax collections to meet the city's budget demands would be severely affected.

After a year of debate within the township of Williston, a referendum was passed to approve the mall. A projected 30 percent cut in Williston's property taxes influenced voters in the small town—a town that had no full-time police or fire department. The results of the referendum did not deter the mall's opponents in Burlington. They sought protection under Act 250—a state environmental law passed to deter unwanted economic development.

District commissions had been set up in Vermont to evaluate the environmental impact of large-scale land development projects. The city of Burlington, along with environmental groups, expressed opposition to the mall to the area's district commission.

The governor, Richard Snelling, also became involved. He appointed a special review committee to assess the state's interests in the case. He even hired consultants, using government funds, to aid in the assessment. The opposition had been trying to raise funds, up to the time of the governor's decision, for the same purpose. The governor stressed that his actions should not be interpreted as opposition to the Williston mall.

The District Environmental Commission studied the evidence and ruled against the mall. The commission did compliment Pyramid, however, on its plans for landscaping, water use, and energy conservation. Governor Snelling applauded the commission's decision. Under its broad definition of the environment, the commission ruled that the mall would have a negative impact on neighboring Burlington by stunting its natural growth and by causing injury to its social fabric. The commission appeared to be strongly influenced by the mall's projected traffic congestion as well. Pyramid had agreed to fund some of the road improvements needed to alleviate the projected congestion, but the commission believed that the congestion that would result on other routes would cost the government more than the value of benefits brought to the area by the mall.

Another report estimated that an additional 5 million gallons of gas would be used annually by area people to go to the mall. This would constitute a waste of energy. Pyramid had argued that any assessment of energy use should be confined to that used to develop the mall. The firm further wondered how gasoline usage could negatively influence the decision since the state actively encouraged visitors to drive through Vermont and enjoy its natural beauty. The firm also questioned whether Act 250, which was passed to limit the exploitation of the environment by ski resorts and condominiums (servicing out-of-state visitors), appropriately applied to mall development.

Robert Congel, the majority partner in the Pyramid Companies, is nothing if not determined. After ten years, Congel's Pyramid tried Williston again, this time with Ben Frank, a Vermont resident, as a partner. But the opposition was still there. Burlington's mayor Bernard Sanders claimed that the mall would cause both traffic and pollution. He called the fight over the mall "the most significant development battle in the history of Vermont— that threatens to destroy our way of life." Ben Frank countered that Burlington officials were "opposed to competition. . . .They've had it all to themselves forever." He pointed out that the mall would provide convenience and easy access. He also noted that half of the 75 acres were reserved for maple trees. Frank claimed that the mall would not be the first construction in the area since it would be placed next to an interstate highway. It also would create 1000 jobs. Critics, however, pointed out that most of the new jobs would pay only minimum wage.

The current governor, Madeline Kunin, seemed to carry forward ex-Governor Snelling's feelings about the "total" environment in Vermont. She proposed a law "to give neighboring towns a voice in regulating large developments." Mayor Sanders, the only socialist mayor in the United States, portrayed the controversy as pitting "private greed versus social responsibility." What the mayor did not mention was that an estimated $31 million in annual retail sales would be drawn away from Burlington by the mall. Mayor Sanders feared that Pyramid would plough money into the campaign funds of candidates for government office who would favor the mall. This is what the firm was accused of doing in Poughkeepsie, New York. "Where they don't like what local government does, they buy local government," warned Mayor Sanders. "They bought Poughkeepsie—they are a somewhat ruthless corporation."

Questions

1. Define societal well-being according to the views of Ben Frank, Bernard Sanders, and Richard Snelling.
2. Evaluate, from a moral perspective, the decisionmaking process of the District Commission applying the standards of Act 250.
3. How does the title of this chapter apply to this case?

Sources

"A law that prevents economic disruption," *Business Week* (October 30, 1978), 38.

"A pall over the suburban mall," *Time* (November 13, 1978), 118–119.

"Developers keep on building," *Chain Store Age Executive* (May 1990), 52, 54, 59.

Randy Fitzgerald, "The job that gave me a future," *Reader's Digest* (July 1990), 109, 110.

Roberta Brandes Gratz, "Malling the northeast," *The New York Times Magazine* (April 1, 1990), 35, 54, 58, 59.

Sam Hemingway, "Negotiating traffic projections Pyramid's biggest challenge," *Burlington Free Press* (October 22, 1978).

Howard Katz, "The mall versus the meadow," *The Washington Post* (National Weekly Edition: June 20–26, 1988), 9.

Nick Marbo, "State," *Times-Argus* (Barre, VT, August 3, 1977), 3.

Christopher Owen, "Pyramid spurns fuel-use findings, *Times-Argus* (Barre, VT, February 6, 1978), p. 1.

Jeffrey A. Trachtenberg, "Five Bonwit stores are slated for sale to mall developer," *The Wall Street Journal* (March 7, 1990), C13.

Notes to Chapter 4

[1]Luigi Bagolini, "Value judgments in ethics and in law," *Philosophical Quarterly* 1 (October 1951), 423–432.

[2]Second Corinthians 3:6. This quotation from St. Paul is probably the original source for the now-familiar contrast between the letter and spirit—despite the fact that the context of the quotation (as well as modern translations) suggests that it is not the "spirit of the law" that St. Paul had in mind but rather the "Holy Spirit."

[3]The best analysis of this issue known to us is contained in Lief Carter, *Reason in Law* (Boston: Little Brown, 1979), pp. 104–165.

[4]Thomas Aquinas, *Summa Theologica*, trans. by Fathers of the English Dominican Province (London: Burns Oates & Washburn, Ltd., 1927), Part II., vol 8, p 5.

[5]Nicholas Ember and Robert Hogan, "Moral Psychology and Public Policy," in William M. Kurtines and Jacob Gewirtz (eds.), *Handbook of Moral Behavior and Development* (Hillsdale, NJ: Lawrence Erlbaum Associates, 1991), vol. 3.

[6]Trevor Gambling and Rifaat Abdel Karim, *Business and Accounting Ethics in Islam* (London: Mansell Publishing, Limited, 1991).

[7]An interesting analysis of business behavior outside the boundaries of what is legal is found in John E. Conklin, *"Illegal But Not Criminal:" Business Crime in America* (Englewood Cliffs, NJ: Prentice-Hall, Inc., 1977). In addition to his analysis of the subject, Conklin provides details of a number of business crimes that led to the conviction of the persons involved.

[8]So far as we know, none of the business actions or practices reported in our cases has actually been found in court to be illegal. But even if a particular action had been found to be illegal, the context of the business values in which it took place would still merit discussion.

[9]W. D. Ross, *The Right and the Good* (Oxford: The Clarendon Press, 1930).

[10]Jean-Paul Sartre, *Existentialism*, trans. by Bernard Frechtman (New York: Philosophical Library, 1947), p. 33.

[11]E. F. Carritt, *The Theory of Morals* (London: Oxford University Press, 1952), p. 115.

[12]Ann Colby et al., *Moral Stages and Their Scoring* (Cambridge, MA: Center for Moral Education, 1980), Part I, p. 25, Table 2.

[13]Thomas Hobbes, *Leviathan, The Second Part* (London: Collier Books, 1969), Chapter 16 (first published in 1651).

[14]Ding-Ho Wang, cited in Boye Lafayette De Mente, *Chinese Etiquette and Ethics in Business* (Lincolnwood, IL: N.T.C. Business Books, 1989).

Chapter 5

Costs / Benefits

Chapters 5 and 6 focus on what has been labeled *postconventional moral reasoning*. Postconventional decisions are freely made; the individual does not feel captive to coercion, reward, group pressure, or law. At the preconventional level of morality (Stages One and Two), the person concentrates on himself or herself, without much regard for anyone else. At the conventional level of moral development (Stages Three and Four), ethical reasoning is strongly influenced by reference group values or legal rules. At the postconventional level, the interests of both the individual and others combine to influence decisions. The individual, when attempting to resolve conflict, acts on personal principles that will benefit others as members of society, apart from their status as members of a reference group or particular political entity. This action embodies the concept of mutuality that was mentioned briefly in Chapter 2.

Determining what is good for people often results in a weighing of costs versus benefits. Not only is the general decision technique known as *cost/benefit analysis* widely used and taught in the business world, but it is a mainstay of decisionmaking in everyday life as well. If we wish to be rational in assessing the best choice open to us in a particular situation, how else should we go about our assessment but by comparing the ratio of costs to benefits of the various options before us? As consumers, for example, we might well choose a particular brand of personal computer because it offers the "best value for the money"—that is, even though a different machine might offer more storage capacity and even though some other machine might be cheaper, the model we should rationally prefer would be the one with the best overall "score" when both the cost and the benefits are taken into account. Yet this apparently "obvious" principle for making choices has been frequently called into question when applied to certain types of business decisions. Ford discovered this when it tried to balance the cost of extra safety equipment against the potential cost of an accident involving its Pinto model. Our goal in this chapter is to help disentangle several of the major issues in this dispute.

Beyond "Law and Order"

At Stage Five in Kohlberg's scheme of moral development, the individual seeks to look beyond and behind the existing laws to discern the reasons for having laws at all. Societal well-being has a broader meaning for the Stage Five adherent than it does for those who use the reasoning processes of Stages One through Four. Society is not limited to individuals, firms, or political jurisdictions, but is defined as all those people affected by the conflict to be resolved. At Stage Five, according to Kohlberg, what is right

> . . . .is upholding the basic rights, values, and legal contracts of a society, even when they conflict with the concrete rules and laws of this society. Hence there is an awareness that people hold a variety of values and opinions and that most values and rules are relative to a specific group. Because they constitute the social contract, these "relative" rules should usually be upheld. However, some non-relative values and rights like *life* and *liberty* must be upheld in any society regardless of majority opinion. . .[Persons at Stage Five] are concerned that laws and duties be based on rational calculation of overall utility, "the greatest good for the greatest number." [1]

If Kohlberg is correct about moral development, basing one's moral decisionmaking on a concern for "the greatest good for the greatest number" is an advance over obeying the law simply because it is a law. If one performs an act that violates the letter of the law, the onus is on that person to show why that act enhances societal well-being. As opposed to the formal legal assumption that a person is innocent until proven guilty, in ethical considerations the person who breaks the law is "guilty" until he or she provides adequate justification for the Stage Five action. If, for example, a person employed by an aerospace firm working on a government missile delivery system signed a secrecy agreement about his or her work, we would expect that individual to honor the agreement. But if that same employee were asked to construct a container that would hold a deadly plague virus to be carried in the missile, would it be ethically acceptable for the employee to expose this assignment to the press? Perhaps, but the burden of explanation and justification would lie on the individual's shoulders. If the employee speaks out and breaks the agreement, he or she would be labeled a whistleblower.

Revealing information that is likely to be embarrassing to the organization for which you work is thus generally referred to as *whistleblowing*. Whistleblowers act out of values that they believe are higher or more important to society as a whole than the value of being a team player. In this sense, whistleblowers act in direct opposition to the group-conformity characteristics that mark Stage Three of moral development. And, since they often risk blame or punishment for their actions (at least from their superiors within the firm—and often from their peers as well), whistleblowers typically are not acting in accordance with Stages One or Two.[2] The circumstances of the particular case determine whether the whistleblower's level of development is at Stage Four, Five, or Six.

To test the ethical defensibility of their position before going public with damaging information, potential whistleblowers might want to ask the following questions:

1. Is what they want their firm to do feasible?
2. Is their firm doing something that is not consistent with its stated goals?
3. Have superiors in the firm been questioned about their behavior sufficiently so that the whistleblowers are reasonably sure that they have all the relevant information?

Problems with Postconventional Reasoning

In a related sense, is ignorance an adequate justification for doing social harm? Kurtines has found in his studies that most people can discern the difference between right and wrong in simple situations by the age of fifteen.[3] Right and wrong in such cases would refer to acts that would, prima facie, benefit or harm others. But what about complicated situations? It would sound innocent to present the claims that "I didn't intend to have that happen," "I honestly didn't consider that alternative," or "I just didn't know." But does ignorance ethically excuse acts that bring about harmful consequences? Plato, in the *Republic*, claimed that ignorance is an aspect of evil since it is the opposite of "Being." Using Plato's line of thought, the right to make normative comments implies a responsibility not to speak from ignorance.

Reflect on the first sentence of Chapter 1, which stated that businesspeople sometimes do bad things for good reasons. A Stage Five person identifies with that statement. But are good intentions enough? Michael Kinsley observed that "Virtually every time someone is described as having 'good' or 'noble' or 'best of' intentions, that person is about to be accused of doing something wrong."[4] The message is that good intentions often go awry and inhibit rather than enhance societal well-being.

Another problem is in the difficulty of sticking to Stage Five moral reasoning. Kohlberg found that no more than one-fourth of us reason at the postconventional level of moral judgment. Even that figure might be too high. Subsequent research has shown that, depending on the pressures of the situation, people have a tendency to revert to lower stages of moral reasoning.[5]

Stage Five behavior implies rights as well as correlative responsibilities. If one goes beyond or against the traditional moral norm in the name of individual autonomous rights, it is his or her concurrent responsibility to reasonably justify his or her actions in terms of enhancing societal rather than personal (Stage Two) well-being. This is the obligation under the social contract of justice that allows such behavior. That justifying explanation is a sign of respect for the system of societal justice in operation. David Gauthier claims that a close reading of Plato, Hobbes, and Locke reveals that each of these philosophers advocated a social-contract approach to morality. The social contract, he further claims, may be the basis from which moral principles may be derived.[6] To think about ethics in this way is to apply a principle or a set of principles to one's views about morality—which leads us to the ethical theory of utilitarianism.

Utilitarianism: Its Appeal

Just as an informal sort of cost/benefit analysis is a common decision procedure in everyday life, thinking along utilitarian lines is fairly common in moral decisions. Some scholars believe that utilitarianism is the most defensible approach to ethics. Certainly, the catch phrases associated with utilitarianism are frequently heard in moral discussions: "The greatest good for the greatest number," "The greatest balance of pleasure over pain," "The best thing to do under the circumstances." It is possible, of course, that such phrases are largely "window dressing"—an attempt to mask a basically self-centered or company-centered orientation that might lead to negative public reaction if it were openly expressed. But it is also possible that such phrases are sincere expressions of the way in which a given person reasons about moral issues. To put this type of moral reasoning into proper prospective, however, we need to become more precise in our terminology.

Utilitarianism, in the broadest and most general sense, is the view that what is morally right or wrong is determined entirely by the consequences that an action has for everyone affected by it. In other words, utilitarianism is simply the general name for the universal form of what the Introduction to this text called *consequentialist* or *teleological* theories of ethics. If an action brings about a greater balance of good over evil consequences than any other action that is open to the agent, then that action is morally right. The question does arise, however, as to whether the greatest balance of good over evil is equivalent to the greatest good for the greatest number. The utilitarian differs from other consequentialists or teleologists by insisting that the consequences for everyone affected must be considered—and be considered equally. In contrast, other consequentialist theories, such as egoism, limit their consideration to the benefits accruing to specific people or groups. The appeal of utilitarianism, according to James Wallace, "lies in its promise to provide for the humane, tough-minded individual a way of resolving complex moral problems and disagreements by rational means."[7]

Not only does utilitarianism contrast with egoism and the other restricted teleological theories, but it also contrasts with what might be called *traditional* or *conventional* morality. The eighteenth-century British philosopher Jeremy

Bentham was particularly vigorous in defending utilitarianism by ridiculing the usual moral thinking of his day. Non-utilitarian moral reasoning, claims Bentham, is either utilitarianism in disguise (that is, some theory in which the consequences for all are the real basis for decision while avoiding the term *utilitarianism*) or reasoning based on what Bentham calls "the principle of sympathy and antipathy." A holder of this latter principle approves or disapproves of particular actions not because of their consequences, but simply because of whatever feelings of approval or disapproval the person happens to find in himself or herself. Such feelings in themselves are claimed to be sufficient reasons for one's moral judgment. Since the holder of the principle of sympathy and antipathy needs only to consult inner feelings, rather than the results that an action is likely to have, this theory has the appeal of being simpler and easier to apply than utilitarianism. In Bentham's view, when people say that they base their moral convictions on "common sense," "a moral sense," "the fitness of things," "the law of nature," or similar phrases, they are usually basing their convictions on mere subjective feelings. The special phrases that they use when talking about their views are simply, according to Bentham, "so many contrivances for avoiding the obligation of appealing to any external standard, and for prevailing upon the reader to accept the author's sentiment or opinion as a reason for itself."[8]

To put it as straightforwardly as possible: the reason why Bentham and so many others prefer the theory of utilitarianism to the alternatives is that utilitarianism seems to offer a relatively clear, simple, and objective way of settling moral questions—a way that is, in principle at least, free from the dominance of mere tradition, prejudice, or personal whim. This general and impersonal method of moral decisionmaking does not presuppose any particular political or religious beliefs. It is a theory that everyone, in principle, might someday come to share in common. It provides us with the one plausible means for settling moral disputes between persons. The adoption of utilitarianism as our theory of ethics is, according to Bentham, the one best way to achieving widespread human happiness. If Bentham is correct, our search for an adequate theory is ended.

Difficulties with Utilitarianism

Theorists have offered many reasons for rejecting utilitarianism. For example, if Kohlberg is correct about the evolution of moral development, persons at lower stages of moral reasoning will be unable to "see the point" of those ethical theories that characterize higher stages than their own. The person whose moral thinking revolves entirely around the question of whether he or she will be punished by those in authority is unlikely to appreciate how "the greatest good for the greatest number" could be so important in the thinking of convinced utilitarians. In other words, to oversimplify a bit, the egoist, the conformist, and the traditional follower of "law and order" may all find utilitarianism confusing and threatening—and will, therefore, reject it for these reasons. If they are steadfast in their reasoning, can an appeal to utilitarian logic suffice to resolve conflicts with them over moral issues?

Also, some suspicions about utilitarianism have stemmed from simple misunderstandings rather than from some individuals' levels of moral development. It is sometimes suggested, for example, that utilitarianism be rejected as an ethical theory because accepting it would be "dangerous" in some ways—perhaps because it somehow would lead to bad consequences in the long run if we based our moral decisions on utilitarian cost/benefit calculations. Note that during his presidency, Ronald Reagan issued an executive order prohibiting federal agencies from taking regulatory action "unless the potential benefits to society from the regulation outweigh the costs."[9] This seems commonsensical enough. Later the same year, however, the Supreme Court held that in the regulations embodied in the Occupational Health and Safety Act, the health and safety of workers should outweigh "all other considerations." The Court added: "Any standard based on a balancing of costs and benefits. . . would be inconsistent with the law."[10]

One area of practical concern for business is the utilitarian calculation regarding corporate contributions to nonprofit causes. From a purely economic point of view, a business exists to make a profit for its stockholders. Contributions to nonprofit causes presumably dilute profits. From a public-image standpoint, however, various stakeholders (as we shall see in Chapter 7) expect the firm to be a good "public citizen." Consequently, several interrelated questions face the corporation:

1. Are there long-term gains to the corporation itself that will justify its contributing to nonprofit "causes"? Is the contribution consistent with its mission?
2. Assuming the feasibility of such corporate contributions, might some major social need justify such contributions even in the absence of demonstrable long-term benefits to the corporation itself?
3. If such corporate contributions are to be made, what should be the criteria for selecting the recipients? Need? Merit? The likelihood that the funds will be judiciously used? The likelihood that the cause's efforts will benefit the firm? The emotional sympathies of the person or persons having the final say in the award? Or, perhaps, the likelihood that public disclosure of the award will not prove embarrassing to the firm?

Obviously, the issue of corporate contributions is far from simple.

The point the utilitarian is trying to make, however, is that long-term consequences of an action must be weighed in reaching a moral decision. Utilitarianism at its best is a very "far-sighted" theory rather than one of short-term expediency.

Problems with Business Utilitarianism

It is now time to bring our discussion of utilitarianism back into contact with the notions of costs and benefits. Since money—dollars and cents—may be the first thing that comes to mind for many persons when business is mentioned, it is not surprising that costs and benefits are often thought of largely in financial terms. It is clear, however, that both the costs and the benefits of a particular business decision may involve much more than just dollars and cents. Such costs and benefits may include time and energy spent or saved, safety risks and potential benefits to health, psychological frustrations and satisfactions, legal sanctions of various sorts, and many other factors in addition to money. If cost/benefit analysis is really to serve as an effective tool for business decisionmaking, however, it would seem that these various factors must be reduced to some common unit so that comparisons and calculations can be made. And since dollar value is a widely recognized unit for comparison, it is certainly understandable that most cost/benefit thinking in business situations is expressed in dollar amounts. This procedure, although understandable and plausible within limits, can lead to some rather questionable results—as some of the cases in this chapter will show. Many philosophers and some business analysts argue that there is simply no clear and objective way to assign a dollar value to such factors as life, safety, and fairness.

A Practical Problem

One relatively common issue with utilitarian implications in practical business life is the need to close plants or to discontinue some other operation on which the people in a particular geographical area have come to depend.[11] Because the social impact of such closings can be great, in some countries plants cannot be closed without government approval. The feeling in such countries is that the devastating consequences of the sudden loss of many jobs should be subject to governmental influence rather than be seen as purely economic decisions. Some questions to raise about such closings include the following:

1. Is the community that provided the workforce and public services "owed" anything in addition to the wages for that workforce and the taxes for the public services?
2. Prior to a decision to close a plant, should the workforce be consulted about possible cost-cutting suggestions, operational changes, or even benefit concessions to make the plant more competitive?
3. After a plant closing, what benefits, if any, should be given to the workers (for example, outplacement services) and the community (for example, assistance in finding a replacement occupant for the vacated premises)?

Again, as with the other practical business issues we have mentioned, the answers to such questions are far from simple. Of the three guidelines—feasibility, consistency, and reasoning—that we suggest as tests for resolving conflicts about moral issues, one stands out as particularly applicable to the issue of plant closings. That is the guideline of consistency. Specifically, has the firm indicated, in words or actions, to those affected by the closing that a plant would not be closed in the manner which the firm chose?

A Theoretical Problem

The approach taken by many utilitarian moral philosophers bypasses the debate about expressing costs and benefits in dollar amounts by identifying the good that is to be maximized as happiness or pleasure (rather than dollars). Bentham, for instance, went so far as to propose a "calculus" for comparing the pleasures and pains caused by an action and thereby deciding in an apparently objective way whether the action is right or wrong. Bentham's proposed calculus required the decisionmaker to consider "dimensions" of the pleasure or pain produced by an action, such as intensity and duration.

What is not clear, however, is the sense in which Bentham's dimensions constitute a "calculus." He says such things as *"Sum up* the numbers expressive of the degrees of good tendency which the act has with respect to each individual. . . ."[12] But just as there are questions about the assigning of dollar values to human life or safety, there are also serious questions about how numerical values can be assigned to several of the dimensions on Bentham's list. A related problem concerns the relative importance of each dimension and who is to assign differential weights to these dimensions.

Bentham's calculus seems to concentrate on human individuals. Yet there are some problems with this approach. One problem is whether the welfare of the environment should be taken into consideration. Some writers with a strong concern for ecology and the environment have suggested that the "greatest good" of the entire ecosystem or biotic community should be taken into account. (We return to this issue in Chapter 10.) The point here is that the exact meaning of *extent* or *greatest number* in utilitarianism needs to be made clear before the theory can really be applied to every situation.

Even if we restrict our concern to humans, however, it is not always clear which humans will actually be affected by a given action. Just as the ripples in a pond may spread out indefinitely, the exact number of individuals affected by one of our actions may be impossible to ascertain.

Finally, it is sometimes suggested that the utilitarian is asking us to do something mathematically impossible: namely, to maximize two variables (that is, the total net amount of good and the total number of beings who will receive this good). Theoretically, at least, there may be cases where the greatest amount of good can only be obtained if this good is restricted to a smaller number of persons. It seems to us, however, that most utilitarians have only meant to say (by referring to "the greatest number") that the good of everyone is to be considered in making a moral decision. Their primary commitment is to increasing the total amount of good in the world. Although everyone is to count, maximizing the number of persons affected is a secondary issue.

Costs and Benefits in Business Situations

Two issues about utilitarianism merit reinforcement: (1) the natural restriction of considering only cost and benefits to the firm in business decisionmaking, and (2) the claim that some factors in business ethics simply do not fit into the cost/benefit structure.

It is understandable that many (even all) of the businesspersons mentioned in the following cases have limited their thinking to comparing the costs and benefits for their own companies in the various decisions they made. After all, a standard claim is that the goal of any business is to increase its own profit. Since we have heard such advice most of our lives—and since as our company profits we tend to profit as well—it is not surprising that many business decisions are made solely with the goal of attaining the best possible consequences for the firm. Cost/benefit analysis from this limited perspective could not be labeled *utilitarianism* since the consequences for other persons and companies are not considered (unless such consequences have an effect on the welfare of one's own society). Of course, some persons hold that what is good for the individual (or the firm) will always lead to what is best for society as a whole. This viewpoint is a version of the laissez-faire theory in classical economics. The laissez-faire theory holds, roughly, that each business seeking to maximize its own profit will lead to the greatest benefit for the society as a whole, and that this maximization of societal benefit is assured by the guidance of an "invisible hand" created by competing firms—each battling to serve consumers. Whether this actually happens or not is much debated in contemporary economics and philosophy. Some theorists note that at times the economic forces within our society react so slowly to change that the invisible hand appears to be inflicted with arthritis.

Apart from the debate over laissez-faire theory, you should remember that cost/benefit analysis of moral issues in business is just one form of consequentialism. The theory behind business decisions based solely on the consequences for one's own firm would be an example of what we, in the Introduction, called *restricted teleological theories*. The label we could invent for this particular theory might be *firmism*—or perhaps *companyism*—the view that the consequences for one's own firm or company constitute the sole basis for deciding what is right or wrong in a particular situation.

Utilitarians would criticize the doctrine of firmism as being too narrow to be morally acceptable; the welfare of others is important in addition to the welfare of one's own firm. Egoists, on the other hand, would criticize firmism for being too broad. According to ethical egoism, the only consequence worth considering is one's own welfare as an individual. The egoist would regard as foolish (and even immoral) anyone who took the welfare of a firm as a whole to be the test of right and wrong. We invite the reader to keep these contrasting theories in mind when reading the cases in this chapter.

Conclusions

The final question to consider is whether teleological theories in general—be they universal or restricted—are adequate for use in all business situations.

According to many philosophers, and also according to Kohlberg's theory of moral development, there is a still-higher stage of moral thinking than any of the positions held by teleologists. Those who use simple cost/benefit thinking in moral situations run the risk of overlooking the possible conflict with such basic universal principles as justice or fairness. In effect, does an emphasis on bottom-line results constitute a principle as inflexible as any promised by rule deontologists? If a situation arises in which the greatest good for the greatest number would lead to some distribution of this good that seems clearly unfair, utilitarianism would not be a totally acceptable theory on which to build our codes of ethics. For example, it is sometimes suggested that the institution of slavery in the Old South led to a greater balance of good over evil for all concerned than any other social or economic system would have. Even though a certain percentage of the population was held in slavery, the need for large numbers of agricultural (and other) workers and the need for capital to accumulate meant that—in those particular circumstances at least—appeals to the greatest good for the greatest number could be used to attempt to justify the institution of human slavery. If the facts cited by someone arguing in this way were correct (which they may not be), a utilitarian would have to admit that slavery was morally justified. But many of us might respond: "But slavery would be morally wrong even if it did happen to produce the greatest amount of good overall; slavery is unfair regardless of whatever good it might do; it is simply wrong for one human being to own another; persons possess an intrinsic value that the institution of slavery denies." Such a position, characteristic of the type of ethical theory that we have called *deontological*, constitutes an alternative to utilitarianism, egoism, and firmism, and will be explored more thoroughly in the next chapter. For the moment, it may be sufficient to be reminded that such an alternative exists. Perhaps there is more to moral decisionmaking than simply weighing the costs of an action against the likely benefits.

To summarize the reasoning process of the cost/benefit utilitarian in Stage Five, that individual is likely to be (1) more motivated by an individualistic viewpoint attuned to societal well-being than by a viewpoint preoccupied with personal well-being, (2) more motivated by consequences that promote civil liberties and public welfare than by consequences benefiting reference groups, and (3) more motivated by social principles than by group norms. His or her motto might be "sin bravely."

Communicative Action for the Stage Five adherent is based on principles directed toward society's general welfare. Strategic or adversarial communication is only the preliminary mode used in conversations; it will later be supplemented by Discursive reasoning. Pointing out weaknesses in the other party's position in terms of enhancing societal well-being can only be the prelude to serious efforts to resolve conflict. Serious negotiation starts with Discursive reasoning that acknowledges the other party's position and principles, but then calls on additional principles that all well-intentioned members of society are thought to respect. These principles are brought forward with utility as the foundation for the legitimacy of their arguments. Stage Five adherents are more open-minded in their approach to communication, for they would be willing to sacrifice elements of their position if their principles were not compromised.

Here are some questions to consider in weighing costs and benefits in the following cases:

1. Can an appropriate mechanism be constructed for weighing the value of human life?

2. Whose costs should be evaluated in ethical decisions?

3. What time period (in terms of future consequences) should be considered in these calculations?

❖ Case Study 5–1 ❖

NIKE

Nike is a name well-known in the sporting world. But its success has had a negative side. Nike's notoriety helped make it the target of a boycott by a Chicago-based equal opportunity organization. That organization, PUSH, claimed that Nike's management profile did not reflect the profile of one large, profitable market segment of the firm's business. The firm had no African Americans on its board of directors or in its vice presidential ranks, and it did little business with African American suppliers. PUSH's efforts to obtain minority-related business information from Nike did not receive a positive response. PUSH then resorted to a tactic that it felt sure would get Nike's attention—a boycott.

The head of PUSH, Tyrone Crider, believed the boycott would gain support in the African American community. PUSH chartered a bus, and a group of protesters traveled to Nike's headquarters in Oregon. When the group arrived, Crider commented that "we will no longer stand by and allow apartheid corporate policies." However, the welcome his group received from local civil rights groups was less cordial than he had expected.

The Black United Front in Portland had asked Nike to open a factory outlet in a predominately black neighborhood. Nike did so, and donated the outlet's profits to a community development corporation. Daryll Tukufu of the Portland Urban League noted that Nike had also donated $100,000 to a local youth program working with minorities. Robert Phillips of Portland's NAACP maintained that PUSH had not done its homework. He felt that perhaps the wrong reasons were used in choosing Nike as a boycott target.

Nike's reaction to PUSH's concerns was adversarial. A Nike spokesperson admitted that the firm's vice presidents were white. The company policy was to promote from within, and each vice president had at least ten years of service with the firm. The spokesperson also stated that while Nike supported neighborhood development, its business was to sell athletic equipment, not to be an economic development organization.

Nike executives questioned PUSH's motives. They wondered if there was a connection between the boycott and an ad placed by Reebok in a PUSH publication. They also raised the issue of a published report indicating that Reebok officials had provided PUSH with financial data about Nike's operations.

PUSH, though, is an activist organization. Its persistency has produced results. Its activists are given credit for persuading firms such as Coca-Cola and Kentucky Fried Chicken to give more business to minority suppliers. Some people, however, questioned whether PUSH was on the wrong course. Columnist William Raspberry thought that addressing the plight of poor blacks was a more important issue. He asked what good it did for the poor if Nike hired an African American vice president.

Nike's relations to the poor had produced unintended results. Nike's gym shoes had become a status symbol among poor black teenagers. In Maryland, fifteen-year-old Michael Thomas was killed by a friend who wanted his Air Jordan basketball shoes. In Houston, sixteen-year-old Johnny Bates was killed by a seventeen-year-old who wanted Bates's Air Jordans. When the Reverend Jesse Jackson, the founder of PUSH, commented on these and similar events, he said that high-priced gym shoes symbolized materialistic values aimed at impoverished people. He felt that the underclass associated Air Jordans with power. He further believed that the company had to be responsible for its advertising and the results produced by that advertising. Jackson also stated that the celebrity endorsers of such products had to accept responsibility for the results produced by their endorsements.

Spike Lee, who directed some of the ads, stated: "The commercials that Michael Jordan and I do have never gotten anyone killed." The public relations director for Nike reacted strongly to criticisms of the firm's advertising. She stated that remarks implying that Nike was exploiting the poor and causing teens to kill other teens for their gym shoes were racist remarks. She further stated, "Our commercials are about sports, they're not about fashion." Ironically, an industry survey showed that over 75 percent of sports shoes bought in this county are not used for sports.

Did PUSH's boycott accomplish its goals? Perhaps so. Nike hired a Los Angles agency, with an African American partner, that specialized in marketing to minorities. Nike's chairman Phil Knight also said that he would appoint a minority to the firm's board, and he did. John Thompson, the African American basketball coach at Georgetown University, was named to the firm's board. Thompson, who had been a consultant for Nike, had praised PUSH for its past activities. He felt, though, that PUSH had not given appropriate recognition to Nike's proactive minority policies. Finally, Knight said that he would add a minority vice president to Nike's executive ranks a year after he named a minority to the board of directors.

Questions

1. From the limited information presented, give a preliminary assessment of the stages of moral reasoning used by the parties mentioned in the case. Explain your assessment.
2. What moral grounds would you personally need to have if you were to participate in a boycott?
3. One issued raised in the case is that the firm and its product's endorsers had a moral responsibility for unintended negative actions supposedly caused in part by the firm's advertisements. Is there any such responsibility? If so, what are the limits of that responsibility?

Sources

Steven M. Colford, "The gospel of advertising from Rev. Jesse Jackson, *Advertising Age* (October 15, 1990), 1, 72.

Matthew Grim, "Push comes to shove as Nike defends its image," *Adweek's Marketing Week* 31 (August 20, 1990), 6.

Eric Harrison and Bruce Horovitz, "Nike feels heat, sets minority goals," *Los Angeles Times* (August 18, 1990), D1, D3.

Chip Johnson, "Nike taps Georgetown's John Thompson for its board in bid to block criticism," *The Wall Street Journal* (May 23, 1991), B8.

"Nike hires an agency with minority interest," *The New York Times* (November 14, 1990), D17.

"Push announces sanctions against Nike athletics," *Jet* 78 (August 1990), 10.

William Raspberry, "When PUSH comes to shove," *The Washington Post* (August 29, 1990), A25.

Rick Telander, "Senseless," *Sports Illustrated* (May 14, 1990), 36–49.

Stuart Wasserman, "Nike's hometown ignores boycott call," *Los Angeles Times* (August 25, 1990), D1, D3.

Isabel Wilkerson, "Challenging Nike, rights group takes a risky stand," *The New York Times* (August 25, 1990), 10.

Wiley M. Woodard, "It's more than just the shoes," *Black Enterprise* 21 (November 1990), 17.

❖   Case Study 5–2   ❖

CITIBANK

David Edwards was a member of Citibank's international staff in Paris. He claimed that he was fired because he called attention to a practice over which he had a conflict of conscience. Specifically, he worried about the propriety of foreign exchange transactions in the Paris office.

Edwards claimed that the Paris office had sent a telex message to the Nassau office, instructing it to buy $6 million in French francs. The Paris office was to supply the francs at the rate of 4.7275 francs to the dollar. The telex then instructed the Nassau office to sell the francs at the rate of 4.7375 to the dollar. The purchase was to be split between the New York and Brussels offices. The profit would be credited to the Nassau office. While Citibank's total earnings were not affected, the transaction could be viewed as lowering the earnings of its Paris office. The taxes on earnings are lower in the Bahamas than they are in Paris.

This type of transaction is called parking, and it was an accepted way of doing business internationally. Citibank denied that it had done anything wrong. One U.S. banker commented on the matter, saying, "Surely it is not in the U.S. shareholders' interest that American companies pay the maximum amount of taxes on their overseas operations." Data show that a number of international banks have established offices in the Bahamas for tax purposes. The Securities and Exchange Commission (SEC) investigated Edwards' charges and decided that the case was not worth further attention.

Peat, Marwick, Mitchell—as Citibank's auditor—reviewed the situation at the Paris office. Its review stated: "We do not think that the French Tax Authorities have determined a fiscal doctrine with regard to transactions on the international money market." Money can be transferred internationally simply through computer messages, and banking regulations covering this phenomenon were vague.

The Paris-to-Nassau transaction was not unique. Similar movement of money was noted between Citibank's Frankfurt and Nassau offices. Again it was the Nassau office which came out ahead. The SEC was asked to look into still another charge that Citibank was moving local deposits from Germany to an office abroad and then back again with different deposit dates. This served to lower the reserve requirements mandated by German authorities. The SEC ruled that this matter was of little interest to Citibank's stockholders, and thus of little interest to the SEC.

Edwards claimed that a second set of books kept by Citibank adjusted for this internal movement of funds. An executive of Citibank replied to

Edwards, charging that Edwards was well aware of the legitimate purpose of the second set of books. It was the way many large corporations did business. The books were kept to "pool rate costs of funds and the allocation of many overhead and operating expenses totally independent of the financial and accounting principles and tax regulations."

An assistant vice president of Citibank then circulated an internal memorandum on handling currency transactions with the Nassau offices. He stated that such transactions could be made with a "tax haven" office but should be kept inconspicuous. Another vice president in the London office warned that central banks in other countries might be severely upset by parking transactions. Peat, Marwick, Mitchell also warned that while there might not be a law against the practice, taxing authorities might question it.

Edwards had blown the whistle and blown it loudly. His charges were conveyed to Citibank officials at three levels—Paris, the New York home office, and the board of directors. His claim was that after his qualms were first voiced, he was denied official performance reviews. He also said that he was transferred to a position that was not typical for his career path. The executive vice president of Citibank then wrote to Edwards and said that allegations of wrongdoing made by Edwards had been investigated by Citibank's Comptrollers Division. He further stated that Citibank had asked Edwards repeatedly for evidence to validate the charges. He believed that Edwards had failed to provide substantive evidence. Edwards replied that he really had not had the opportunity to present his case. The exchange of letters between the two appeared to include a mixture of both Ordinary and Strategic communication. Little sympathy or empathy seemed to be expressed by either party for the other's position. Citibank's final report on the matter concluded that there was no "substantive, factual corroboration of the allegations."

Edwards was not satisfied. He then wrote to the chief partner of Peat, Marwick, Mitchell; to members of the board of directors; and to the chairman of Citicorp's (Citibank's holding company) audit committee. At that point, Edwards was fired. Coincidentally, the treasurer of Citibank's Paris operation, whom Edwards had accused of wrongdoing, resigned shortly thereafter to accept a senior position with another bank. The treasurer of the Brussels office, who directed the bank's foreign exchange operation, also accepted a position with another bank.

Citicorp has a policy manual covering ethics situations. This manual is distributed to all its offices. After the Edwards incident, it developed an ethics training session based on different moral conflicts that its employees might face. Teams of Citicorp employees attempt to resolve conflicts in a manner acceptable to management. A group of managers sits in on each training session. If a team questions a "correct" answer to a scenario, it may appeal to the management group. That group can override the "correct" training session answer if the challengers' rationale is thought to have merit. During the training session, the employees are told that Citicorp does have an ethical ombudsman who can be consulted about ethical problems without going through the normal chain of command.

Questions

1. What stages of moral reasoning appear to be used by Edwards and by the officials at Citibank?
2. Does Citibank's justification of the practice of parking meet the normative guidelines of feasibility and consistency?
3. What would you have done differently to resolve the conflict if you were in Edwards' place and in the executive vice president of Citibank's place?

Sources

"Citibank's activities being probed by SEC due to charges in suit," *The Wall Street Journal* (July 27, 1975), 13.

"David Edwards vs. Citibank: The trading room, part II, *MBA* 12 (August–September 1978), 11, 55.

Karin Ireland, "The ethics game," *Personnel Journal* 70 (March 1991), 72, 74, 75.

"Jitters from the Citibank case," *Business Week* (August, 21, 1975) 94.

Karin Lissakers, "Citibank must obey the rules," *Challenge* 25 (November–December 1982), 60–63.

"Parking lots," *The Economist* (September 29, 1984), 82.

Roy Rowan, "The maverick who yelled foul at Citibank," *Fortune* 107 (January 10, 1983), 46.

Alexander L. Taylor, "Playing the money game," *Time* (March 1, 1982), 67.

Thomas C. Theobald, "Offshore brands and global banking—One Bank's View," *Columbia Journal of World Business* 16 (Winter 1981), 19–20.

❖   Case Study 5–3   ❖

ZENITH

BUNK!

*That's our answer to people who say that the
American worker isn't as good as he used to be.
He's good enough to work at Zenith.*

Those were the opening lines in an advertisement that appeared in the
nation's magazines. This ad for Zenith's televisions caught the public's
attention. Whether one perceived its tone as aggressive or defensive, there
was still an industry story to be told. In the 1950s, over 175 manufacturers
of televisions existed in the United States. Over the next forty years, that
number dropped to 3: Zenith, RCA, and General Electric.

Zenith's eye-catching ad ended with these words: "The American
worker? He's as good as they come."

That worker may have been good, but he was expensive. And evi-
dently he had become too expensive for Zenith. Zenith abruptly pulled the
ad from circulation. As it did so, the firm announced that it would trim its
U.S. workforce by 25 percent. Production was to be shifted to Mexico and
Taiwan.

Prior to the layoff, Zenith's domestic workforce numbered 21,000.
Following the lead of other American television producers, it was transferring its manufacturing plants to countries with a lower labor cost. The
employees did not expect the cutbacks since the firm was making money.
But Zenith was losing market share, and competitive pricecutting was
shrinking the profit margins.

In a letter to employees, the chairman of Zenith explained that low-
priced televisions from abroad were making strong inroads into the
American market. Like RCA and General Electric, the firm believed jobs
had to be moved to low-labor cost countries. He stated: "We think Zenith
has tried longer, has tried harder, and has tried more successfully than any
other company to protect the jobs of its American employees." He added
that without the cuts, "it will be impossible for us to protect the interests of
our stockholders. . . ." The original 25 percent cut eventually grew much
larger, to the point that most of Zenith's productive capacity was moved
abroad. Later, justifying the transfer of jobs to Mexico, Zenith's chairman,

Jerry Pearlman, said that instead of making a profit, "We would have lost $250 million and gone out of business."

Aside from large cities like Chicago, smaller cities especially felt the impact of the Zenith layoffs. One thousand workers were initially let go in Springfield, Missouri; another thousand followed later. Still another thousand lost their jobs in Watsonville, Pennsylvania, while eight hundred were let go in Sioux City, Iowa. The economic devastation in Sioux City typified the problems experienced in the other cities. When Zenith, the city's largest employer, shut down its operations, a strong ripple effect resulted. Three of the area's homebuilders went out of business, and small local firms that supplied Zenith with parts had to close or lay off employees. The decision to shut down the Sioux City operation left many of the workers bitter. They felt that they had been allowed no input to the decision. To find alternative work, most had to leave Sioux City and move elsewhere.

Zenith's larger suppliers wondered what would happen if the firm shifted its engineering and procurement personnel abroad as well. Bill Ehrsom, of National Semiconductor, supplied sockets for Zenith's television sets. He felt that if Zenith's designing were shifted to Taiwan, "you bet your bottom dollar that the Japanese will go after that business." His greater fear, though, was that Zenith would sell the business. He noted that when Japan's Matsushita bought Motorola's Quasar's television business, they set up their production process in such a way that he could not compete to be their supplier.

Japanese aggressive marketing tactics are what caused Zenith to move offshore in the first place. Zenith accused the Japanese of predatory pricing and of "dumping" their TVs in the United States. However, a ten-year court suit brought by Zenith against Japanese television manufacturers was dismissed by the Supreme Court. Zenith's reaction to losing its battle with Far Eastern rivals was to join forces with one of its Korean competitors, Lucky-Goldstar. Goldstar bought 5 percent of Zenith's stock. Zenith chairman Pearlman "conceded that if he couldn't beat 'em, he would join 'em."

Questions

1. Did Zenith have any moral obligation to consult with or negotiate with its workers before it transferred productive facilities abroad?
2. Zenith obviously did a cost–benefit analysis before it transferred operations. Can the cost–benefit analysis be justified by the ethical (not economic) theory of utilitarianism?
3. Some might say that the executive decision at Zenith to transfer operations abroad was an example of pure deontology at work. Just what ethical obligation could have provided underpinning for the Zenith decision?

Sources

"Bunk," *Time* (May 16, 1977), 49.

Robert Z. Chew, "U.S. worker ads ended as Zenith shifts work abroad," *Advertising Age* (October 3, 1977), 2, 92.

"Court ends Zenith's TV suit," *The New York Times* (April 28, 1989), 12.

Andrew Czernek, "Parts production to follow Zenith tv shift offshore," *Electronic News* (November 14, 1977), 38.

Andrew Czernek, "Zenith shifting tv output abroad; 5600 jobs affected," *Electronic News* (October 3, 1977), 1, 80.

Jaclyn Fierman, "Facing up to hard times at Zenith," *Fortune* (July 24, 1985), 67.

"New Zenith dumping filing," *TV Digest* 29 (January 2, 1989), 12.

Robert L. Rose, "Zenith sells a 5% stake to Goldstar," *The Wall Street Journal* (February 26, 1991), A3.

Lois Therrien and Laxmi Nakarmi, "Zenith wishes on a Lucky-Goldstar," *Business Week* (March 11, 1991), 50.

"Workers at 8 plants of Zenith Radio to get federal aid," *The Wall Street Journal* (December 8, 1977), 4.

"Zenith production moving to Mexico," *The New York Times* (October 1990), D4.

"Zenith to lay off 25% of workers within a year," *The Wall Street Journal* (September 28, 1977), 2.

Notes to Chapter 5

[1]Ann Colby et al., *Moral Stages and Their Scoring* (Cambridge: Harvard University Center for Moral Education, 1980), Part I, p. 25, Table 2.

[2]Two helpful discussions of this issue are found in: Sissela Bok, "Whistleblowing and professional responsibility," *New York University Education Quarterly* 2(4) (1980), 2–7, and Norman Bowie, *Business Ethics* (Englewood Cliffs, NJ: Prentice-Hall, Inc., 1982), pp. 140–149.

[3]William Kurtines, "Sociomoral Behavior and Development from a Rule-Governed Perspective: Psychosocial Theory as a Nomatic Science," in William M. Kurtines and Jacob L. Gewirtz, *Moral Development Through Social Interaction* (New York: John Wiley & Sons, 1987), pp. 149–194.

[4]Michael Kinsley, "In defense of good intentions," *Time* (June 1, 1992), 90.

[5]Dennis L. Krebs et al., "Structural and Situational Influences on Moral Judgment: The Interaction between Stage and Dilemma," in William M. Kurtines and Jacob Gewirtz (eds.), *Handbook of Moral Behavior and Development* (Hillsdale, NJ: Lawrence Erlbaum, Associates, Publishers, 1991), p. 113.

[6]David Gauthier, *Morals by Agreement* (Oxford: Oxford University Press, 1986).

[7]James D. Wallace, *Moral Relevance and Moral Conflict* (Ithaca, NY: Cornell University Press, 1988), p. 12.

[8]Jeremy Bentham, *An Introduction to the Principles of Morals and Legislation,* Chapter II, Section 14. Many editions. First published in 1789.

[9]Executive Order 12291, *Federal Register,* February 10, 1981. Quoted in "The Limits of Cost-Benefit Analysis," *Report from the Center for Philosophy and Public Policy* (College Park, MD: University of Maryland, Summer 1981), vol. I, Number 3 , p. 9.

[10]U.S. Supreme Court decision, June 17, 1981. Quoted in "The Limits of Cost-Benefit Analysis," p. 9.

[11]A particular example of this which was much-discussed in recent years was the decision to close the General Motors assembly plant in Flint, Michigan. Many people not directly affected by this decision came to have a sense of its poignancy through the film *Roger and Me,* the controversial documentary that drew attention to the Flint situation.

[12]Bentham, Chapter IV, Section 6.

Chapter 6

EQUITY, JUSTICE, AND FAIRNESS

The words are familiar enough to all of us. *Justice*, along with *liberty*, is part of our Pledge of Allegiance. *Fairness* is something we have all grown up hearing praised. *Equity*, while less familiar, is also a concept that many have been taught to honor. Just what these concepts amount to, however, or just how they apply to business, is more elusive. Are they moral goals that lead to societal well-being? Are they requirements for a lasting resolution of conflicts over moral issues?

Many of us may suspect, of course, that what is just, fair, or equitable will vary from culture to culture and from one historical period to another. As we become more aware of cultural differences, we may tend to doubt that words like *justice* refer to objective, universal truths or values at all.

On the other hand, commitment to some basic sense of fairness is deeply rooted in virtually all of us. This is well illustrated by a hypothetical conversation between a student and an ethics teacher:[1]

STUDENT: Values are relative and one person's are as good as another.
TEACHER: No, some people's are better.
STUDENT: No, values are relative, and no one can impose personal values on another.
TEACHER: Values are not relative, and if you do not agree then I will flunk you.
STUDENT: That would not be fair.

TEACHER: Are you trying to impose your view of what is fair on me?
STUDENT: I think I see your point.

This story casts doubt on a glib relativism and suggests that beneath our occasional skepticism about the claims of morality lies what might be called a *moral presupposition* that has to do with fairness.

Nature of Equity

The concepts of equity, justice, and fairness are interrelated. Since it may be the least familiar of the three notions, however, let us begin with *equity*. The word derives from the same Latin root as *equal*, and thus refers to a condition where some type or degree of equality exists between two or more parties. It differs significantly from literal equality, however, by suggesting that what is to be made equal is a certain minimum level of something, not a total amount. To put this another way, equity has been achieved when two parties are "on an equal footing," not when they are equal in every respect.

Our legal system is based on *equality before the law*. This does not mean, however, that each person in a society must be made equal in every way. The equality we prize in our society is in opportunity rather than in results. Although some people have maintained that all persons should be made equal in every respect, such propositions have typically been abandoned in the face of the observation that human beings do not remain equal for long even after they have been artificially made so. And because total equality in this sense is simply not a feasible goal, it has tended to be replaced by the more achievable goal of equity. In one sense, this is just an example of the traditional ethical maxim *ought implies can*. Since total (or "radical") equality cannot be had, it cannot be the case that total equality is what we ought to strive for.

Another argument against the feasibility of total equality rests on Robert Nozick's analysis of the concept of self-esteem.[2] Nozick points out that equality, contrary to the claims of some of its advocates, does not produce more self-esteem—since self-esteem is based on criteria that differentiate people. But, insofar as this is true, it could be argued by a radical egalitarian that self-esteem in this sense is not a good thing to have or seek.

Self-esteem, however, is most credibly built on what is felt to be a level playing field. Is the business playing field level when men and women compete? The answer may depend on whether ethics are viewed from a justice perspective or from a view based on empathy. Carol Gilligan notes that the value of justice is more comfortable to men than to women. Men have been nurtured on it from childhood. Women, however, have been taught an ethics based on caring or empathy.[3]

Our business culture, though, appears to associate ethics more closely with justice than with empathy. This association, claims William Damon, has caused women "to incorporate the elements of justice reasoning associated with role morality" into their evaluation process when they compete in the workforce.[4]

The net result is that little or no difference has been observed between the moral reasoning of men and women.[5]

An Application

One of the practical business issues related to this point is usually referred to as the question of *comparable worth*. The issue, of course, is whether the members of different identifiable groups (typically "women" as contrasted with "men") are receiving equal pay for equal work. Much of the evidence that has been published concerning the salaries of men and women suggests that women are frequently paid less than men. The question that usually arises at this point, however, is whether the work being done by the women in question is *equal*. That is, do the workers have *comparable worth?* How, then, does one measure the comparative worth or value of the work done in a particular job? The physical or mental effort put forth in a job seems to be a poor gauge. In our more-or-less *meritarian* business culture (discussed later in this chapter), skill is a more widely accepted measure than effort. But even skill is hard to measure directly, so we tend instead to adopt the classic economic law of supply and demand. In brief, we expect the "market" to determine the relative value of two jobs and the comparable worth of the persons who fill them.

Suppose, now, that one worker claims he or she is being treated unfairly by being paid less than a worker in a similar position. In addition to the factors mentioned in the last paragraph, one issue that frequently surfaces in such cases is seniority: in some businesses, certain positions were essentially closed to members of one sex (or to certain minorities) until recent decades, so although seniority *is* a generally accepted gauge for rewards in business, applying it in cases like this may simply compound earlier injustices. Perhaps the best that can be done in such a situation is to apply the normative guidelines for conflict resolution that we have already posited. This means that the parties concerned should seek a resolution that is *feasible* (in the light of all the various factors affecting the situation), supported by the best *reasons* available, and *consistent* with both the company's stated policies and the moral standards of the community. Applying these general guidelines does not mean that a resolution will be easy. In fact, our belief is that a fourth guideline must be added to the decision process to resolve business issues with equity implications satisfactorily.

Kant's Equity Criterion

The fourth normative guideline that we offer is *universalizability*. This is the claim that taking the moral point of view requires that we be willing to allow others to do the same types of things we consider morally acceptable for ourselves. For example, if a person claims that some type of difference in pay is acceptable from the point of view of morality, that person must be willing for others to differentiate in the same manner in similar circumstances. This process is sometimes referred to as willingness to *universalize* what one does. The requirement is not that anyone else (much less everyone) actually do the act in question, but simply that the agent be willing for it to be done by others. (This same general notion is contained in what is sometimes called the principle of *reversibility*. Reversibility simply requires that we be willing for others to treat us in the same way we treat them—in other words, that we be willing to reverse our relative positions.) The recognition of this requirement of universalizability in thinking about morality will serve to resolve some— perhaps many—of the conflicts we find ourselves in. Immanuel Kant referred to this concept as the *Categorical Imperative*, and believed that universalizability was sufficient by itself to resolve moral conflict.[6] We are not convinced that one criterion alone is a moral panacea, but we believe that universalizability is at least a necessary criterion in testing resolutions to conflict concerning equity, justice, and fairness.

Asking ourselves whether we are willing to have others do as we do helps us put our behavior in a new perspective, the perspective of its acceptability from the moral point of view. Each stage of moral development that we have distinguished thus far has a particular approach for trying to settle the ethical conflicts that arise between us. Universalizability—along with feasibility, consistency, and reasoning—provides the common ground for testing the equity resulting from attempts to resolve those conflicts.

Equity Limits

Conflict of interest, the subject of the next chapter, is a natural feature of human life, one that cannot be entirely avoided. Because of this, there will always be potential temptations to upset those "fair" and "equitable" social arrangements that human beings work out among themselves. Yet even though human conflict and temptation often make states of equity potentially unstable, equity seems nonetheless possible, and therefore is a feasible moral goal. Equity is, in fact, a way of setting minimal limits for all. It may be a necessary compromise if the interests of all are to be advanced. After all, insofar as the members of a group believe that a state of equity does not exist among themselves, their social order tends to break down. And insofar as social order breaks down, we find ourselves in something like the tooth-and-claw state of nature described by Hobbes and discussed in Chapter 4. This state of nature, in our opinion, is precisely what the institution of morality is designed to help us avoid.

Applying Universalizability

Another practical business issue relevant to equity is the concept of a fair price. In the economic sense, receiving a fair price for its goods or services rewards a business for the risks it takes in bringing a product to market (as well as for the costs of its raw materials, etc.). In a broader sense, however, both short-term and long-term factors need to be considered. Suppose, for example, a company has developed a new drug that can save many lives. In the long term, a variety of market factors will tend to keep the price of a drug within socially acceptable bounds. In the short term, however, with a new product and no competition, the concept of a fair price might require a perspective in addition to the traditional one of supply and demand, especially where (as in the present example) this product is essential to preserving lives. To help resolve this conflict, we might turn to our fourth moral guideline—*universalizability*. In addition, we might want to consider the corollary to that guideline, the principle of *reversibility*. That is, would we want others to do to us what we propose doing to them if our positions were reversed?

If equity is intended to ensure certain minimal limits or baseline starting points for all persons in a given social group, to what qualities do these limits or starting points apply? That is, what sort of things must everyone be provided with if each is to have a fair chance to perform in a job or to compete in life? Obviously, certain things are necessary for mere survival. Since money is the usual means to these things in our society, a certain minimum income has often been maintained to be the essential ingredient in any equitable social system. A case can be made, however, for the claim that the possession of a certain minimum amount of information is more important in achieving equity.

Many issues arise concerning equity in business. One recurring question is just what constitutes equity in a selling situation. As individual consumers, most of us feel at a disadvantage when we shop for infrequently purchased, high-price goods. For example, what does the average person know about the durability of roofing shingles? What about state-of-the-art music sound systems? Do we as customers expect the law to protect us from our ignorance? Certainly we have some responsibility to educate ourselves, but is this feasible or reasonable when the purchase involves technologically complex products?

We fear that salespeople will use their expertise, the fifth type of power mentioned by French and Raven, to exploit our ignorance.[7] Here is where the normative guideline of universalizability comes into play. What would the salesperson deem acceptable practice if roles were reversed in the transaction? In this role reversal, would you as the salesperson-turned-customer abide by the invisible-hand concept mentioned in the last chapter? Would you heed Hobbes's warnings about the dangers of power, mentioned in the first two chapters?

The reader will consider in Chapter 9 how much harm can be done by the withholding or distortion of necessary information. Even though information itself is far less tangible than food, shelter, or money, in our complex society it is often an essential means to the satisfaction of those other needs. This seems particularly true in the business community, where profits are often directly tied to being "in the know."

Of course, there are still other things of value that the businesses may distribute equitably. An example would be the perquisites or "perks" that reward those who are successful in their professional lives. The company car, the private secretary, the corner office, may all be distributed either fairly or unfairly.

These last examples, however, appear to be items that go somewhat beyond the concept of equity as we are using it in this chapter. If equity aims at providing a baseline or starting point from which individuals may then compete, what role does the concept of fairness have to play? After all, fairness is a venerable concept in philosophical ethics as well as a presupposition in our everyday thinking.

Justice as Fairness

The contemporary philosopher who has done most with the concept of fairness is John Rawls. In a series of papers that culminated in his book *A Theory of Justice,* Rawls developed an approach to ethics that has come to be known as *justice as fairness.*[8] The starting point of this view is Rawls's observation that in any society where the generally accepted rules and practices are likely to lead to the (long-term) benefit of all participants, some will be tempted to disregard the rules when it is to their own advantage; at the same time, these people are benefiting from the fact that most of the other members of the society are obeying the rules. We might call such persons freeloaders, or (more emotionally) parasites. The economic term would be *free riders.* Rawls does not deny that individuals can sometimes succeed in promoting their own interests by taking advantage of the socially cooperative behavior of others. But such a refusal to play by the rules is a perfect example of what it means to be unfair or unjust. As Rawls writes, "We cannot preserve a sense of justice and all that this implies while at the same time holding ourselves ready to act unjustly should doing so promise some personal advantage."[9] Part of Rawls's point is psychological: one cannot (psychologically) maintain a sense of justice while always making an exception for oneself. And part of Rawls's opening point is logical: universalizability, the willingness to allow others the same behavior as oneself, is (logically) part of the concept of morality.

Neither this observation nor the anecdote of the teacher and the student, however, shows very clearly exactly what justice or fairness actually is. That specific question can best be approached, we think, by briefly examining two of the other major views of justice in contemporary thought. These are (1) the meritarian view and (2) the Marxist view.

Approaches to Justice

In Plato's *Republic,* there are at least three interpretations of justice, ranging from meritarian to egalitarian. The meritarian view of justice is that the good things of life should be distributed in accordance with the merit of the recipient. Those who work hard, one might say, deserve or merit more than those who do not. Justice, according to this view, consists of rewarding persons in proportion to their merit. This is the prevailing view for distributing business rewards in our country.[10] Although this is a popular view, and no doubt contains an element of truth, whether it should be accepted or not seems to depend on the criterion of merit being used. Do members of one union, for example, "merit" more than members of another union? Such views have been widely held. Do those with higher intelligence deserve more favorable treatment just because of that intelligence? Are family connections a criterion of one's merit? The use of such qualities seems to many persons today to be unjust on its face. The reason that hard work was appealing as a criterion of merit probably has to do with work being regarded as a virtue in our culture. So perhaps virtue itself is a plausible criterion of merit. The main problem that has been raised with this view is that many feel it would not be fair to make virtue so central unless all the individuals being considered had had an equal chance at achieving this virtue. One contemporary philosopher, William Frankena, has expressed this viewpoint as follows:

> Before virtue can reasonably be adopted as a basis of distribution, there must first be a prior *equal* distribution of the conditions for achieving virtue, at least insofar as this is within the control of human society. This is where equality of opportunity, equality before the law, and equality of access to the means of education come in.[11]

So, underlying the feelings which some persons have about the importance of merit seem to be more basic feelings about equality of opportunity. We made this point earlier in the chapter when discussing equity and equity limits.

The second basic account of justice to be considered, the Marxist view, is usually summed up in the expression, "from each according to his ability, to each according to his needs." Even non-Marxists will acknowledge that it is wrong to demand more of someone than his or her abilities permit—but this is because (as we have mentioned before) "ought" implies "can." And most of us will agree that someone's needs are relevant to how we should treat that person. For example, we are usually considered justified in giving special treatment to handicapped persons. Also, apart from its Marxist context, this egalitarian view underlies the values of many cultures in this world. Their position is that the rich should share their wealth with the poor. This admonition is a message found in the Judeo-Christian scriptures that most of us have been exposed to. But what evidence is there that the basic aim in distributing the good things of life should be to arrange them proportionally to abilities and needs? Our basic concern seems to be to make an equal contribution to the chances that each person has to live a good life. And having extra help is surely necessary if handicapped persons, for example, are to have an equal chance in life. If the above claims are correct, only equality of opportunity, not equality of outcome, appears to be at the heart of what we (in our culture at least) mean by justice. Most of us accept part, but not all, of the Marxist's claim.

This is a good point at which to return to John Rawls's theory of justice as fairness. His concept of justice ties together certain aspects of equity. Our sense of what is just or fair is often based on the way, manner, or procedure followed in reaching a decision rather than on the outcome itself. The notion of due process of law is one example of this. The concept of the fair toss of a coin is another.

Types of Justice

Rawls distinguishes three types of procedural justice, two of which are directly relevant to business ethics. The first of these, which he calls *perfect procedural justice,* is illustrated by the following example. Several persons are to divide vacation time within the firm. Each person would like to have as much of the time for himself or herself as possible. In this case, says Rawls, there is both an independent criterion for what would be a fair division of the time and a procedure guaranteed to produce that division. The fair division, as the reader may already have guessed from this introduction, is for the time to be divided equally. The procedure that will ensure this equal division is to have one person divide the time and be the last person to select his or her portion. Making the periods as equal as possible will be the best way for that person to end up with the greatest possible time. This is very clever, but there are few situations in the business world where perfect procedural justice can be employed. As Rawls puts it, "perfect procedural justice is rare, if not impossible, in cases of much practical interest."[12] The problem in the business world is that there is often no agreement on which outcome would really be fair. And, in addition, there is often no agreement on which procedure itself would be a fair one. These two difficulties give rise to Rawls's two further types of procedural justice, both of which may be directly applicable to business.

Contrasting with what Rawls calls perfect procedural justice is what he refers to as *imperfect procedural justice.* Here, the justice of the procedure itself is agreed on, but, for various practical reasons, it is impossible to achieve perfectly just results. Rawls's example is the conviction and punishment of criminals. The ideal, of course, is that all guilty persons would be punished and no innocent persons would be. In our society, trial by jury and the various forms of due process are the ways we have worked out to try to achieve this— and we can agree that these procedures are just or fair even though they are not infallible in producing just results. Sometimes the guilty escape punishment and sometimes the innocent are punished by mistake. Still, most of us believe, our system is the best one that we can devise. Imperfect procedural justice is the type of justice most in line with the theory underlying the free enterprise system.

The final type of procedural justice distinguished by Rawls is called *pure procedural justice.* Justice in this case is solely a matter of following the correct procedure. Contrast this with the two types discussed above: in perfect procedural justice, both the procedure and the results could be independently recognized as just. In imperfect procedural justice, the procedure is recognized as just but the results are (unavoidably) sometimes unjust. In pure procedural justice, following the procedure itself establishes or defines what a just result would be, so that justice depends purely or solely on the procedure rather than the results. In other words, in this case there is no independent test of a just outcome apart from whether or not the established procedures have been followed. An example of this pure procedural justice would be the procedures involved in setting up a fair game of chance. If a state lottery, for instance, is run in an honest manner, the lottery may be referred to as "fair" even if the lucky winner is both wealthy and selfish.

The importance of these distinctions between various forms of procedural justice is that in typical business situations, it is procedural justice that is often most useful in resolving or avoiding conflicts. Imperfect procedural justice might apply, for example, in the case of the manufacturer whose ideal is that all of his or her products be free of defects. Since completely achieving this ideal is impossible, for practical reasons, the manufacturer typically sets up some type of quality control to discover those defects that can reasonably be found before distribution. Just as in the case of the punishment of criminals, an occasional mistake may be made, but the procedure used may still be just—since it may well be the best and fairest procedure available.

Analogous to the lottery example, a business may set up procedures for promoting its employees or for awarding contracts to its suppliers. Assuming that these procedures are followed in a fair and honest manner, they may define what constitutes a fair decision in a particular situation—as in Rawls's concept of pure procedural justice.

Moral Development

Particular situations, of course, need fair decisions, often immediately. But the recognition that moral behavior may require reflection and choice, even choice in the absence of certainty, is characteristic of much of the best writing about ethics. Lawrence Kohlberg, for example, describes the thinking typical of Stage Six, the most highly developed of his stages of moral reasoning, as "self-chosen ethical principles. . .which are used to generate particular decisions."[13] The principles used at this final stage are not simply derived from "what other people expect of us" or answers that can, so to speak, be "looked up in the back of the book." The principles used at this stage must be ones we have chosen ourselves, which we would be willing for others to follow as well, and which in fact guide our behavior. While we acknowledge that there can be exceptions to codified rules, we allow no exceptions to self-chosen principles other than that caused by prioritizing principles which are in conflict.[14]

An individual who uses Stage Six reasoning will make judgments based on self-governing principles that are directed toward enhancing societal well-being. Society is understood by the Stage Six person as all those who are directly or indirectly affected by the decision. Equity and impartiality toward those affected by a decision are cornerstones of the principles of conscience that depict this stage of moral reasoning.

The individual at Stage Six is likely to engage in what Habermas labels *Discursive Communication* to resolve conflict. This form may be contrasted to Ordinary or self-serving Strategic Communication. Kurtines[15] has isolated separate types of Discursive Communicative action that flesh out Habermas's concept:

1. Reflective action by which we make explicit to the other party our understanding of the facts underlying that person's position.
2. Reflective action by which we state in explicit terms to the other party what we understand are the principles underlying that person's position.
3. Integrative action by which we attempt to establish a new shared mutual understanding with the other person, based on facts and principles.

Conclusions

The approach to resolve conflicts over moral issues with a Stage Six person is sequential. The initial step is to attempt to reason to an alternative position that is different than the original positions held by each party. This alternative position must be consistent with the original principles espoused by both parties. If this proves difficult, the second step is to identify another principle that the Stage Six person holds as strongly as the original principle. This may not be as difficult as one might fear, given W. D. Ross's qualms about rank ordering deontological principles.[16] From this alternate principle, the task is to test still other positions until one is judged appropriate—that is, until both parties believe the solution has not violated their principles.

The Discursive reasoning used by the Stage Six person, in brief, shows that person to be (1) more motivated by autonomously arrived-at personal goals with a societal orientation than by imposed social rules or totally self-focused concerns, (2) more motivated by long-term consequences than by short-term consequences, and (3) more motivated by universal principles than by calculations of utility. With these characteristics in mind, some of the general questions that you may wish to reflect on in reading the cases in this chapter are as follows:

1. Do the major parties in each case seem to resemble the student in *The Wall Street Journal* story in presupposing some sense of justice or fairness?

2. Under what conditions would preferential treatment of either employees or firms be justified when merit is not an issue?

3. What changes would be made in our business system if equity and fairness were explicitly guaranteed by the Federal Trade Commission?

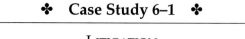

❖ Case Study 6–1 ❖

LITIGATION

Litigation has entered the world of science and technology. Contrary to the image of jurors who are supposedly openminded and impartial, today's cases are tried before juries carefully selected to match predetermined profiles. Jury selection counseling has become a big business. One firm that handles a variety of large corporate accounts is a division of BBD&O Advertising. That group is managed by a statistician and a public relations specialist. Other firms in the field include Jury Analysts, Decision Research Corporation, and Jury Behavior Research, Inc.

The methods used by these services are based on the results of social science research. One consultant, in a suit against General Motors, advised his client's lawyers to base their jury selection on physical attributes such as large irises, wide-set eyes, thin lips, and turned-up noses common to emotional people. His rationale: emotional people like helping others. Other litigation counselors use marketing research techniques to create case-specific jury profiles. Litigation Services generates test juries whose age, income, education level, and sex are similar to those in the actual trial venue. As many as twenty-five of these panels may be created for a single case. The jurors are exposed not only to the facts of the case but also to planned courtroom strategies.

Jury Behavior Research, Inc. takes the process even farther, relying not only on research but on technology as well. Using a tool called a Perception Analyzer—a hand-held device that measures the subject's response to verbal stimulus—researchers measure surrogate jurors' emotional reactions to proposed arguments. Those who score well in pretrial tests are incorporated into the courtroom strategy; those who fail are eliminated.

Decision Research Corporation (DRC) uses focus-group interviews to develop jury profiles. When SCM brought a patent protection suit against Xerox, DRC gathered small groups of people to listen to the facts of the case and discuss their feelings. The discussions were taped and analyzed to determine patterns among potential jurors. Analysis found that women were generally sympathetic to SCM's case, while men and white-collar workers who had followed the progress of Xerox over the years were more likely to side with the opposition.

Surprising or not, results of such investigations are effective. Based on research findings, SCM's lawyers struck both men and white-collar workers from the jury panel and established a final jury of nine women and three men. The profile-matched jury members found in favor of SCM. The costs for such services are quite high, but the payoff is often much higher. In the SCM case, Decision Research received a fee of over $100,000. SCM, who won the case, received an award of $100 million.

Attorneys and clients have been taking advantage of social science and marketing research techniques for more than twenty years. The most widely publicized of these cases was perhaps the Watergate trial against former Attorney General John Mitchell. Concerned that emotions triggered by the Watergate scandal might damage their client's chances of acquittal, Mitchell's attorneys hired Marty Herbst, president of a "communications think tank" to determine the kind of jurors most likely to support their case.

The profile Herbst created defined the ideal juror as a Roman Catholic, conservative, blue-collar worker who earned an income slightly below the national average and read the *New York Daily News*. According to Herbst, "We wanted people who were home established, to the right, more concerned with inflation than Watergate" and who would associate John Mitchell with John Wayne.

The information provided by such studies gives defense attorneys a strong potential advantage when questioning prospective jurors. How the trial judge assigns preemptory panel challenges—that is, the right to strike a prospective juror from the panel without cause—provides a means of making that potential advantage real. The more challenges the defense has, the more likely it is that attorneys can construct their "ideal" jury. And the more unevenly juror challenges are divided, the more likely it is that the defense can keep the opposition from doing the same thing.

This was clearly the case in the Mitchell trial. Judge Lee J. Gagliardi initially awarded the defense twenty challenges and the government ten, but later reduced the government challenges to eight because of pretrial publicity. The defense used all twenty of its challenges; the prosecution used only seven. The result, a jury that with one exception fit perfectly into the mold created by the defense through pretrial research. The verdict: not guilty.

Critics of jury research claim that the system undermines the objectivity on which the legal system was built. According to John R. Wing, chief prosecutor in the Mitchell case, "If the jury is not selected fairly, then everything that follows may be of little or no importance." His own experience provided a case in point. As a fellow prosecutor commented later, "The case was lost in the 'voir dire,' or examination of prospective jurors."

Advocates of pretrial jury research counter these arguments with claims that jury profiles actually improve the advocacy system by insuring that the better-prepared argument in a court case wins. This process may even have advantages for the public. High jury awards against large corporations result in higher insurance costs for the companies. Increased insurance costs, in turn, result in higher costs to the consumer. If corporations can cut their losses through pretrial jury research, others may benefit as well.

There is little doubt that recent developments have changed the face of America's judicial system. As one New York City judge put it: "And what is the purpose of jury selection? To find 12 people who are fair, impartial and open minded to reach a just decision? Any lawyer who does that should quit."

Questions

1. Contrast the application of the terms *fair and equitable* as they apply to jury profiling.

2. Is the society improved by the practice of profiling?

3. Relate jury profiling to the concepts of power and justice.

Sources

Aaron Abbott and Adam Davis, "Pre-trial assessments make witness testimony pay off," *Risk Management* 36 (June 4, 1989), 22, 23, 26–29.

Martin Arnold, "How Mitchell–Stans jury reached acquittal verdict," *The New York Times* (May 5, 1974), 1, 41.

William Booth, "Courtroom tinkering," *The Washington Post* (May 14, 1990), A3.

Lana J. Clark, "Jury evaluation and how to use a shadow jury," *Legal Assistant Today* 8, 4 (March/April 1991), 98–99.

Amitai Etzione, "Science: Threatening the jury trial," *The Washington Post* (May 26, 1974), C3.

Richard Greene, "Jury tempering," *Forbes* 134 (November 1984), 214, 218.

"Jury selection viewed as "weeding" process," *National Underwriter: Property and Casualty* 88 (April 20, 1984), 28.

Ray Marano, "Mock jurors give lawyers real benefits," *Pittsburgh Business Times* (January 22, 1990), S1, S14.

"Psychodrama," *The Economist* 312 (July 8, 1989), 75, 78.

Jay Schulman et al., "Recipe for a jury," *Psychology Today* (May 1973), 37–44, 77–84.

Curt Schleir, "Lawyers court help in jury selection, legal cases," *Advertising Age* 56 (November 14, 1985), 30–32.

❖   Case Study 6–2   ❖

SANDOZ

Schizophrenia affects more Americans than does any other psychotic disorder. Less than half of the two to three million schizophrenics in this country are helped by traditional medical remedies. The illness usually appears when the victim is in his or her late teens or early twenties. Irrational fears, social withdrawal, unusual sleeping hours, and regression to infantile behavior patterns are symptoms of this ailment.

Thorazine, a drug from the 1950s, brought only partial relief from the illness. Then came the discovery of Clozapine. Clozapine was developed in Europe by Sandoz, a Swiss pharmaceutical firm. Sold under the name of Clozaril, it found an eager market in the United States. But its use is tightly monitored because of deadly side effects experienced by a few patients. The effects are a loss of white blood cells—a condition called agranulocytosis.

For those not experiencing agranulocytosis, Clozaril is truly a wonder drug. Witness the following testimonials.

- One woman thought she was God and shifted in and out of mental institutions. A few weeks after she started the Clozaril treatment she no longer experienced delusions.
- Another woman spent most of her twenties believing her parents were witches. Clozaril treatments brought her back to normal.
- A man in his early thirties had been haunted by the spirit of an executed murderer before his Clozaril treatments took effect.
- Still another man believed that historical figures lived at home with him. Clozaril straightened him out.

Estimates are that up to 200,000 Americans could be helped immediately by treatment with Clozaril—but only those who could afford it. When first introduced, the treatment protocol cost about $9,000 a year. The major element in the cost is a continual blood monitoring test for agranulocytosis. Forty-three patients have died from the side effect, and this potentially fatal possibilty has forced Clozaril from some foreign markets. Said Gilbert Honigfeld of Sandoz: "We are critically concerned about patient safety—not only for the welfare of the patients who could die, but also for continued accessibility [of the drug]."

Sandoz's initial solution to this problem was to require the Clozaril Patient Management System (CPMS). The CPMS requires continual patient monitoring. However, this costs money. That cost bothered some members of the medical community, who described it as blackmail and ransom. The real problem with the price of CPMS is that many schizophrenics are financially indigent. Their treatment must be paid for with public dollars. Oregon's mental health commissioner feared: "As we pay for Clozapine, we have to shift individuals on other psychotropic medications, because we don't have enough money to pay for that."

A faculty member at Harvard Medical School decried Sandoz's CPMS as monopolistic. One U.S. Senator introduced legislation to take the monitoring out of Sandoz's hands. The argument is that local hospitals could provide the same patient monitoring at a much lower cost. Part of the reason for the complaints is that some state Medicaid offices had balked at paying the price of CPMS. Many private insurance firms also balked at paying for Clozaril treatment.

Sandoz's concern was the legal liability if patients suffered from the negative side effects of Clozaril after they were removed from the CPMS regimen. But, heeding public criticism, the firm agreed to let outside parties do the monitoring. That would reduce the cost of the drug to $4,160 per year, with the monitoring being extra. But critics were not satisfied. They noted that the cost of the monitoring program supervised by outside professionals under Sandoz's guidelines might cost as much or more than the CPMS system.

To view this problem from a financial perspective, a National Institute of Mental Health analysis calculated that schizophrenia costs the nation $50 billion a year. A *Time* magazine report estimated that close to one-fourth of the country's hospital beds are filled with people with schizophrenia. Clozaril can help reduce those costs. But the drug and the related monitoring would have to be available at a lower price. Sandoz is aware of these costs, but it is also aware of the costs of doing business. Dr. Gilbert Honigfeld of Sandoz noted that it costs at least $150 million to bring a drug like Clozaril to market. And even then, its patent life is limited.

Until the time that alternative drugs such as risperidone are approved as alternative treatments, Clozaril is the only hope for many sufferers, and only a fraction of those who need it can afford it. Nor do states and veterans' hospitals have the budgets to allow for more than a small number of patients to receive subsidized treatment. In the words of a parent whose daughter suffered from schizophrenia: "The miracle of Clozapine has turned into a mirage." She adds, "You can see it, you can read about, but you can't get it."

Questions

1. What obligations, if any, does Sandoz have to consider a schizophrenic's ability to pay when pricing the Clozaril treatment?
2. Is Sandoz being fair?
3. How would you resolve the dilemma between the patient's need for the drug treatment and the firm's need for profit? Does your solution meet the four criteria for conflict resolution?

Sources

Paul M. Barrett, "Sandoz Settles FTC Charges Over Clozaril," *The Wall Street Journal* (June 21, 1991), B3.

Judy Folkenberg, "Balancing hope with safety," *FDA Consumer* (June 1990), 17, 18, 21.

Peter Huber, "The lawyers versus the homeless," *Forbes* 146 (July 9, 1990), 92.

Deborah Pinkney, "Drug's monitoring system draws physicians' fury," *American Medical News* (June 1, 1990), 1, 12.

Andrew Purvis, "Way out of reach," *Time* (October 1, 1990), 79.

"Sandoz alters drug pricing," *The New York Times* (January 15, 1991), D18.

"Sandoz unit reports first in U.S. death linked to Clozaril," *The Wall Street Journal* (January 3, 1991), B4.

Chris Spolar, "New schizophrenic drug arouses furor over cost," *The Washington Post* (July 31, 1990), WH7.

Claudia Wallis and James Willwerth, "Awakenings," *Time* (July 6, 1992), 52–60.

Ron Winslow, "Sandoz price cut on Clozaril welcomed, but concerns continue over continued safety," *The Wall Street Journal* (December 7, 1990), B5.

Ron Winslow, "Sandoz sets rule for use of drug but move may fuel controversy," *The Wall Street Journal* (March 1, 1991), B2.

❖   **Case Study 6–3**   ❖

PROPOSITION 13

Proposition 13 was the end product of a rebellion by California property owners. Faced with spiraling property taxes, Californians were given the opportunity to cap their property taxes and stabilize the assessments on their land. The cap was set at 1 percent of the cash value of the property. Assessed value was to increase no more than 2 percent per year and would change to fair market value—that is, selling price—only when the property was sold.

When Proposition 13 went into effect, almost $6.5 billion was cut from property taxes. Homeowners saw their taxes reduced by over $2 billion. Residential rental property owners welcomed a cut of over $1 billion. Almost $3 billion of the cut was enjoyed by owners of nonresidential property. The governor of California, when evaluating the tax savings for businesses, stated that they had a "moral obligation" to create more jobs in the state with that money. Prior to the passage of the Proposition, some business supporters of Proposition 13 indicated that the public would benefit from their commercial tax savings.

Howard Jarvis was the prime sponsor of Proposition 13. He realized that renters would have to support the bill if it were to have a chance of passing. Jarvis was the director of a group of apartment-house owners in Southern California. He assured renters that their rents would be reduced upon passage of Proposition 13.

Proposition 13 became law but rent reduction did not follow. A woman in Palo Alto requested that her landlord rescind a planned rent increase because of the benefits he would receive from the new law. The landlord's answer was: "We empathize with your position. We understand it is hard for a single woman to make it on her own. Would you please vacate the premises by September 3."

One newspaper sought out landlords who had cut rents because of Proposition 13. In the first three days of its search, it could find no one who had. The governor and state workers then phoned landlords to persuade them to roll back rents. The governor admitted that the effort wasn't too successful. Howard Jarvis then tried to get landlords to lower their rents. Some did, but for a reason other than that of an "equitable distribution of savings." The rationale, according to one property manager, was to avoid threatened rent control measures put before city councils.

A renter's hotline, put in operation at that time, showed that despite the savings generated by Proposition 13, average rental rates rose more than 10 percent. Howard Jarvis expressed anger toward the landlords whom he felt had gone back on their word. But the most anger was expressed by the municipalities that had counted on property tax revenue and those who bought homes in the years after Proposition 13 went into effect.

Reductions in governmental tax revenues meant cuts in public spending. The results included reduced hours of operation for libraries and less frequent street cleaning. A recent estimate of the effects of Proposition 13 comes from Los Angeles. The county expected to lose $250 million due to property tax limits—money that helped fund the offices of the district attorney, public defender, and sheriff.

New buyers of homes, in turn, expressed outrage at the inequities caused by Proposition 13. Two cases serve to illustrate the perceived inequities. Stephanie Nordlinger bought a home in the suburbs of Los Angeles and paid $1,700 in property tax. Her assessed property value was based on the purchase price she had paid. Her neighbor, who lived in a larger house, paid only $358 a year in property taxes. He had lived in the house for thirteen years. Another buyer in Santa Monica received a tax bill for $4,650. This was sixteen times the $270 paid by his neighbor who had lived in a similar house for over ten years.

Proponents of Proposition 13 countered that any change in the assessment procedure would hurt the elderly. Most of the elderly had not changed residence since the passage of Proposition 13. The law protected people on fixed incomes. The price for that protection was a cut in government services. A University of California study gauged that property in the state was underassessed by 45 percent because of the law. The cost in lost taxes rose to $13 billion a year.

When the law was challenged in the Supreme Court, it was found to be constitutionally legal. However, Justice Blackman, who wrote the majority opinion which supported the law, still labeled Proposition 13 as "distasteful" and "unwise."

Questions

1. Has justice been served by Proposition 13? Explain your answer.
2. Upon what basis can the governor project a moral responsibility onto businesses? What school of moral thought and stage of moral reasoning seem to be depicted by his statement?
3. Create arguments both for and against the claim that equity has resulted for both rents and property taxes by Proposition 13.

Sources

Mary Barnett, "No relief for renters," *The Progressive* 42 (November 1978), 33–36.

Thomas D. Elias, "Proposition 13 haunts California four years after passage," *The Atlanta Journal and Constitution* (January 31, 1982), 28A.

Ralph Frammolino, "Study finds property in state undervalued by half," *Los Angeles Times* (March 11, 1993), A16.

Philip Hager, "State justices reject property tax case," *Los Angeles Times* (March 1, 1991), A35.

John Quirt, "Aftershocks from the great California taxquake," *Fortune* (September 25, 1978), 75–77, 80, 92, 84.

Tom Redburn and Nancy Yoshikara, "Landlords' tax break from Proposition 13 may backfire," *Los Angeles Times* (February 4, 1979), II, 1.

Stephen J. Sansweet, "Companies' big saving from Proposition 13 is slow to reach public," *The Wall Street Journal* (February 13, 1979), 1, 22.

David G. Savage, "U.S. justices uphold Proposition 13 tax structure," *Los Angeles Times* (June 19, 1992), A1, A30.

William Trombley, "Legislature ponders problems of Proposition 13," *Los Angeles Times* (July 15, 1990), A3, A31.

Ben Wiberman, "Howard Jarvis' new crusade," *Forbes* (September 24, 1984), 43–44.

Notes to Chapter 6

[1]This pass-along story may have had its roots in a *Wall Street Journal* article from the 1970s, but we have not been able to track down the original source.

[2]Robert Nozick, *Anarchy, State and Utopia* (New York: Basic Books, Inc., 1974), pp. 239–246.

[3]Carol Gilligan, *In a Different Voice: Psychological Theory and Women's Development* (Cambridge, MA: Harvard University Press, 1982).

[4]William Damon, *The Moral Child: Nurturing Children's Natural Moral Growth* (New York: The Free Press, 1988), p. 100.

[5]Lawrence J. Walker, "Sex Differences in Moral Reasoning," in William M. Kurtines and Jacob Gewirtz (eds.), *Handbook of Moral Behavior and Development* (Hillsdale, NJ: Lawrence Erlbaum Associates, Publishers, 1991), vol. 2.

[6]Immanuel Kant, *Ethical Philosophy: The Metaphysical Principle of Virtue*, trans. by James E. Ellington (Indianapolis: Hackett Publishing Company, 1983). First published in 1797.

[7]John R. P. French and Bertram Raven, *Studies in Social Power* (Ann Arbor, MI: Institute for Social Research, 1959).

[8]John Rawls, *A Theory of Justice* (Cambridge, MA: Harvard University Press, 1971). See especially Chapter 1.

[9]Rawls, p. 569.

[10]Morton Deutsch, "Equity and Economic Efficiency: Is There a Trade-Off?" in N. Eisenberg and E. Staub (eds.), *Social and Moral Values* (Hillsdale, NJ: Lawrence Erlbaum Associates, Publishers, 1989), p. 142.

[11]William K. Frankena, *Ethics,* 2nd. ed (Englewood Cliffs, NJ: Prentice-Hall, 1973), p. 50.

[12]Rawls, p. 85.

[13]Ann Colby et al., *The Measurement of Moral Judgment* (Cambridge, MA: Center for Moral Education, Harvard University), vol. I, Part 1, Table 2, p. 80.

[14]John Martin Rich and Joseph L. De Vistis, *Theories of Moral Development* (Springfield, IL: Charles C. Thomas Publishers, 1985).

[15]William M. Kurtines, "Sociomoral Behavior and Development from a Rule-Governed Perspective: Psychosocial Theory as a Nomotic Science," in William M. Kurtines and Jacob L. Gewirtz (eds.), *Moral Development through Social Interaction* (New York: John Wiley & Sons), 1987.

[16]W. D. Ross, *The Right and the Good* (Oxford: The Clarendon Press, 1930), pp. 18–22.

Part Two

CONFLICT RESOLUTION

Chapter 7

CONFLICT OF INTEREST?

Throughout the first six chapters of this text, we emphasized the point that *conflict of interest* comes closest to the heart of what ethics is all about. As we mentioned in the Introduction, some philosophers have defined morality as a human institution that aims to resolve or "harmonize" conflicts of interest. This statement coincides with the definition of ethics that we offer— "a set of normative guidelines directed toward resolving conflicts of interest, so as to enhance societal well-being." Regardless of whether you accept conflict resolution as part of the definition of morality, conflicts of interest are surely a typical stimulus for persons to think seriously about moral or ethical questions.

In a broad sense, business in a free economy is based on conflicts. Two such conflicts include the conflict between different firms (which we call *competition*) and the conflict between the firm's need for profit and the desire of the public to obtain maximum benefits for minimum costs. This broad view raises two general questions: "What constitutes "fair" competition?" and "What is the proper role of business in relation to the public?" The ethical perspective that regards competition as conflict rests on the notion that competition is more constructive than destructive.[1] Constructive competition offers the possibility that all parties to a conflict can benefit. That is, competition fosters efficiency and provides an incentive for us to work "harder and smarter." Destructive conflict, in contrast, offers more questionable benefit to society. Its means can be brutal, given the mindset of "I win only when you lose." Its results, in turn, may well lead to quasi-monopoly market conditions under which there are few incentives to innovate. This type of conflict is more likely to raise moral questions because of the negative consequences both for competitors and for the publics served by those businesses. In our opinion, the total resolution of conflict is not always possible. Consequently, some effective process is necessary to control or manage conflict so that it does not prove destructive to the stakeholders involved.

Stakeholders in Conflict Resolution

A less abstract view of conflict concerns the role of business in relation to its publics or stakeholders. Philip Kotler defines a *public* as any group that has an actual or potential interest in or impact on an organization's ability to achieve its objectives.[2] Given this definition, there are obviously many different types of publics in a company's environment. Conflict resulting from a questioned business practice will involve one or more of these publics.

There is, first of all, the *general public* composed of those who are aware of the firm. The general public, however, is unlike many of the other publics in that it does not act toward the company in any organized way. For example, we in this country are aware of the harm but have done little about the destruction of the Brazilian rain forest.

Second are the *local publics*. Within a particular geographical area, local publics have a variety of special interests. Included in this definition would be those whose physical or financial well-being is directly influenced by the firm—for example, a supplier who delivered an invoiced shipment minutes before the customer declared bankruptcy.

Third are what might be called *citizen action publics*. These are groups—for instance, minority groups, consumer groups, and environmental protection groups—that have been organized in an attempt to gain influence on matters that concern their members.

Fourth are the various *media publics* such as radio and television stations, networks, newspapers, and magazines. Conflicts may arise when a particular company and a particular media outlet have differing views on political or economic issues. Fifth are the various *government publics*. Governments and governmental agencies—from local to state to national—all are potentially involved in influencing business organizations. Therefore, the possibility of conflict always exists.

Sixth are what might be called the *financial publics*. Banks and investors who hold stock, bonds, or commercial paper in the enterprise (for example, depositors in the Bank of Credit and Commerce [BCCI]) are the most visible members of this public.

Last are what Kotler calls *internal publics*. In a typical company, these would include the officers, managers, white-collar workers, and blue-collar workers. The personal values of these individuals may not always mesh with the values of the firm.

Given our final clause in our definition of ethics—"to enhance societal well-being,"—it is rare when an ethical issue in business does not affect at least one of these publics.

Examples

Perhaps the most difficult types of ethical conflict involve internal disputes that affect individuals at work in a company. Such conflicts might be called *conflicts of conscience* if this phrase is interpreted broadly. A worker, for example, may experience a major conflict between feelings of loyalty to the company and a conviction that some policy or product of the company is morally wrong. This type of conflict may give rise to the action we called "whistle-blowing" (see Chapter 5).

For the most part, the actual or potential conflicts we have distinguished involve a conflict between two or more legitimate interests. For instance, a worker may be torn between a legitimate feeling of company loyalty and a legitimate concern with doing what is felt to be morally right.

Imagine that you are the chief accountant in a small branch office of a highly profitable multinational firm. A valued employee who served the firm well retired two weeks ago. This employee chose a retirement plan with high salary and low insurance benefits. Last week, that employee suffered a moderate stroke. The employee has no savings, no family, and will be turned out of the hospital onto the streets next week. Your boss asks you to draw from the firm's petty cash account to pay for this week's hospital bills. He also asks you to change the employee's retirement benefit plan choices to one designating low salary and high insurance benefits. The original forms have not left the local office yet. What will you do? Use the four normative guidelines to explain your action. Which public's interests, if any, would you consider in this case? Your answer should be related to how broadly or narrowly you define the society whose well-being you seriously consider in your decisions. That definition, in turn, will help you identify which of the six stages of moral reasoning you are using.

If we accept the viewpoint that parties and publics affected by a business transaction may have a legitimate interest in that transaction, it then becomes important to determine whether and how resulting conflicts with moral ramifications can be resolved.

Moral Development and Conflict Resolution

While Kohlberg set the stage for examining moral development, his colleagues have modified and expanded his approach.[3] They believe that Kohlberg's cognitive approach falls short in adequately encompassing the motivation behind moral actions. They also feel that emotion as well as reason has a motivating role in moral action. Thus, efforts to resolve conflict should not discount the emotional needs of the parties involved. In addition, they wonder if the fifth and sixth stages of moral development, given the different social conditions in which people live, really evolve in the natural progression that Kohlberg has claimed.

Even with these perceived flaws, the format of developmental stages provides us with an excellent tool to examine the ways in which businesspeople attempt to resolve conflicts from their own moral vantage points.

Habermas's View

Integrating conflict resolution and moral development has been a focal point in the work of Jürgen Habermas. Although Habermas's egalitarian political philosophy may cause some in business to shutter, there is much to be praised about his efforts to settle conflict through negotiation. He assumes that all reasoning persons will be driven by at least some similar underlying principles or goals. His thought is that a mutually arrived at consensus is possible through a communication process structured around those common goals. However, conflict resolution does not come easily.

Conflict resolution in the form of consensus is threatened when obstacles to the communication process arise. Such obstacles arise when

- the words or expressions used by either party do not readily lead to mutual comprehension;
- the speaker does not intend to communicate all the pertinent facts;
- the honesty of the speaker is questioned; or
- the statement of the speaker leads to a less than optional resolution of the conflict, given the norms of the parties and the options available.[4]

Apart from these procedural impediments to successful communications, there are more humanly mundane obstacles impeding conflict resolution. These include

- feared injury to pride
- perceived sacrifice of ideology
- perceived loss of power bases
- perceived loss of flexibility
- confusion over motives and goals if we are seen to be moving away from our original position.

To overcome these obstacles when dealing with the other party, a strictly adversarial mode of communication (Strategic Communication) may prove less successful than a cooperative (Discursive Communication) mode.

Resolution by Strategic Communication

Sometimes verbal coercion proves to be a useful mode for overcoming both procedural and human obstacles to successful communication. We described this method in Chapter 1. When one party to the conflict has the power to impose its will on another (regardless of whether this power is political, economic, or physical), it is very tempting to resolve the conflict at one level by the simple use of coercion. Such temptations can be very seductive, as most of us know. But there is one overwhelming problem with this means of conflict resolution: it has a built-in tendency to backfire. The logic of the situation was analyzed by Thomas Hobbes in the *Leviathan*. Hobbes declared that using brute force to settle conflict leads to "the war of everyone against everyone," a condition that he also referred to as "the state of nature."[5] Humans find themselves in this combative situation whenever they lack the structures of government, law, and morality to regulate their dealings with one another. Chaos results when such relationships cannot be "harmonized." If one person or group were so strong, however, that his/her/its power could not be successfully challenged, social stability could be achieved simply through the use of brute force. In a sense, this is true. Some firms within selected business environments do seem to operate under these conditions at times. But the resentment that results from the experience of being dominated by brute force will tend to be expressed, in the long run at least, in various acts of rebellion. These acts of rebellion can do grave harm, even to those persons or groups whose power appears irresistible.

Those who need to react to the power of Strategic Communication have options other than to submit to verbal coercion. The party under attack may simply withdraw from the exchange, or, as we sometimes figuratively put it, may "take his ball and go home." A second option is to deny the conflict and talk around the situation—engaging in what Habermas calls Nonsignificant Communication.

In response to these nonsubmitting reactions, the wielder of coercive power may shift the thrust of persuasive efforts to rely on power in the form of rewards, expertise, or legitimate authority. These responses are within the definition of Strategic Communication (we briefly discussed these methods in Chapters 2, 3, and 4). The underlying goal behind each of the four types of power is simply to prevail with one's position—to win the party with the conflicting point of view over to one's position.

As we explained in Chapter 2, persons at Stage Two of moral development will consider only the consequences produced for themselves in weighing the amount of good gained by an action or type of action. Holders of such a view are called *"restricted" consequentialists*—since the consequences or results considered relevant in making an ethical judgment are restricted in some way. Other consequentialists using higher stages of moral reasoning take all consequences of an action, regardless of the person or group to whom they occur, to be relevant to an ethical judgment. Holders of this view are called *"universal" consequentialists*—since all consequences (throughout the "universe") are considered relevant.

An Example

Overcoming obstacles through the form of Strategic Communication that focuses on consequences is apparent in the following example. Consider the case of a telephone company employee who will be financially rewarded for all of the extra telephone services he or she sells. Imagine this employee feeling tempted to play on the fears of an elderly low-income customer through verbal coercion by saying, "Of course you need a phone in each room of your three-room apartment. What if someone were trying to break in and you needed to call the police right away?" (This conversation was actually overheard by one of the authors in a branch office of the telephone company.) The egoist reasoning at the second stage of moral development will weigh the personal consequences of taking advantage of the customer in this way against the personal consequences of not doing so. But the egoist might also consider the consequences of performing various alternative actions. Since an indefinite number of possibilities exists for every situation, the egoist may well be able to think of several creative alternatives to taking advantage of the customer. In any case, however, the personal consequences for the employee would be the only factors relevant to the rightness or wrongness of the act from the egoist's perspective.

On the other hand, the utilitarian at the fifth stage of moral development would look at the consequences for everyone for each various possible action. *Everyone* here means all the publics affected in any way by the action. According to the utilitarian, the "pros" and "cons" of each possible action for each person affected need to be considered. Even though it might often be literally impossible to do this, the method remains the utilitarian ideal. And insofar as our moral reasoning approaches this ideal, the utilitarian would say, our conflicts of interest will be settled by the superior authority of a universal morality. This utilitarian stance is more representative of Discursive Communication than of the adversarial counterpunching found in Strategic Communication. Table 7-1 illustrates some of these relationships.

Resolution by Discursive Communication

Strategic Communication will not always be successful. It may, in fact, exacerbate a conflict rather than resolve it. If we cannot walk away from a conflict, the only realistic option is Discursive Communication. A synopsis of Habermas's Discursive Communication process appears in the procedures suggested by Roger Fisher and William Ury.[6] Their work summarizes the conclusions drawn from the Harvard Negotiation Project, and they present a sequential five-step procedure for resolving conflict.

1. Separate the principles behind both parties' positions from the positions themselves.
2. Obtain agreement on mutual goals regarding the principles.
3. Understand and support aspects of the other party's reasoning and position.
4. Calculate consequences of each act versus the principles.
5. Yield to principles but not to pressure.

**Table 7–1 Process for Resolving Conflict
at Different Levels of Moral Reasoning**

Preconventional Level (Stages 1 and 2)	Conventional Level (Stages 3 and 4)	Postconventional Level (Stages 5 and 6)
Personal Perspective		
Personal natural identity	Social role identity	Identity of true self
Span of Concern		
Personal natural and social environment	Primary reference group or members of political community	All interacting associates or all human as private individuals or all people as members of a world society
Goals		
Maximize personal pleasure and avoid pain through obedience or reciprocity	Acquiescence to concrete morality of primary reference group or secondary references groups	Civil liberties and public welfare or Moral freedom or Political freedom
Behavioral Norms		
Understand and follow behavior expectations with respect to actions and consequences of actions	Understand roles and follow legal/social norms	Understand and apply universalizable personal principles
Negative Sanctions		
Punishment	Shame	Guilt
Types of Communication		
Incomplete interaction emphasize subjective instrumental purpose	Complete interaction emphasize system maintenance or group conformity	Discursives communication emphasize utility or Social contract or Universal principles

Source: Adapted from Jurgen Habermas, *Communications and the Evolution of Society.,*
Boston, Beacon Press, 1979, pp. 68, 76, 77, 81, 83, 89

Giving credence to Fisher and Ury's operationalization of Habermas's theory, Daniel Druckman's experiments confirm the difficulty of attaining conflict resolution when the parties cannot separate their original positions from the principles that spawned them.[7]

The goal of Discursive Communication, according to Habermas, is to obtain a consensus position that would embody the highest stage of morality. In more practical business terminology, Dean Pruitt has interpreted this consensus to mean an "integrative agreement." An integrative agreement occurs when "the participants are all satisfied with their outcomes and feel that they have gained as a result of the conflict".[8] Pruitt notes that integrative agreements result from integrative bargaining. Such bargaining has a utilitarian aspect in that it results in benefits for more than just the bargainers.

The Discursive Process

The steps within the process of integrative bargaining embody the crux of Habermas's Discursive Communication without drawing on the theoretical base of why and how those steps lead toward a consensus. Some of these steps, as detailed by Richard Walton and Robert McKersie, are as follows:[9]

- Find personal points, not related to the issue, in common.
- Use similar language.
- Agree on common problems.
- Isolate "superordinate" goals which are acknowledged by and compelling to both parties.
- Focus on mutual success.
- Deemphasize differences.
- Increase interaction between the parties.
- Emphasize common fate.
- Emphasize common background.
- Try to solve substantive problems of the other party.
- Try to strengthen the opponent's position within the organization.
- Confer status on the opponent.
- Separate yourself from dislike of the other person.
- Reward opponent's behavior with compliments and expressed appreciation.
- Remind opponent of role obligations.
- Assist opponent to work through feelings.

James Wall has labeled these bargaining tactics as the joint problem-solving debate.[10] These tactics flesh out the broad guidelines set out by Fisher and Ury in presenting the recommendations of the Harvard Negotiation project team. This process is summarized in Habermas's moral negotiation terminology in Table 7-2. Before proceeding any farther, let us stop to remind ourselves that this is not an esoteric exercise in philosophy. Our purpose in applying Habermas's Discursive Communication method to ethical issues in business is not so much to analyze theoretical discourse about what is true as to focus on practical discourse about what is right.[11]

Theoretical Legitimacy

Socrates and Plato held that an ethical person is a reasoning person. They also observed that moral issues arise when there are conflicts of interest. These observations underpin the work of twentieth-century philosophers such as Baier and Perry, who concentrated on conflict resolution as the focal point of

Table 7–2   Resolving Conflicts of Interests

Strategic Communication	Discursive Communication
Holds personal reason for position	Identifies similarities between positions
(in accord with)	*(in accord with)*
Closed-minded conviction while listening to opposition	Open-minded approach while listening to opposition
(leads to)	*(leads to)*
Identifying contradictions	Separating principles from positions
Focuses on differences in original positions	Calculates consequences of new position
(then)	*(then)*
Takes adversarial stance	Tests against principles
(then)	*(then)*
Offers counterevidence based on own interest and custom of habit	Seeks mutual integration based on agreement and convention of reason
(relying on)	*(relying on)*
Power or manipulation	Shared analysis

morality. And it is this train of thought in moral thinking that leads us to Discursive Communication as a means to resolve moral conflicts. In turn, *feasibility, consistency, reasoning,* and *universalizability* are appropriate normative guidelines to test whether a position that has been advanced to resolve a moral conflict really does enhance societal well-being.

From the comparisons in Table 7-2, we determine that we should search for some method of conflict resolution without the drawbacks associated with Strategic Communication. Ideally, such a method would be *rational,* in that it would appeal to the reasoning abilities of human beings; and it would also be *universal,* in that it could in principle apply to all persons, regardless of their particular circumstances. This approach can be taken regardless of the individual's particular desires, point of view, or code of ethics. It may be that such an ideal method does not actually exist. On the other hand, perhaps it does. Only further investigations can settle this question.

Is there any way to resolve conflicts of interest rationally? At least two different, general approaches attempt to do so. The first of these is what might be called a *scientific* approach. It includes applying the methods recommended in such fields as decision science and decision theory. Such an approach tends to rely heavily on mathematical models of how decisions can be made under various circumstances (limited knowledge, for example). Mathematical models, when combined with the findings of the social sciences (psychology, for example), may enable one to form clearer ideas about how disputes tend to be resolved between people. Negotiators can make use of such theories and information, sometimes operating more or less intuitively, in trying to resolve conflicts—or as Fisher and Ury's book put it, in "getting to 'yes'." Such studies and methods are the subject of the *Journal of Conflict Resolution,* the leading publication in this area. Although most of us have developed some skills in conflict resolution through trial and error, specific reading and training can develop and refine these abilities.

As was suggested above, however, there is a second type of approach to the rational resolution of conflict. This latter method attempts to get an individual to think carefully about a situation in the light of one's ethical theory, or, as some would put it, "from the moral point of view." Of course, since our views of ethics and morality differ, there is no guarantee that such thinking will resolve all—or even most—conflicts. Some conflicts, however, do seem to resolve themselves once we take the moral point of view, and there are others that move closer to resolution when we do adopt this method. After all, if this were not the case, Thomas Hobbes's suggestion that morality might help us avoid "the war of each against all" would not make any sense.

Conclusions

From the standpoint of those who define morality as an instrument for producing social harmony, conflict in general is a bad thing—something to be always eliminated if possible. In our opinion, however, that is not feasible. Conflict—whether between the interests of the same or of different persons or groups—is a natural phenomenon. Rawls noted that since we must associate with others, there is an advantage to cooperating with them.[12] This is self-evident in a business environment. But we are naturally sensitive to the possible inequitable distribution of benefits resulting from that cooperation. Potential conflict then arises from the tendency to cooperate while trying to protect personal interests. The point is not to try to eliminate that conflict but to manage it so that it will not be destructive.

Aristotle held that all persons naturally desire to know. That is probably true. It seems to us, however, that persons naturally desire to grow, to reach out beyond their present situations, and to test the limits both of their own abilities and of their social settings. Such testing will, of course, tend to result in conflict. How much money can I make? How high can I rise in my company? How much can I get away with? Such questions are as natural as the social codes and sanctions that aim at keeping us from violent and unrestricted conflict.

Such codes are usually internalized during the course of maturation. Business values develop in a similar way. And once these values have developed, the behavior they lead to may persist even without direct supervision by someone in authority. For this reason, it is far more efficient to impart the values of the company to the individual workers, letting the workers make decisions so that they may act from these values than it would be to have the CEO constantly meddling in the activities and decisions of each worker.

Just as society at large may be said to have a culture, so may a corporation. In some business situations, this corporate culture is strongly influenced—even determined—by the CEO. In certain respects, the influence of the CEO is parallel to the influence of the parents in a family: there are parents whose influence over the values of family members rests on the threat of force. Other parents influence through the power of example. Still other parents influence (often with negative consequences) by abdicating any leadership role in the family at all. In any case, the atmosphere in a family and the parents' influence on it will parallel the culture of a corporation and the CEO's influence. The appeal to brute force, as we have suggested, seems not to work well in either the family or the workplace. (Reflect, for example, on such statements as these: "I don't know why my kid's so bad; I beat her every day" and "I threaten every day to fire him; how come he makes so many mistakes in his work?")

The CEO can often be a catalyst in the development of the business values that make up a given corporate culture. This corporate culture, of course, is one aspect of what we referred to earlier in this chapter as an *internal public*. And our earlier comments about the possibilities of conflict resolution still apply. What we will address in the following chapters is a set of procedures for overcoming the communication obstacles that impede conflict resolution.

In ending this chapter, consider the degree to which company values have been successfully imparted in the cases that follow. Take into account the following questions:

1. Are corporate values readily identified by actions of the employees?

2. Does the behavior of those employees generate internal conflict?

3. Would those businesspersons invite others, particularly those with whom they transact, to adopt the same set of behaviors and values?

❖   Case Study 7–1   ❖

OHIO EDISON

Pipe bombs exploded at a Pacific Gas and Electric Company facility near Cupertino, California. The group that took credit for the bombing identified itself in a letter to the police, calling itself the Eugene Kuhn unit of the New World Liberation Front. Eugene Kuhn was a man who became the center of public controversy in Ohio after he had frozen to death. His case is not unique: deaths under similar circumstances have occurred in Indiana and Connecticut. The situation is perhaps best explained if we track events over a thirteen-month period in Ohio.

In March, the first month of this period, an elderly woman appeared before the Public Utilities Commission of Ohio (PUCO). She stated that she and her husband had worked hard during their fifty years of marriage. Their mortgage was paid off, and they prided themselves on their financial independence. However, they lived on a fixed income and did not know how they were going to cope with rising prices. Of particular concern was the proposed rate increase in their electric bill.

The PUCO public information director stated that the Commission was aware of the potential life-threatening dangers that could result if people could not afford to pay their utility bills. PUCO had created and disseminated guidelines to utilities concerning the protocol to be followed before electric services would be turned off because of overdue payments. The director said: "In a couple of other states people froze to death because utilities had been turned off, and we didn't want that to happen here."

The PUCO guidelines mandated a three-step process. First, the utilities were asked to try to establish a time payment plan with individual customers who had difficulty paying their bills. Second, the utility was asked to make a concerted effort to communicate personally with customers before power was cut off. Third, PUCO established a toll-free telephone service that customers could use to get advice on payments.

Need for these aids became evident when Ohio Edison formally requested a 40 percent rate increase in October. The 22 cities that were affected countered with a proposal to accept just a 16 percent increase. PUCO's staff studied both the request and the counteroffer and came up with a compromise rate hike of 24 percent. The cities rejected the compromise. The 40 percent rate increase originally proposed by Ohio Edison was in line with profit margins accepted by PUCO in its previous hearings on rate hikes. That increase translated into an 8.5 percent return on assets.

In January of the following year, seventy-four-year-old Eugene Kuhn was found dead in his bed in Mansfield, Ohio. He had died of exposure. The temperature in Kuhn's bedroom was under ten degrees. Eight days before he was found, Ohio Edison had disconnected his electric power. Kuhn, a retired factory worker, had not paid his electric bill since the previous September. The amount he owed Ohio Edison was $18.38.

Under Ohio law, a utility could disconnect power if a customer was more than a month in arrears in paying a bill. Ohio Edison's policy was to extend that cut-off date to sixty days. In Kuhn's case, Ohio Edison had carried him for over ninety days.

The utility had tried to contact Kuhn but had received no response. Ohio Edison even contacted the county welfare office to inform that department of the impending cut-off of services to Kuhn. The welfare office sent a letter to him, but he never retrieved it from his mailbox. In reaction to Kuhn's death, no disconnection of power supply was allowed by the company for the rest of the winter.

One Cleveland official had forebodings of what would happen in the spring. He believed that utilities would begin mass power cut-offs that would affect those who had not kept up with their bills. A consumer counselor outlined the problem in dollars and cents. Comparing one mother's welfare income versus her bill for rent and power, the bottom line showed a one dollar deficit. "How can she pay it and still eat?" was his comment. He further wondered if those who faced disconnection would be able to pay off their electric bills before cold weather returned the following October.

Two months after Kuhn's death, PUCO reached a resolution on Ohio Edison's request for the 40 percent rate increase. It paired down that number and approved a 26 percent increase, over the objections of the cities affected. Seven months later, Ohio Edison announced that it would seek an additional rate increase totaling $57 million. Part of the justification was to fund air-pollution control measures in Mansfield. During this period, Ohio Edison's net return on assets was approximately 4.6 percent.

Questions

1. List in rank order the moral responsibilities of Ohio Edison. To whom is the company responsible?
2. Is there an ethical justification for turning off the electricity of people who have not paid their power bills?
3. Construct a negotiated policy between PUCO and Ohio Edison so that future conflicts might be avoided.

Sources

William R. Diem, "Utilities ordered to serve nonpaying homes," *Plain Dealer* (Cleveland, January 27, 1977), 1.

Robert Fernandez, "Edison halts rate hike plan till July 1990," *Akron Beacon Journal* (Akron, OH, March 17, 1989), 1.

Robert Fernandez, "Ohio Edison puts on a sunny face," *Akron Beacon Journal* (Akron, OH, April 9, 1989), 1.

Jennifer French, "Utilities are lending a helping hand," *Times Herald-Record* (Middletown, NY, September 8, 1987), 1.

William Hershey, "Edison talks stall; rate hike hearings seen," *Akron Beacon Journal* (Akron, OH, October 8, 1976), 1.

Jesse Leavenworth and Marc R. Crowe, "Report on death issued," *Hartford Courant* (Hartford, CT, November 8, 1986), 6.

Douglas McCormick, "Bar some utility shut-offs," *Cleveland Press* (January 14, 1979), 14.

Deena Mirow, "Utilities pinch," *Plain Dealer* (Cleveland, March 8, 1976), 5.

Moody's Public Utility Manual (New York: Moody's Investors Service, Inc., 1978).

"Patient on life support dies after power is cut," *The New York Times* (September 24, 1989), Sec. 1, 14.

"Terrorists adopt victim's name," *The New York Times* (January 28, 1977), Sec. 1, 17.

Pauline Thomas, "Ohio Edison seeks big hike," *Plain Dealer* (Cleveland, October 11, 1977), 3.

❖   **Case Study 7–2**   ❖

MARY CUNNINGHAM

Mary Cunningham is brilliant. She is also an admitted idealist. After a short but eventful career in business, she founded a nonprofit support group to help pregnant working women. This support group, called the Nurturing Network, has attracted over fifty corporate sponsors. The Nurturing Network aids pregnant women in their search for affordable medical care and even temporary employment. She feels that her work with the Nurturing Network is motivated by the same goals that she had while working at Bendix. But at Bendix she felt that her goals were misunderstood. In her words: "I thought that you could establish wonderful societal reforms through organizations, not only by how you handle your employees but by supporting a CEO who had those policies."

Cunningham is a Phi Beta Kappa graduate of Wellesley with a genius-level IQ score. She met her first husband, a Harvard Business School student, while at college. After graduation, they moved to New York where she found employment as an officer at Chase Manhattan Bank. Her marriage started to show signs of stress when she returned to Massachusetts to attend the Harvard Business School. Perhaps a victim of her idealism, she said of the break-up, "We were more focused on the message we were sending to society than on our marriage."

After graduating from the Harvard Business School, she took a job as executive assistant to Bill Agee, Chairman of Bendix. She saw in Agee the same motivation and goals that drove her life. Agee was likewise impressed. Cunningham was promoted to Vice President for Corporate and Public Affairs and then to Vice President for Strategy Planning—all in less than three years.

Agee credited Bendix's strategic changes to Cunningham's planning ability. He is on record as saying that she was the most important person in the company. However, the fact that the two executives were together on many occasions became the topic of disparaging gossip. The rumors about their relationship became so widespread that Agee felt he had to take action. He decided that a public statement in front of Bendix personnel was appropriate. In that statement, he denied that Cunningham's promotions were due to any personal nonbusiness relationship.

What exacerbated the situation was that Agee's marriage had been coming to an end. His wife had not cared for the social role demanded of the spouse of a corporate chairman. They had talked about divorce for some time but had waited until their children were older and more independent. Cunningham, according to one report, had helped build up Diane Agee's confidence and self-sufficiency so that she could handle the break-up.

Part of Cunningham's problem at Bendix was her method of translating strategic planning into action. Executives within Bendix felt that she went too far in presenting her suggestions as joint Agee/Cunningham decisions. Bendix president William Panny criticized Cunningham's behavior within the firm and let her know his feelings. Panny also made Agee aware of those feelings, questioning her action's effect on plant morale. Agee's reaction was to ask Panny to resign. Questions were asked by other Bendix employees as well. One complaint was that Cunningham was so determined to suggest changes that she believed were needed that she sometimes bypassed line authority.

Cunningham sensed this criticism, as well as the rumors about her relationship with Agee. She contemplated a leave of absence but rejected the suggestion that she resign. Her rationale was that resignation would send the wrong message to young women in the corporate ranks. Agee and Cunningham independently denied that they were romantically involved. Bendix's board of directors, though, believed that the situation had gotten out of hand and told Agee that Cunningham would have to go. Cunningham resigned and blamed the rumor campaign for her departure.

Working women have long perceived the concept of a glass ceiling in America. Many of them question what it takes to be promoted to corporate executive levels. Some reacted to Cunningham's resignation by wondering if being both attractive and intelligent was an impediment to a woman's success in business. Others felt that Cunningham should have been more sensitive to the natural resentment directed toward successful women in corporations.

Cunningham went on to accept the position of Vice President of Seagram's wine group. In fact, she created the strategic plan to form the wine group within Seagram. In her free time, she continued to advise Agee about operations at Bendix, and he acknowledged her role as his key confidant. When

Bendix's subsequent takeover attempt of Martin Marietta turned sour, Agee resigned. He then took the position of chairman and chief executive officer at Morrison Knudsen. Cunningham, in turn, took over the task of administering the Morrison Knudsen's charitable foundation. She even made use of an office next to the chairman's. When Agee initiated changes within the firm, morale problems cropped up. While there are those who criticized Agee, his wife depicted his actions as examples of enlightened management. But morale problems usually revolve around criticism, and some of that criticism at Morrison Knudsen was directed at the chairman's wife, Mary Cunningham Agee.

Questions

1. What moral justification can a firm offer to restrict the personal behavior of its executives? What would you prohibit? Why?
2. Can you identify any ethical problems in this case?
3. If you had been brought into Bendix as a consultant to resolve the conflict surrounding Mary Cunningham when it first emerged, what would you have done?

Sources

"Bendix Battle: Mary Cunningham's farewell," *Time* (October 20, 1980), 78.

Peter W. Berstein, "Upheaval at Bendix," *Fortune* (October 18, 1982), 157–165.

Harlan S. Byrne, "Bill Agee to the rescue? Beleaguered Morrison Knudsen calls ex-Bendix boss," *Barron's* (August 15, 1988), 14–15.

"The Cunningham story," *Newsweek* (October 27, 1980), 82–83.

Tim R. Ferguson, "A working woman's network into motherhood," *The Wall Street Journal* (September 4, 1990), A15.

Christopher Knowlton, "Bill Agee gets a second chance," *Fortune* (March 27, 1989), 94–96.

Mary Makarushka, "Mother Mary: life after Bendix," *Savvy* (October 1988), 16.

Hugh D. Menzies, "The boardroom battle at Bendix," *Fortune* (January 11, 1982), 54, 56, 57.

Richard Meyer, "Bill Agee comes to Morrison Knudsen," *Financial World* (September 6, 1988), 14–15.

Annetta Miller, "Confronting a corporate 'stigma'; a top working woman's pregnancy-support group," *Newsweek* (April 4, 1988), 48.

Thomas Moore, "Why Martin Marietta loves Mary Cunningham," *Fortune* (March 16, 1987), 66–70.

Nancy J. Para, "Mary Cunningham's new network," *Fortune* (August 31, 1987), 92–93.

Roy Rowan and Thomas Moore, "Behind the lines in the Bendix war," *Fortune* (October 18, 1982), 157–165.

Gail Sheehy, "Storm warnings at Bendix," *The Washington Post* (October 14, 1980), B3.

Richard L. Stern and Reed Abelson, "The Imperial Agees," *Forbes* (June 8, 1992), 88–92.

❖   **Case Study 7–3**   ❖

LONRHO

Lonrho was impressed with the negotiation skills of Roland "Tiny" Rowland. Rowland was recruited to oversee the operations of the London-based mining firm after he had worked for a competitor in southern Africa. Lonrho representative Angus Ogilvy approached Rowland about joining the firm. Rowland accepted the proposal and merged his local African firm into Lonrho.

Rowland envisioned a future role for Ogilvy in Lonrho and offered him favorable terms to subscribe to stock options. Ogilvy agreed and wrote to Roland: "I only hope you realize how grateful I am. It'll make a tremendous difference to my personal life." Ogilvy later traded his stock option for a percentage of Rowland's own Bahamas-based firm, Yeoman Investments.

Because of the political turmoil in southern Africa, Rowland, with Yeoman Investments acting as intermediary, bought a Rhodesian firm for Lonrho's South African operation. It was not a direct purchase because of exchange controls placed on Rhodesia (now Zimbabwe). To facilitate the purchase, Yeoman bought a Swiss mining firm. That firm loaned money to a second firm, Borma Holding. Lonrho and Borma Holding then jointly bought the Rhodesian firm. Borma subsequently sold its share to Lonrho South Africa. Rowland, when later asked about the rationale behind this convoluted method of purchase, replied it had to do with Ogilvy's need for funds.

Rowland's personal firm, Yeoman Investments, made 590,000 pounds on the deal. Ogilvy's share was 60,000. Ogilvy claimed, however, that he had had no knowledge of the transaction. He also claimed that he would have opposed the transaction if had he known about it. Why would he make this disclaimer? Ogilvy had married Princess Alexandra of the British royal family. Since the British government had imposed sanctions on firms dealing with Rhodesia, public exposure of Ogilvy's stake in Yeoman

Investments would prove embarrassing for the government. A British government report on the Yeoman–Borma affair did indeed question Ogilvy's judgment relevant to government policy, given his financial relations with Tiny Rowland. But no legal penalties issued.

Rowland knew the power of connections and influence. Lonrho's finance director, Fred Butcher, was among a group of executives charged with fraud as they sought full control of a partly owned Lonrho subsidiary in South Africa. It would take influence to finesse this situation. Butcher, on behalf of Rowland, approached a man with such influence, Duncan Sandys. Sandys was a former British Commonwealth Secretary who served as a consultant to Lonrho. Sandys accepted Lonrho's chairmanship, but not at the suggested pay of 35,000 pounds. He demanded and received an annual salary of 130,000 pounds. This was an extraordinary sum by British standards. Lonrho's board of directors was not told of the compensation package for fear they would reject it.

Sandys's employment served its purpose. After meeting with and writing to various South African government officials, Sandys could announce that charges against Butcher had been dropped. But this resolution had its price. Sandys's compensation package, which included tax-free monies funnelled through the Cayman Islands, came to light. Although the compensation plan was not illegal in British law, it caused a furor.

A majority of Lonrho's board of directors asked for Rowland's resignation. They accused Rowland of both deception and self-serving financial dealings. The matter was then brought to Lonrho's stockholders. Leaders of African nations where blacks were in power rallied to Rowland's side. Lonrho had become the largest food producer in Africa. Rowland had sent grain to draught areas of Mozambique and to those who sought to establish the independent nation of Zimbabwe. The presidents of Kenya, Malawi, and Zambia counted themselves among his friends. Said President Kenneth Kaunda of Zambia: "Tiny Rowland is a capitalist with a human face." When other European firms abandoned operations in Africa, Rowland had expanded Lonrho's interests. The newly independent countries appreciated both his investments and his efforts to establish peace on the continent.

Lonrho's stockholders also appreciated his performance. They voted in his favor and against the board of directors. He was viewed as a "roguish hero" who defied the shackles of social conventions. His management style, which enabled the firm to prosper, gained him appreciable favor among the British public.

But controversy continued to follow Rowland's actions. Just as the United Nations was poised to vote sanctions against Muammer Gaddafi's Libyan government, Rowland sold part of Lonrho's Metropole hotel group to a Libyan governmental agency. A Lonrho spokesman acknowledged the criticism but noted, "We've got to think about getting the best deal for our shareholders." Rowland's position was more straightforward: "To me, Gaddafi is a super friend. This is not the only deal we will do with him. At my age, I can say anything I like. Don't talk to me about morality and proper behavior. Gaddafi and Lonrho are a perfect fit."

Questions

1. Evaluate both Angus Ogilvy's and Duncan Sandys's stages of moral reasoning and deontological/teleological approaches to ethics.
2. Which of Roland Rowland's methods of resolving conflicts had ethical ramifications?
3. Just how would you have attempted to resolve the Rhodesian company's purchase, given your personal moral values and the British government's sanctions about dealing with Rhodesia?

Sources

Nigel Dudley, "The last throw of the dice," *Profiles* (March 1993), 31–32, 34.

Pranay Gupte, "Inside Lonrho today," *Forbes* (March 21, 1988), 100, 102, 104.

"Lessons of Lonrho," *The Economist* (July 10, 1976), 71–72.

Richard A. Melcher and John Templeman, "Found: a suitor who suits Tiny Rowland," *Business Week* (December 28, 1992), 38.

Richard Melcher, Geoffrey Smith, and Mike McNamee, "'Tiny' Rowland's colossal woes," *Business Week* (April 13, 1992), 33.

"Mr. Ogilvy to resign directorships after Lonrho report criticizes him," *The Times of London* (July 7, 1976), 1.

"The Lonrho affair," *The Sunday Times of London* (July 11, 1976), 52–53.

"Tiny and the elephants' graveyard," *The Economist* (November 12, 1988), 5.

"Tiny's lucky shamrock," *The Sunday Times of London* (July 25, 1976), 39.

Peter Wilsher, "Lonrho: curb, don't kill," *The Sunday Times of London* (July 11, 1976), 14.

Notes to Chapter 7

[1]Kenneth Boulding, *Conflict and Defense: A General Theory* (New York: Harper, 1962).

[2]Philip Kotler, *Principles of Marketing* (Englewood Cliffs, NJ: Prentice-Hall, Inc., 1980), p. 52.

[3]Their work is cited in the anthologies completed by Kurtines and Gewirtz, Beckowitz and Oser, and Likona—all referenced frequently in this text.

[4]Jürgen Habermas, *Communication and the Evolution of Society*, trans. by Thomas McCarthy (Boston: Beacon Press, 1979).

[5]Thomas Hobbes, *Leviathan* (London: Collier Books, 1969), p. 100. (This book was first published in 1651.) In this same year Hobbes also published *Philosophical Rudiments Concerning Government and Society* (the English translation of his *De Cive*, which he wrote in Latin).

[6]Roger Fisher and William Ury, *Getting to Yes* (New York: Penguin, 1981), pp. 21–29, 70.

[7]Daniel Druckman, Benjamin J. Broome, and Susan H. Korper, "Value Differences and Conflict Resolution," *Journal of Conflict Resolution* 32 (3) (September 1988), 489–510. In those experiments, conflicting positions—when interwoven with specific values—were resolved much less frequently than when the opposing parties could discuss their respective values apart from their initial positions. In turn, the greater each party's understanding of the other party's underlying set of values, the less rigid were those parties in sticking to their original positions.

[8]Dean G. Pruitt, *Negotiation Behavior* (New York: Academic Press, 1981), p. 17.

[9]Richard E. Walton and Robert B. McKersie, *A Behavioral Theory of Labor Negotiations* (New York: McGraw-Hill Book Company, 1965), pp. 226–261.

[10]James A. Wall, *Negotiation: Theory and Practices* (Glenview, IL: Scott, Foresman and Company, 1985), Chapter 12.

[11]William M. Kurtines, Margarita Azmitia, and Mildred Alvarez, "Science and Rationality" (Miami: Florida International University Working Paper, 1989).

[12]John Rawls, *A Theory of Justice* (Cambridge: Harvard University Press, 1971), p. 7.

Chapter 8

INTERNATIONAL VALUES

onflict has many causes. According to Habermas, the first cause is the simple failure of one party to comprehend the other party. An initial step toward conflict resolution suggests reviewing the language, concentrating not just on grammar and accents, but also on the words, phrases, and sentences used by the other party. Language is our medium for understanding. It serves to maximize the cooperation that we need if we are to complete business transactions successfully. It also can serve to enhance societal well-being by minimizing the potential for "naked domination"[1] of one person by another.

The language of the party with whom we have conflicts over business ethics should be analyzed in three contexts:

- The environment in which that party operates. For example, it is important to consider the political, cultural, and economic differences *within* as well as *between* countries.
- The verbalization of that party's intentions.
- The other party's interpretation of the norms regulating his or her relation to the people with whom business is involved; this is a point over which expectations may differ by culture and country.

Cross-Cultural Misunderstandings

If language causes problems in domestic business dealings, the problem can be magnified when international transactions are involved. Michael Blumenthal has explained how difficult it is to formulate an international code of business ethics.[2] He has noted that the definition of key terms—such as *bribery*—pertinent to a code of ethics varies between countries because of cultural values and customs.

Our task, especially in international transactions, is to ask questions so that everything—from environmental perspectives to abstract phrases—becomes clear to us. We can start by asking for paraphrases, for more detailed explanations, and even for literal translations that will give us an understanding of the other party's position. These same questions can also provide information about the principles underlying the other party's position; we can even begin to speculate about the party's intention to act on those principles.

To comprehend the other party's meaning, we need to look for clues. Do the other party's words match his or her behavior? Do the person's words match the symbols associated with the position stated? To understand what we mean, think about the following example. One of the authors of this book was invited to speak about business ethics at a symposium on poverty in the developing world. Sponsored by a developing nation, the conference was held at a luxury hotel in the United States. The meals that were served were gourmet delights, and each participant from that nation was obviously highly educated, fashionably dressed, and a member of the privileged class. Ironically, the strongest speech on the lack of concern about poverty was delivered by a legislator who arrived late, carrying a full shopping bag from the expensive department store next to the site. These symbols of affluence left some doubt about the sincerity behind the words of the speakers. Nonetheless, this author's observations could be considered a miscomprehension, based on his cultural expectations.

Problems of miscomprehension occur frequently within multinational corporations. It is hard for American employees to realize that in some countries, especially in the Orient, it is characteristic for a businessperson to speak in vague terms with nuances that only experience can help decipher. Irene Park claims that purposeful vagueness dominates the language of business negotiators from mainland China.[3] The point is that even if we believe that we fully comprehend the words, intentions, positions, and principles of our colleagues abroad, we are still left to decide which criteria to use for resolving ethical conflicts in international transactions.

Do Ethics Cross International Borders?

Multinational corporations have discovered that domestic decision procedures will not necessarily solve problems abroad. An ethical decision may encounter resistance from that same firm's representatives in other countries.

Given varied cultural backgrounds, it is understandable that the beliefs and actions of managers in individual host countries differ from those at the home office. Nonetheless, a partial consensus sometimes will emerge when executives from various countries have sufficiently identified with the beliefs and attitudes of the international business community. Some businesses have learned to use internationally recognized criteria as filtering devices when promoting employees to positions that entail decisionmaking responsibility.

Disinvestment Decisions

The difficulties multiply, however, when a decision involves public input. Here the likelihood of a total consensus on any moral issue (short, perhaps, of a general condemnation of unprovoked murder) becomes unlikely. Take, for example, the concept of disinvestment. For an individual investor, the decision to disinvest in a firm entails acting on personal beliefs. Is it feasible, though, to project that decision as a moral obligation for businesses or governments? Should firms curtail their operations in mainland China because *we* personally disapprove of China's use of prison labor to produce goods for the international market? If a country's internal political processes are not compatible with your own moral values, would you advocate that a firm in which you hold stock disinvest in that country? Would you consider who would be hurt and what would be gained by the decision? Or would you reject this consequentialist approach and claim that some deontological principles such as the free mobility of labor in the China example override situational balancing of benefits and detriments?

For those who seriously consider the normative guideline of consistency between beliefs, words, and actions when attempting to resolve ethical conflicts, is disinvestment the only position compatible with personal principles? Other options exist if the goal is not just to express anger about conditions in another country but also to act so as to enhance the well-being of that country's citizens. Witness the actions of Levi Strauss at the beginning of this decade: it pulled out of Burma and threatened to do the same in Bangladesh because the company's standards of conduct prohibit its worldwide suppliers from employing children under the age of fourteen. To comply with their contracts, suppliers in Bangladesh would have had to fire forty children. The children's families needed those wages, however, so Levi Strauss negotiated an agreement with the suppliers, setting terms that enabled the children to receive both wages and a formal education. The company arrived at this agreement through the process of Discursive Communication. The method made it possible for the parties to change their positions without sacrificing the principles directed toward enhancing societal well-being.

Can Corporate Values Cross International Borders?

Although the existence or nonexistence of public consensus on an issue is *a* factor in ethical thinking in business, simple appeals to the attitudes and opinions of any actual group do not settle the issue of whether a given practice is morally right. Such appeals could only settle debates about what is considered right at a particular time, in a given place, and by a majority of people. Within multinational corporations, it is unlikely that the companies will be able to appeal to a common tradition, whether moral or religious. This is not a new concept: writing of Europe in the seventeenth century, Pascal claimed that "conscience is one thing south of the Pyrenees, another north."[4] The differences are even more striking when all continents and all centuries are included.

As we mentioned in Chapter 3, business leaders recognize the problems of applying American moral values to their overseas operations. Consider the comments of some Fortune 500 executives:

- Although every businessman should have high moral principles and mercantile morality it is utterly foolish to require that other peoples live by the same standards in order to do business with the U.S.
- Altogether too much righteous indignation and too little common sense is exhibited by our legislative and regulatory bodies in dealing with the exceptional customs of other peoples.
- As a matter of fact, being only 200 years old makes the U.S. a novice at civilization management when compared to other countries such as Japan.[5]

Even if a particular moral or religious tradition could be cited in support of a code of ethics for multinational corporations, the question of what is universally or actually right would still remain—along with the more basic question of how to justify answers deemed right. Business leaders, however, must provide answers and justify responses to differing publics. Business exists to "satisfy" some of society's needs. Furthermore, if a given business system does not satisfy society's needs, it is likely that an alternative system will be tried. The economic and political changes in Eastern Europe since 1990 seem to illustrate this phenomenon. If for no other reason than for public goodwill, international businesses need criteria upon which ethical decisions can be made and justified. The question is whether those criteria should take the form of general guidelines or of specific codes.

Codes of International Ethics

Written codes of ethics are not prevalent in a large number of countries, and to expect a uniform code to be widely accepted may be somewhat unrealistic.[6] This is the case despite efforts at constructing such a code by the International Chamber of Commerce, the International Confederation of Free Trade Unions, and the U.N. Centre on Transnational Corporations.

We are not yet at the stage where all exporters agree about the fundamentals of international business morality. At present, no consensus exists about rights and responsibilities in international business transactions. In describing Japan, Boye De Mente claims that loyalty and the responsibility of fulfilling obligations come before all else in moral evaluations.[7] Bar-Tal concurs, noting that in some cultures, friendship appears to outweigh nondiscrimination or making judgments based on merit.[8] Magnis-Suseno found that in Java, the culture expects Stage Three morality rather than behavior based on "higher" stages of moral reasoning.[9] Nissan's intercultural studies confirm that "at least some specific moral norms are culture dependent and not structurally (self-constructed general principles) derived."[10] Nor are the hopes for an international code of business ethics bolstered by Liebert, whose examinations of anthropological literature show no support for universal moral principles. He, like Nissan, found that norms and standards about what is right and moral vary widely between cultures.[11]

Becker and Fritzsche analyzed opinions held by businesspeople from France, Germany, and the United States. Their study determined that views on the feasibility of a Code of Ethics depended on the businessperson's native culture. They concluded that personal integrity takes on slightly different meanings in different cultures.[12] Managers in western Europe and the United States were uniformly guided only by some simple view of natural law (such as the idea of a right to life). In contrast, managers in other countries tended to express more *firmist* views in conflicts of interest and were less concerned with ethical ramifications than Americans seemed to be. De Mente[13] in turn noted that the concept of truth, as understood among Japanese businessmen, is related to harmony and is colored by obligations and circumstances. Harmony or *wa* is the cultural value upon which trust is built and economic progress made. Harmony takes precedence over truth.

Codes of ethics are merely facades of integrity unless they match the values of the individuals involved and thus show benefits for each party. When societal values are centered on factors other than economic equity, there may well be a problem with the enforcement and acceptance of codes. This is most likely to occur when there is little trust in the political/social system. In many underdeveloped countries, the issues of family security and survival may well overrule the precepts of any code. In such situations, the trust necessary to make cooperative endeavors work could be eroded.

Most codes read like the biblical Ten Commandments, with a heavy emphasis on "Thou Shalt Not." The longer they become, the less flexibility they allow. Formal strictures such as the Foreign Corrupt Practices Act (FCPA) may be too rigid in that the Act projects U.S. values onto international transactions as operating standards. It is not clear at this point, however, whether the FCPA has been abided by or skirted abroad. Xerox's attitude toward this situation, for example, is that foreign operations are expected to uphold the same standards that prevail in the company's U.S. operations. By contrast, Nestlé companies are charged to respect the laws and customs of the countries where they operate.[14]

An Example

In the case of questionable foreign payments, our ability to use Discursive Communication to negotiate a resolution to the conflict is severely limited by the Foreign Corrupt Practices Act. In effect, the Stage Four moral reasoning mandated by the Act legally constrains our actions. But if we break the law, would postconventional moral reasoning see us through? The burden of proof is on our shoulders because we would have done a bad thing—break the law— for what we perceive to be a good reason. Not only would we have to show that our action was well-reasoned, but we would also have to show that it was feasible, consistent, and universalizable—especially universalizable. The moral justification for our act would be most likely tied to the principle of benefi- cence. To assume a universal set of canons of morality is highly risky in inter- national transactions. In fact, Nielsen states that any assumption of international moral norms is invalid, given the unique aspects of different cultures.[15]

Stewart gives credence to Nielsen's position by isolating differences between the operating values found in different countries.[16] These include the following:

individual, independent choice	versus	group, dependent consensus
individual responsibility	versus	group responsibility
immediate and future consequences	versus	traditional principles
accomplishment	versus	survival
material achievement	versus	self-actualization
exploitation of abundant resources	versus	reallocation of scarce resources

The existence of these differences raises doubts about the feasibility of an international code of ethics. The differences point to discrepancies not just in positions but in the core values upon which such a code would have to be built. In light of these findings, individual discursive negotiations, rather than reference to a deontological code, may provide the most feasible means to resolve moral conflicts between firms from different cultures.

One Position on International Values

If we are truly part of an interdependent global economy, then at the very least our reference group for values must include the partners and suppliers in the countries with whom we do business. But how do we handle conflicts over values between suppliers, producers, and consumers? Especially at issue are the values related to rights and responsibilities.

Kenichi Ohmae, the leading business strategist in Japan, has offered a posi- tion on these issues of conflict. His position has found sympathy in the indus- trialized world. His is a clear and cold message.

Ohmae prefaces his message by stating that only one billion of the world's five billion people enjoy the advantages of linkage among the world's advanced economies. If the developing economies wish to join this interlinked economy, these countries would have to pay the high price of acceptance of the global- ized business values shared by members of what he calls the interlinked econ- omy (ILE). He proclaims that this set of values holds more weight than local or national affiliation.

Ohmae's implied promise is that economic problems will be dissipated over time if developing countries adopt the shared values that mark the interlinked economy. He notes that the interlinked economy "will encompass most East European countries, most of Asia's newly industrialized economies (NIEs), and some Latin American countries, if they adopt ILE policies."[17]

What type of behavior is called for if business operations are to provide the vehicle to lift a society from the deprivations of poverty? A partial list, based on our interpretation of Ohmae's work, would include the following:

- A meritarian rather than an egalitarian approach to social justice, by which each right has a corresponding responsibility.
- Local firms joining in partnership with multinational firms while suppressing local and national values in favor of specific, globally shared business values.
- Cooperation and trust being valued over individual autonomy.

In terms of the stages of moral development, what is being suggested by Ohmae is a value system that operates at the conventional level of development, particularly at Kohlberg's Stage Three. Individuals at this level define what is ethical not in terms of direct, personal rewards (in these cases, rewards for their country) but in terms of what is valued as good for the group (in these cases, members of the ILE). This level of moral development may not represent the customary morality within a given society. For example, a company may have to change its methods of awarding contracts or hiring personnel; it might have to shift its decision criteria to place less stress on friendship and more on capability.

A closer look at Ohmae's position might also uncover facets of Stage One as well. Residents of developing countries may feel that the financial power of ILE firms has forced them to adopt the ILE set of business values. The fear of being left out of an emerging global economy, with its associated rewards, can be a strong motivating force.

Do the shared values of an international, interlinked economy meet the tests of the four normative guidelines, as summarized in Chapter 6, to resolve conflict of interest with ethical dimensions? Three of the tests are met:

- Certainly, the ILE proposition about shared values is tightly *reasoned.*
- The proponents of shared values are *consistent* in their behavior, for what they believe is what they say, and what they say is what they do.
- The proponents welcome *universalization* of their shared values.

A problem, however, exists with the fourth criterion. We need to question whether the operationalization of shared values is truly *feasible* in developing countries that hold widely divergent values. Mandating a set of ILE-shared values seems to be an example of Strategic Communicative Action rather than Discursive Communicative Action. Such a mandate may cause more conflict than it resolves. Full comprehension of the opposing party's position is the first requirement for the consensus needed to attain a lasting resolution of conflict. Do multinational firms put forth a concerted effort to understand not just the words but also the cultural context behind the words used by businesspeople from developing countries? Or are the other party's values dismissed out of hand as primitive and dysfunctional to an efficient business operation? Do we, ourselves, act in such a manner when we evaluate the positions of disadvantaged subcultures here at home, let alone abroad?

Ethical Decision Criteria For Multinationals

To some extent, the theories of ethics that we discussed in previous chapters each offer a potential decision procedure.[18] The utilitarian, for example, would urge that business decisions (international as well as national and personal) aim at "the greatest good for the greatest number." Businesses operating under government control, especially in socialist countries, might be expected to adopt such a position. The egoist, in contrast, would employ the "self-interest" criterion, regardless of the country in which he or she might be located.

As we have mentioned before, many Americans can be classified as being at Stage Four in Kohlberg's scheme of moral development. The typical type of moral position associated with Stage Four is a simple kind of rule deontology, an affirmation perhaps of "American values." When faced, often for the first time, with a culture that resists accepting this type of moralizing, an executive will usually search for some new understanding of morality.

Kohlberg has pointed out that growth in moral development is often stimulated by confrontation with a moral situation that one's existing moral theory cannot handle. Accordingly, a person with a Stage Three, culture-based moral view in which friendship predominates might develop a Stage Four form of rule deontology in which merit prevails.

But another type of development associated with individual situations is also possible. For instance, an executive may look at the contrast between typical American business values and those of another country, to conclude that values are totally relative to that culture. The executive may then turn to some version of act deontology and base moral judgments directly on his or her intuitions concerning the situation. But elevating merely personal feelings or choices to the status of moral truths presents an example of what Jeremy Bentham, quoted in Chapter 5, criticized as "the principle of sympathy and antipathy." Advocating that feelings of approval or disapproval are themselves the basic reason for something being morally right or wrong seems unlikely to provide an approach to ethics that could be shared by a group, whether that group be an individual firm or the worldwide business community.

Warnock's Principles of Moral Ethics

The contemporary British philosopher G. J. Warnock has offered a set of criteria to resolve ethical issues for multinationals.[19] Warnock argues that ethics are social action-guides that are designed to help people resist the temptation to do things that are likely to lead to harm. Within this general framework, Warnock defends four independent moral principles, each of which could have some application in business ethics: nonmaleficence (do not harm), beneficence (do good), nondiscrimination, and nondeception. Beneficence and nondiscrimination are discussed in this chapter; the other two topics are explored in Chapter 9.

These principles might be particularly appropriate for one ethical issue that is currently of concern in international business: the issue of questionable payments. To clarify this example, could these principles be invoked if questionable payments are being paid to a customs official of a foreign country in return for permission to allow needed medical supplies to enter that country? The medical supply firm will profit from the sale of these items, and the residents of that country will benefit. Perhaps even lives will be saved. However, none of these benefits will occur unless a questionable payment is both made and afterwards covered up. What should be done in this case? Does beneficence toward the residents outweigh nonmaleficence and nondeception in this situation?

Warnock admits that because his four moral principles are independent of each other, they may come into conflict in particular situations. When this happens, there is no fixed or absolute way to resolve the conflict. The moral agent must simply consider all of the factors involved and then make a decision that he or she believes is the best choice. As Warnock writes, "It seems to me quite impossible to exclude the possibility that predicaments may arise which are, literally, morally insoluble."[20]

Beneficence

But Warnock makes an interesting point in discussing beneficence: for various practical reasons, one's beneficence should normally be focused on oneself or on those persons to whom one is particularly close. This is not necessarily an endorsement of Stage Two egoism or some other restricted teleological theory. Rather, if one's goal is really to "maximize the good consequences" in the world as a whole through one's actions, in most circumstances the most effective way to do this will be through benefiting oneself and/or those in one's immediate environment. Ordinarily, the individual is the best judge of what consequences will be best for himself or herself. Also, there is a certain efficiency in individuals and groups taking primary responsibility for benefiting themselves and meeting their own needs. This appears to be suspiciously similar to the reasoning behind laissez-faire economic theory. As Warnock writes, "In normal circumstances, if everyone embroils himself persistently, however well-meaningly, in other people's concerns rather than his own, a considerable measure of chaos and cross-purposes is likely to ensue."[21]

This does not mean, however, that when great benefit can obviously be done to other persons, one is not required to help. It is simply a practical point regarding decisions in relatively normal conditions. It means, for example, that a business firm wishing to contribute to the betterment of the world might well begin by looking close to home (or to its several "homes," in the case of multinationals) for practical ways to be beneficent or helpful.

Nondiscrimination

Another aspect of Warnock's view is his concept of fairness in the form of nondiscrimination. Human beings are naturally tempted to discriminate in favor of persons who are like themselves or who are connected to them in some way. But when we routinely give in to this temptation, situations are likely to become worse than they would be if we could resist this temptation. For example, it is not discrimination to give preference to the most qualified candidate for a job, even if that candidate happens to be a personal friend. In some circumstances, especially where there are only vague or uncertain criteria for evaluating the actual correctness of a decision, it will be appropriate to avoid even the appearance of wrongdoing by adopting and following rules that are even more stringent than might otherwise be required. (For example, some firms prohibit the hiring of one's relatives even in cases where the relative is likely to be the best-qualified candidate). But here again, morality often requires a balancing or judging between potentially conflicting principles or prima facie duties. Note the potential conflict between Warnock's advocacy of nondiscrimination and his admission that beneficence is normally directed towards those people to whom we are close.

In a few countries, such as the United States and India, versions of affirmative action plans have been legislated into existence. These plans serve two purposes. The first is to encourage nondiscrimination. The second is to set target goals regarding the racial/ethnic makeup of the workforce. These purposes are admirable in the abstract, but may come under criticism in specific cases of application. The ethical questions to consider are these: Do you hire or promote a member of a minority group when a member of the majority group appears better qualified? To what degree is it the responsibility of the firm to train a member of the minority group so that that person becomes qualified to handle the job? Do such actions constitute reverse discrimination? Your answers to these questions are likely to depend on how you have defined the third component of the definition of ethics—the question of "societal well-being." Your answers are also likely to be strongly influenced by your stage or level of moral reasoning. While there are legal constraints to your actions, this issue, unlike the example concerning medical supplies, leaves some room for negotiation. Refer to the Royal Dutch/Shell case at the end of this chapter. Using Discursive Communication, briefly outline how you would attempt to arrive at an appropriate resolution to the conflict in that case. Does your resolution meet the four normative guidelines?

Multinational companies face the potential for various kinds of discrimination that purely domestic companies do not. In some countries, the wealthier party, especially a foreign firm, is expected to give more than it gets in a negotiated transaction. Within domestic businesses, the Equal Employment

Opportunity Commission (EEOC) and various federal laws act to encourage nondiscrimination. We suspect, though, that this moral principle does not travel well in the world of international commerce. In countries where there is little trust in government to provide either stability or economic safety nets, businesspeople tend to rely on a network of family and friends. The welfare of this network's members takes precedence over nondiscrimination when opportunities for advancement arise. Just how many countries can you list where nondiscrimination is prevalent in business decisions? Is it feasible to think this condition will change?

Conclusions

In Chapter 1, we suggested that *feasibility* is one of the appropriate criteria for an acceptable ethical theory or position. If we insist that ethical principles such as Warnock's be codified and universally accepted, we are likely to be disappointed. Former U.S. Secretary of Commerce Michael Blumenthal has pointed out the great extent to which international laws are disregarded. In the light of this disregard, it would be naïve to suppose that all firms, domestic and international, would ever cooperate in following a single standard in any one business situation.

Still, it is our contention that any person's approach to ethical issues must pass the same tests, whether applied to a national or an international level. These tests, which we have presented and discussed in previous chapters (namely that decisions be feasible, reasonable, consistent, and universalizable), can lead to conflict resolution. But will they lead to the enhancement of societal well-being? For the normative guidelines to lead to conflict resolution, an understanding must first be reached about each party's position and the principles underlying that position. But that understanding is only one requirement for a lasting resolution to the conflict. The remaining requirements concerning factual disclosures and honesty have yet to be discussed. Before our discussion continues in Chapter 9, consider first the following questions as you read the cases at the end of this chapter.

1. Who within the firm should be involved in and take responsibility for ethical decisions with international consequences? Why?

2. If there is a conflict between the ethical criteria used to evaluate decisions, what do you believe the hierarchical order of their importance should be? Why?

3. Now that you are nearing the end of this text, it is time for you to set up your own ethical criteria. Can you justify the application of your own criteria in the following cases?

✤ Case Study 8–1 ✤

ITT

Rand Araskog of ITT has had profit on his mind for over a decade. When he took over the chairman's job from Harold Geneen, his task was to improve the company's bottom line. Araskog sold off some of the conglomerate's assets and improved the debt-to-capital ratio. But the financial community still pressed for better performance. This stress on operating performance was nothing new at ITT. Harold Geneen had faced similar and, some would say, more difficult problems.

Perhaps Geneen's greatest difficulty came from a situation in Chile. ITT owned over 70 percent of Chilteco, the Chilean telephone company. The investment was worth at least $150 million, and Geneen believed that the investment was threatened. Salvador Allende was campaigning for the presidency of Chile; his popularity worried Geneen because Allende was supported by the Chilean communists. A communist president might not be a good thing for a capitalist firm from the United States.

ITT would most likely fare better if a more conservative candidate won the presidency. Jorge Alessandri Rodriguez was the candidate whom Geneen preferred. For help and guidance, Geneen approached an American organization that had insights into political situations in Chile. That organization was the Central Intelligence Agency (CIA). According to the CIA agent who met with Geneen, the ITT chairman offered to set up a fund to support Allende's opponent. The CIA agent at that time thought it inappropriate to support a candidate in the election.

But situations change. A few months later, William Broe of the CIA approached Edward Gerrity, an ITT vice president, with a counterproposal. By that time, the election had been held and Allende had won more votes than anyone else—but not a majority. The election was to be decided at a later date by a vote in the Chilean Congress. The crux of the Broe–Gerrity meeting was that economic pressure could be put on Chile to show some of the problems that could occur if Allende were elected president.

Among the options discussed in the meeting were not renewing credits to Chilean banks and stalling shipments of goods and parts to Chile. When these suggestions were brought to Geneen, he rejected them as not feasible. Geneen had hoped for more "constructive" rather than destructive help from the CIA. John McCone, an ITT director and the former head of the CIA, corroborates Geneen's explanation. McCone stated that Geneen's original offer, contrary to some people's suspicions, was not intended to cause economic disruption in Chile.

Geneen felt let down by the U.S. government. He believed that the United States had backed off from its longstanding policy of supporting a democratic government in Chile. He stated that the U.S. government had encouraged American businesses like ITT to invest in Chile to foster a healthy capitalistic system. The focus on ITT's bottom line was a motivating force behind Geneen's concern about the firm's Chilean investment. In his words, "For every dollar we took out, we put in six dollars or eight dollars. Why would we try anything but to keep it going? We thought we had the right to go to our government and ask for help when Chile was going to take our properties." He also claimed that ITT stockholders wrote to complain that Geneen had to do something to protect their investment in the company.

Allende was elected president by the Chilean congress, and U.S. firms felt the effect. Allende's political economic philosophy was quite simple. His words meant "Imperialists, go home." And he viewed imperialists as the multinational corporations that dominated the economies of underdeveloped countries. The Chilean congress nationalized copper mines in which U.S. firms had a financial interest. Anaconda, Cerro, and Kennecott estimated their Chilean assets at over $600 million. Chile claimed that the U.S. firms had made too much profit in Chile and had damaged the worth of the mines. No compensation was to be awarded to the copper firms. Chile expropriated ITT's assets as well. As was the case with the copper firms, no compensation was awarded.

Questions

1. Place yourself in Harold Geneen's shoes just prior to Allende's election. With the benefit of hindsight, what actions could you have taken to preclude the conflict and expropriation that occurred?
2. What circumstances, if any, would give you moral justification for interfering with free elections in another country?
3. You, instead of Harold Geneen, are the chairman of ITT at the time of the Chilean elections. Whose well-being are you personally most concerned with? Why?

Sources

"Allende scoffs at funds For I.T.T.," *The New York Times* (April 11, 1973), 8.

Jack Anderson and George Clifford, *The Anderson Papers* (New York: Random House, 1973), pp. 109, 116–118.

"And meanwhile on the political front," *Fortune* (June 1975), 113.

Robert M. Bleiberg, "ITT and Chile—a panel of arbitrators set the record straight," *Barrons* (November 11, 1974), 7.

Martin L. Bowles, "The organization shadow," *Organization Studies* 12: 3 (1991), 387–404.

Brian Bremmer and Jonathan B. Levine, "It's a new day for ITT's Rand Araskog," *Business Week* (July 2, 1990), 50, 51.

"Fresh light on U.S. role in Chile," *U.S. News & World Report* (April 9, 1973), 66.

"Geneen concedes fund offer to CIA to block Allende," *The New York Times* (March 23, 1973), 1.

"Harold Geneen talks about. . ." *Business Week* (November 3, 1973), 44.

"ITT: the view from inside," *Business Week* (November 3, 1973), 44.

Gary MacEoin, *Chile: The Struggle for Dignity* (London: Anchor Press Ltd., 1974), pp. 64, 65.

Anthony Sampson, *The Sovereign State of ITT* (Greenwich, CT: Fawcett Publications, Inc., 1975), pp. 18, 278, 280.

Eileen Shanahan, "C.I.A. aide says he gave anti-Allende plan to I.T.T.: fund offer to block Allende," *New York Times* (April 3, 1973), 1, 13.

Eileen Shanahan, "McCone defends I.T.T. Chile fund idea," *The New York Times* (March 22, 1973), 1, 6.

"Somebody is lying," *Newsweek* (April 9, 1973), 36–7.

❖   Case Study 8–2   ❖

CHIQUITA BRANDS

People in the United States eat more bananas than any other fruit. Chiquita Brands, which does a large volume of business in this country, sells about one-third of the world's supply of bananas. Founded in the last century under the name United Fruit, the company became United Brands before renaming itself Chiquita in 1990. It has been a profitable firm under its chairman Carl Linder, but profit hasn't been easy to come by. Its size and drive for earnings have made the firm unpopular in areas of Central America, where much of the firm's product is grown.

Unfavorably labeled *el pulpo* (the octopus) in Central America, the powers of Chiquita are formidable. Under a previous chairman, Eli Black, the firm attempted to improve its image from one of Yankee imperialism. The firm embarked on a program to build schools and homes for its employees. The homes, which the firm owned, were offered for sale to employees at a nominal price. The firm also provided expertise to local producers so that Chiquita could reduce its own role in the production side of the business. Eli Black's philosophy was both practical and humanistic. He thought that multinational corporations had social responsibilities in the developing countries in which they operated. He also believed that improved living and working conditions would result in greater worker productivity.

A country in which Chiquita's presence has been felt is Honduras. Honduras is one of the world's leading exporters of bananas. A significant portion of that country's foreign exchange earnings comes from that fruit. At a time when there was an oversupply of bananas, Honduras and other countries in the area formed a production cartel. The cartel countries supplied about two-thirds of the world's bananas. The cartel explored tax alternatives, and Honduras decided to levy a fifty-cent tax on every container (approximately 40 pounds) of bananas.

Black was disturbed about the tax since he believed it violated an existing agreement with Honduras. His humanitarian nature led him to understand Honduras's need for tax revenue, and he thought a negotiated agreement could be reached. At about the same time, a Chiquita vice president was approached by a Honduran official. The official implied that the tax could be reduced if a private lump sum payment were made. Black was told about this offer, but rejected it. He did ask the vice president to report the offer to his immediate superior for that region. The superior acted on the proposal and authorized a $1.25 million payment to Honduran officials. The banana tax was then reduced to 25 cents per container.

The firm filed its 8K report with the Securities and Exchange Commission (SEC). The report mentioned that negotiations with the Honduran government resulted in a 25-cents-per-box tax. The reduction in the tax was estimated to have saved the firm over $5 million a year. At that time, the $1.25 million payment was not illegal under U.S. law. SEC examination of the matter brought forth volunteered information from Chiquita about the lump sum payment. This information became public.

When word of the payment got back to Honduras, it affected subsequent negotiations between the government and Chiquita. The chief Honduran negotiator wanted "retribution for a national scandal." He got it. Chiquita agreed to give the government its rail tracks plus harbor facilities for a nominal payment. The chief negotiator also got Chiquita to agree to an annual 5-cents-per-container tax for five years.

After this episode, Chiquita kept a lower profile in Honduras. But trouble brewed again. Local growers rebelled against Chiquita's dominant position in the market. They wished to sell their banana crop to Fyffes, a British company. Fyffes was willing to pay 40 percent more for the bananas. Chiquita, though, had a long-term contract with the growers.

A Chiquita representative said: "We can't afford to let Fyffes get that fruit." His fear was "If people realize Fyffes can induce producers to break contracts, then everybody will do it." Chiquita claimed that Fyffes had entered negotiations with the Echeverri family, a large independent grower in

Honduras. Chiquita further claimed that Fyffes offered to pay the Echeverri family $2.5 million to sell the bananas to the British firm, thus breaking the contract with Chiquita. The contract still had two more years to run.

Fyffes obtained the bananas, but obtaining doesn't mean shipping. A train of Fyffes bananas derailed when it hit an obstruction. Officials said that the obstruction was deliberately placed on the tracks. Those bananas that did make it to port found another obstacle. Armed private guards blocked the bananas from entering the dock facilities. The bananas were confiscated. Commented Fyffes shipping manager: "This is what happens in a banana republic."

Questions

1. From the limited information given, estimate the stage of moral reasoning used by the individuals mentioned in the case.
2. Evaluate from an ethical perspective the $1.25 million private lump sum payment made by Chiquita to reduce the proposed banana tax. Are your ethical beliefs projectable to behavior stemming from different cultural values?
3. Ethically resolve the conflict between Chiquita and the Echeverri family.

Sources

Kenneth H. Bacon, Mary Bralove, and Steven J. Sarsweet, "United Brands Paid Bribe of $1.25 Million to Honduran Official," *The Wall Street Journal* (April 9, 1975), 1.

"Banana Bribes," *The Economist* 255 (April 19, 1975), 74.

Mary Bralove, "Was Eli Black's Suicide Caused by the Tensions of Conflicting Worlds?" *The Wall Street Journal* (February 14, 1975), 1.

Jose de Cordoba," Honduras Farm's Sales to a Rival of Chiquita Spark Bitter Struggle," *The Wall Street Journal* (June 7, 1990), 1A, 10A.

Judann Dagnol, "Chiquita: United ties broadening established brand-peel," *Advertising Age* (March 2, 1987), 66.

Patricia Gallagher, "United Brands pays Panama tax," *Cincinnati Enquirer* (April 1, 1988), p. 12.

Kerry Hannon, "Ripe Banana," *Forbes* (June 13, 1988), 86.

"Honduran Bribery," *Time* 105 (April 21, 1975), 74.

Penny Lernoux, "The Great Banana War," *The Nation* 218 (June 29, 1974), 813–817.

"New Top Banana," *Time* 105 (May 26, 1975), 72–74.

David Pauly and Rich Thomas, "The Great Banana Bribe," *Newsweek* 85 April 21, 1975, pp. 76, 81.

Raul Romero, "United Brands Polishes Its Image in Latin America," *Management Review* 64 (March 1975), 25–30.

Eben Shapiro, "Revitalized Chiquita Seeks Growth," *The New York Times* (September 11, 1990), D1.

"The Banana Rebellion," *Time* (June 11, 1990), 49.

Eleanor Johnson Tracy, "How United Brands Survived the Banana War," *Fortune* 94 (July 1976), 144–151.

❖   **Case Study 8–3**   ❖

RoyaL Dutch/SheLL

The state of New Jersey withdrew Shell Oil's permission to operate service stations along the New Jersey Turnpike. This denial may have cost Shell about $50 million in annual revenue. In announcing the decision, Governor Florio declared: "New Jersey can't do business with such a company." Florio's decision was in reaction to the urgings of civil rights groups and organized labor. Those groups decried Royal Dutch/Shell's business operations in South Africa. Shell is highly visible in that country since it operates the largest refinery in South Africa.

Of particular concern to the critics were Shell's anti-union activities in South Africa and its sale of petroleum products to the South African police and military forces. The AFL-CIO even encouraged a national consumer boycott of Shell products beyond the boundaries of New Jersey because of the company's business in South Africa. A spokesman for the United Mine Workers in Washington said: "We launched this [New Jersey protest] to target Shell as the worst corporate collaborator with the apartheid regime."

A spokesperson for Shell believed that the only ones who would be punished by the New Jersey decision would be U.S. citizens who owned and worked in the service stations along the turnpike. Governor Florio, in contrast, thought that his sanctions would have a positive effect. His opinion however, was not accepted by many who are sympathetic to the plight of black South Africans. Their reasoning is that such actions, while well-intentioned, actually hurt black South Africans. Helen Suzman, a well-known liberal South African, feared that sanctions only made the South African government more steadfast in its policies.

Mangosuthu Buthelezi,the chief of the six-million-member Zulu tribe, concurred. He believed that sanctions and disinvestment worsened the position of the blacks. James Ngcoya of the South African Black Taxi Association was more specific: "I ask you to listen to our voices before you decide what is good for us, before you decide that black children must go hungry so you can be on the right side of history." Ngcoya dismissed the argument that black South Africans suffer so much that they wouldn't mind suffering a little more if sanctions could change government policies.

Sanctions certainly had an effect on the South African economy. When Ford and General Motors sold off their assets, 6500 employees lost their jobs. Black unemployment rose by 200,000 a year as foreign sanctions took place. More squatter camps arose around large cities. To support the growing population, it is estimated that 1700 new jobs would have to be created every working day from 1990 to the year 2000. More than 200 U.S. businesses left South Africa, and sanctions have cost South Africa over $20 billion. Some South Africans, like 87-year-old Daisy Davids, did not want the U.S. firms to leave. "My Americans, they looked after me," she said. U.S. firms had provided over $200 million in aid to black South Africans in the form of education, training, housing, and legal aid. When the U.S. firms left, the aid started to dry up. This had been the fear of Harry Oppenheimer, chairman of the Anglo-American Corporation. Oppenheimer felt that race discrimination could be defeated by more, rather than less, foreign investment. A growing economy could only aid the lives of the blacks. The South African budget minister agreed and reasoned: "No declining economy in history has ever delivered democracy."

But others were willing to suffer the economic pangs of sanctions. Michael Qwesha, an African National Congress (ANC) supporter, stated: "We aren't ashamed of sanctions. It is our contribution to the struggle." Another supporter of the economic measures, Mkhuseli Jack, stated that the sacrifices caused by sanctions were the price of victory. This was also the opinion of Bishop Desmond Tutu, who was awarded the Nobel Prize for his humanitarian efforts.

The sanction supporters point to a number of laws that restricted the rights of black South Africans. The Population Registration Act, the Natives Act, the Group Areas Act, and the Apprenticeship Act restricted life activities ranging from employment to where a person could live. The homelands policy, in turn, allocated 13 percent of the country's land to blacks. The rest of the land, which included all the gold and diamond mines, was allocated to the white minority. Whites account for less than 20 percent of the population.

To those who aimed to overturn these discriminatory policies, action was called for. Shell was a highly visible target. Nelson Mandela of the ANC struck San Francisco off the list of U.S. cities he was to visit. The reason? Shell was sponsoring an art exhibit of Dutch masterpieces in San Francisco. Across the Atlantic, protestors in Holland tried to frighten consumers away from Shell service stations to call attention to the firm's dealings with a government that pursued an apartheid policy.

A Shell spokesperson put forward the company's position very succinctly: "Were Royal Dutch/Shell to withdraw from South Africa, a strong voice against apartheid would be silent." The company pointed to an independent survey that showed how a majority of the population wanted foreign-based firms to remain in the country. Selling out would simply result in a few of the privileged white ruling class obtaining Shell's properties at bargain basement prices.

Questions

1. What is the ethical justification for one country imposing its ethical standards on another country through the use of sanctions?
2. Whose actions enhanced societal well-being more—Ford by pulling out of South Africa or Royal Dutch/Shell by remaining? Explain.
3. How would you resolve the conflict entailed when a firm is pressed to make a decision to remain in or leave South Africa?

Sources

"Anti-apartheid group, AFL-CIO launch boycott of Shell products," *Platt's Oilgram News* 64 (January 13, 1986), 5.

"Anti-apartheid groups plan campaign against Shell," *Platt's Oilgram News* 64 (January 13, 1986), 1.

Derek Bamber, "Exploration could take off," *Petroleum Economist* (March 1991), 35, 37, 38.

Paul Hoffman, "Group in South Africa advises U.S. business about apartheid," *The New York Times* (June 28, 1971), 1.

Peter Kerr, "Citing South Africa ties, Florio barring Shell oil from turnpike," *The New York Times* (February 12, 1991), B1, B4.

Michael Kimmelman, "Museums hear a knock on the door: politics learning to face the lions of public opinion," *The New York Times* (July 15, 1990), Sec. C, 1, 29.

Elizabeth Kurylo, "Atlanta, colleges keep sanctions," *The Atlanta Journal/The Atlanta Constitution* (July 11, 1991), C6.

Marshall Loeb, "What the U.S. must do/South Africa," *Fortune* 118 (July 18, 1988), 88–90.

Harry Oppenheimer, "Investment not violence," *Business Week* (October 9, 1978), 27.

Kathleen Telsch, "Wide drive against U.S. trade with South Africa is expected," *The New York Times* (February 7, 1971), 2.

Roger Thurow, "Price of victory," *The Wall Street Journal* (September 24, 1990), A1, A10.

Ray Vicker, "Some U.S. firms ignore urgings to leave S. Africa, instead seek to upgrade status of blacks," *The Wall Street Journal* (September 22, 1971), 38.

Roger Vielvove, "Shell and apartheid," *Oil and Gas Journal* (May 27, 1989), 30.

Notes to Chapter 8

[1]W. Wilson, "A Moral Community of Strangers," in Richard W. Wilson and Gordon J. Schochet (eds.), *Moral Development and Politics* (New York: Praeger 1980).

[2]Michael Blumenthal, *Hearing before the Committee on Banking, Housing U.S. and Urban Affairs, 95th Congress S. 305* (Washington, D.C.: U.S. Government Printing Office, 1977).

[3]Irene Park, cited in Boye Lafayette De Mente, *Chinese Etiquette and Ethics in Business* (Lincolnwood, IL: N.T.C. Business Books, 1989), p. 8.

[4]Blaise Pascal, *Pensées,* Paragraph 294, trans by John Warrington (London: J. M. Dent & Sons Ltd., 1960). (This book was first published in 1662.)

[5]Warren French, John Granrose, and Sandra Huszagh, "Exporting business morality," *Marketing Comes of Age: Proceedings of the Annual Meeting of the Southern Marketing Association* (1984), 197.

[6]Robert M. Liebert, "What Develops in Moral Development?" in William M. Kurtines and Jacob L. Gewirtz (eds.), *Morality, Moral Behavior, and Moral Development* (New York: John Wiley & Sons, 1984); Ronald E. Berenbeim, *Corporate Ethics* (New York: The Conference Board, Inc., 1987).

[7]Boye Lafayette De Mente, *Japanese Ethics and Etiquette in Business,* 5th ed. (Lincolnwood, IL: NTC Business Books, 1988).

[8]Daniel Bar-Tal, "Sequential development of helping behavior: a cognitive learning approach," *Developmental Review* 2(2) (1982), 101–124.

[9]F. Magnis-Suseno, cited by Otfried Hoffe, "Autonomy and Universalization as Moral Principles: A Dispute with Kohlberg, Utilitarianism and Discourse Ethics," in Marvin W. Berkowitz and Fritz Oser (eds.), *Moral Education: Theory and Application* (Hillsdale, NJ: Lawrence Erlbaum Associates 1985).

[10]Mordecai Nissan, "Content and Structure in Moral Judgment: An Interpretation View," in William M. Kurtines and Jacob L. Gewirtz (eds.), *Morality, Moral Behavior and Moral Development* (New York: John Wiley & Sons, 1984), p. 213.

[11]Robert M. Liebert, "What Develops in Moral Development?" in William M. Kurtines and Jacob L. Gewirtz (eds.), *Morality, Moral Behavior and Moral Development* (New York: John Wiley & Sons, 1984).

[12]Herbert Becker and David J. Fritzsche, "A comparison of ethical behavior of American, French and German managers," *Columbia Journal of World Business* 22 (Winter 1987),

[13]De Mente, 1988.

[14]Ronald E. Berenbeim, *Corporate Ethics* (New York: The Conference Board, Inc., 1987); The Ethics Resource Center, Inc., "Xerox Programs in Business Ethics and Corporate Responsibility," in *Corporate Ethics: A Prime Business Asset* (New York: The Business Roundtable, 1988).

[15]Kai Nielsen, "Anthropology and ethics," *The Journal of Value Inquiry* 5(4) (1971).

[16]E. C. Stewart, *American Cultural Patterns: A Cross-Cultural Perspective* (Yarmouth, ME: Intercultural Press, 1972).

[17]Kenichi Ohmae, *The Borderless World: Power and Strategy in the Interlinked Economy* (New York: Harper Business, 1990), xii.

[18]This section is based on John Granrose, "Multinational corporations and the ethics of questionable payments," *Business and Professional Ethics* II, Nos. 3/4 (Spring/Summer 1979), 5–6.

[19]G. J. Warnock, *The Object of Morality* (London: Methuen & Co., 1971), pp. 80–93.

[20]Warnock, p. 88.

[21]Warnock, p. 81.

Chapter 9

INFORMATION

A lasting resolution of conflict is most feasible when parties understand each other in the context of their respective environments. Reaching that understanding depends to a certain extent on how each party evaluates the other person's intentions. Does the other person intend to be totally honest when presenting data? Does he or she plan to present all the pertinent data needed to make a decision? Habermas claims that valid, successful communication rests on an open acceptance of both these intentions.[1]

We tend to gauge the validity of the other person's intentions by the information he or she gives us. Does what the other person says match what we think is the case? In addition, does the way in which he or she expresses or asserts a position make it easy for us to trust him or her? Are we being deceived? As we listen to the words of the other party, we make two judgments: one about whether the presenter is relating the facts as we see them and the other, about the presenter's honesty. If both of our judgments turn out to be positive, then the probability of resolving conflicts is greatly enhanced.

What we ask from others is also required from us. We have to establish truth in a cognitive way by paying attention to the logical flow of the information we give to others. That means we should try to back up each of our claims with empirical evidence. Our evidence should not be atypical but should fit the pattern predicted and expected by some underlying theory or set of principles. That theory or set of principles provides the bedrock upon which we have built our position. To establish the credibility of our argument, it also helps if our position is corroborated by people recognized as authorities on the subject.

Yet our claim and supporting evidence provide only the starting point in negotiations on ethical issues. They simply constitute the position that we take—a position that conflicts with the position held by the other person. When we are determining whose position truly enhances societal well-being, our first instinct is to use adversarial, Strategic Communicative Action to find holes in the other person's position so that our position holds sway. But do we even really win arguments by attacking another person's position? Put another way: how many times are we willing to admit that we have lost an argument? Maybe the best approach to conflict resolution is not through Strategic Communication but through Discursive Communication.

Discursive Communication

It may be argued that the most important part of communication involves uncovering the principles that underlie the other person's position. It is easier to reach consensus by modifying positions through Discursive Communication if the parties in conflict feel that they have not sacrificed their principles. The belief that personal principles have not been compromised lowers barriers between the conflicting parties and makes it easier to reach agreement about pertinent facts relating to conflict. This agreement about facts would ideally lead to a common or mutual interpretation of how facts match objective reality. This matching process could entail the selective use of Strategic Communication to gauge the appropriateness of new, modified positions.

Agreement on facts is but one condition for successful communication, and it must happen in tandem with an acknowledgment that each party intends to be open and honest. Recall from the last chapter that there are some societies in which the concept of honesty is less important than the concept of saving face. Our truthfulness can be difficult to establish once it is questioned and is no longer taken for granted. Assuring the other party that his or her suspicions about our honesty are unfounded may not be a simple task. But a three-step process on our part may help to allay the other party's fears:

1. We can refer to our past behavior as a consistent indicator of our current behavior. In addition, we can point to consistency (integrity) between what we have said and what we have done. As an aside, this is why we stressed in Chapter 2 and through subsequent chapters that consistency is one of four crucial criteria to legitimize our communicative efforts to resolve conflict.

2. We can provide testimonials from credible sources concerning our past statements and behavior and the consistency between them.

3. We can be proactive rather than reactive by offering to engage in mutually agreed upon actions that the other party believes would help restore trust.[2]

This three-step process—or similar efforts—may be necessary simply because we have come to accept degrees of deception as more than an uncommon occurrence in business.

Deception

Caveat emptor—"let the buyer beware"—is an old maxim. But just because it is old and frequently cited does not necessarily make it correct or acceptable from the moral point of view. *Caveat emptor* suggests that the total responsibility for carefulness and sensitivity in seeking and providing information between buyer and seller rests with the buyer. This doctrine seems to suggest that whatever the seller can get away with is acceptable. But business leaders would argue that such is not the case. They point to a series of laws passed since 1960 that set guidelines on passing information between producers and consumers. *Truth in packaging, truth in lending,* and *truth in advertising* are some of the euphemistic names of acts and issues pressed on Congress by the Federal Trade Commission to protect the public.

Deliberately giving misinformation is generally called *lying,* and it is condemned under most circumstances. Persons unsympathetic to business frequently tend to cite practices in advertising, selling, and promotion as examples of blameworthy lying. From our perspective, however, a reasoned judgment about the information that business disseminates will require a more subtle and sophisticated definition of such words as *deception* and *misinformation* than is often used.

Radical Nondeception

Take *deception,* for example. A whole continuum of practices needs to be kept in mind if deception is to be understood. At the one extreme is what might be called *radical nondeception.* This would exist in an ideal state where:

1. There is no intention to deceive—not even an unconscious intention.
2. Everything said or implied—both verbally and nonverbally—is true.
3. Everything even remotely relevant to the issue at hand is fully revealed to all parties concerned.

By calling this example an "ideal" state of affairs, we mean to suggest that it is a hypothetical construct—and one whose existence in actual life may not often exist. Yet it embodies the conditions that Habermas claims are necessary to resolve conflict. Whether radical nondeception is feasible in business is a question to consider.

Complete Deceptiveness

At the other end of this continuum is what might be called *complete deceptiveness.* This too is a construct, one in which:

1. There is a conscious intention to deceive—regardless of the consequences for the person(s) being deceived.
2. Everything said or implied—both verbally and nonverbally—is false.
3. In addition to the falsehoods being proclaimed, many relevant facts about the issue in question are being concealed.

In practice, of course, total deceptiveness would not be very useful to the person in business or to anyone else. If a person continually makes false statements, it is likely that some of the falsities will be noticed. Surely this factor will discredit the rest of what the person has said. In practice, therefore, a mixture of false statements among true ones is likely to achieve the maximum "benefits" of deceptiveness. This obvious fact has not gone unnoticed!

The simple omission of only one minor, though possibly relevant, fact may make the person appear to be practicing nondeception. We define *relevant* here as "would make a difference in resulting decisions." Paradoxically, a condition marked by only minor omissions may result in the most effective deception. The "relevance" of various facts to business issues is sometimes difficult to determine, however.

Nondeception

One of Warnock's principles, *nondeception,* provides another way to look at the deception/nondeception continuum. Note, however, that here—as in nearly all other ethical situations—there are possible questions about the *degree* of deception. For example, one advertising campaign might be blatantly misleading, another only slightly misleading, and another only misleading when considered from a single (perhaps unusual) point of view. Surely such differences need to be considered in any moral appraisal.

If Warnock's view only told us that deception was morally wrong—at least prima facie or typically—we might justifiably reply: "Why is this new?" However, Warnock's theory goes beyond simple moral truisms such as "Don't deceive!" by explaining just what it is that is wrong about deception. Warnock points out that deception is very tempting for those of us with somewhat limited sympathies for other people—that is, it is very tempting for nearly all of us to try to benefit ourselves by using deception in various ways. Warnock writes:

> It is possible for a person, and often very easy, by doing things, and especially in the form of saying things, to lead other persons to the belief that this or that is the case; and one of the simplest and most seductive ways of manipulating and maneuvering others persons for the sake of one's own ends is that of thus operating self-interestedly upon their beliefs. [3]

Once this basic point has been made plain, it should be easy to see both the source of the temptation and the source of the moral wrongness in a wide range of business situations. In addition to the temptations to use misleading advertising of other sorts, there will be temptations to withhold safety-related information at times, temptations to use deception to play on the fears that we all already have about becoming victims, temptations to use deception in situations where human greed has been aroused, and temptations to use deception in appealing to human vanity and the desire for prestige and status. How easy it is to use deception to support such attempts to enrich oneself at the expense of others.

In the examples considered in the last paragraph, it seems fairly clear that deception is considered to be directly damaging to those persons who are deceived. Warnock points out, however, that there is also a way in which deception can be damaging indirectly—even when the false belief that the deceiver has implanted is not harmful in itself. It is, writes Warnock,

> . . .not the implanting of false beliefs that is damaging, but rather the generation of the suspicion that they may be being implanted. For this undermines trust; and, to the extent that trust is undermined, all cooperative undertakings, in which what one person can do or has reason to do is dependent on what others have done, are doing, or are going to do, must tend to break down. . . .The crucial difficulty is precisely, I think, that deception is so easy.[4]

Whenever deception is discovered, Warnock would claim, there is a lessening of trust in the deceiver. As trust lessens, cooperation becomes more difficult. Thus, even when the deception is not directly harmful to those deceived, the process seems to be morally objectionable. And, of course, in the typical case the deception itself *is* directly harmful to those deceived. Hence, Warnock would argue that deception is wrong in either way.

Nonmaleficence

As we mentioned in Chapter 8, one of the four moral virtues defended by Warnock is *nonmaleficence*—the disposition to abstain from deliberate and unjustified harm to others (as well as to oneself). Having this disposition is, as Warnock remarks, "not, in a sense, very much of a virtue."[5] In other words, if a person's only claim to being a moral person is that he or she does not deliberately harm others, the person's qualities might not appear at first to be remarkable or unusually praiseworthy. But nonmaleficence "is still very clearly of fundamental importance; for it is obvious what a gangster's world we should find ourselves in without it."[6]

In the business world, of course, few persons would condone doing physical harm to others, not even to their most serious competitors. Physical harm—or even the threat of physical harm—is seldom sanctioned. And such behavior would rarely be productive. The case is somewhat different with what might be called *financial harm:* it is generally accepted as one of the costs of doing business that one's business decisions may result in financial harm to one's competitors. A third type of harm might be called *social harm:* this would include damaging a competitor's reputation, for example.

The relaying of information can cause financial and social harm in several ways. Many businesspersons would frown on harming a competitor by disseminating erroneous information about that firm. But those same persons would not consider it morally wrong to present accurate but incomplete information about a competitor so as to create a more positive impression of their own firm. Of course, as mentioned before, the fact that certain actions are not considered wrong does not automatically settle the question of whether they are or are not actually wrong. This is one area in which further thinking may be required. The question that immediately comes to mind is, "How far do we have to go, morally, in providing full information to others, especially in those cases where providing such information seems likely to be harmful to us or to our firm?"

To further connect the concept of nonmaleficence to the subject of this chapter—information—note that there is an inverse relation between the amount of harm a decision might cause and the amount of information possessed by a well-meaning decisionmaker.

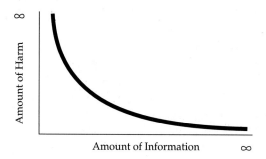

Admittedly, even without any information, an intuitive judgment may result in no harm. Conversely, even with massive amounts of information, harm could be caused because of the inability to process that information or because of a faulty decision rule. But a businessperson would look not just at the above chart when making his decision but would also calculate the cost of obtaining and/or disseminating information and compare this to the cost of the harm. Thus, in the above diagram the word *amount* would be replaced by the word *cost*. This is a tangible demonstration of the cost–benefit approach that we discussed in Chapter 5. The businessperson's decision involves identifying a demarcation point on the graph's line at which he or she is willing to operate. The difficult task is not so much picking that point as it is calculating the cost of harm in terms of probabilities and dollars.

In some instances, the Federal Trade Commission has taken this decision out of the businessperson's hands. The FTC has general guidelines about deception but has refrained from issuing widespread mandates about what information must be divulged in a transaction. Rather, the FTC has focused on situational rulings concerning "necessary" information, and has concentrated on issues such as seeing that used-car dealers divulge the true mileage of the vehicles for sale.

Expected Information

One characteristic is common to many ethical conflicts in business: the violation of expected or projected responsibilities. In these cases, at least one party has not performed to the level expected by the other party—a level benchmarked to custom, contract, or perceived interpersonal commitment. The cause of that violation is most likely to be one of omission rather than commission, and that which was omitted was information.

The cases in this chapter revolve around issues of information and expectations. Some of these issues are clear and familiar. For example, should limits be placed on the common advertising practice of "puffing" a product—that is, exaggerating its benefits? Does the advertising or selling of products that carry with them hidden or unknown risks to health or safety impose any special obligations or responsibilities on persons in the business world? Do we have any obligation to protect people from their own ignorance? If so, in what situations would this obligation apply?

Some information-related issues, however, are even more subtle. For example, does a belief in the moral importance of equality require that the same information be held by two parties in a business transaction? In the absence of equal information, can two parties be said to be on an equal footing? Do the obvious benefits to a seller being freed from burdensome regulations about information outweigh the value of the more rational decisions which a buyer might make if he or she were given full information? Are there situations in which a legal and socially acceptable product should not be advertised or sold at all (to children, for instance)?

The following example will reveal whether you can negotiate a resolution. Action for Children's Television (ACT) is an advocacy group that questions the persuasive means used to advertise to children. Their claim is that younger children do not have enough experience in life to make reasoned judgments; children's limited experiences do not qualify them to judge the truth of claims let alone to consider a wise allocation of their parents' resources. As the manufacturer of an action toy using slot cars (miniature cars that run within slots on a track), you advertise only on Saturday mornings during cartoon shows. Imagine that your slot car track is portrayed in "virtual reality" and that the proportions depicted in the ad are such that it appears that the viewer is on the racing track. The dimensions of the racing cars that move in grooved slots around the track have been adjusted accordingly. To a young child who might be using a pre-conventional level of reasoning, the action is exciting. But ACT's position is that your ad is deceptive: the information given and the action depicted in the ad are factual, but the proportions are out of line with reality. How would you use Discursive Communication to resolve this conflict with ACT? The principle underlying ACT's position is to promote freedom from emotional harm. Can your resolution satisfy the four normative guidelines directed toward resolving conflicts of interest so as to enhance societal well-being?

Information and Privacy

Another issue concerns the security of company records in relation to an individual's privacy. Virtually all of us treasure privacy in our personal lives. The question is to what extent should this value be extended to the business world? Since a company's records disclose its activities and plans, to what extent do companies have a right to keep such records from the public? The criteria that we set out in Chapter 5 to justify whistleblowing provide a partial answer to this question. Business in this country turns on competition, and the competitive advantage clearly depends in part on keeping some data and plans out of the hands of one's competitors. Hence, the issue of secure company records involves a potential conflict between the need for the free flow of information (information that will keep all parties on an equal footing) and the need for security essential to healthy competition. So the question is one of somehow harmonizing or balancing these different needs.

Proprietary Information

The concepts of security and equal footing also underlie the prohibition of insider trading on the stock market. Paradoxically, our economic system rewards the person who takes every effort to obtain all information relative to a financial transaction. However, obtaining and using proprietary information relevant to price changes in a stock can have serious ethical implications. The classical economic model of competition assumes the general availability of all information pertinent to a business transaction. Using proprietary information for personal gain—proprietary information that is purposefully kept from the public—violates the economic assumptions that legitimize the market exchange as an effective and efficient means for enhancing societal well-being. The long-term feasibility of trading on insider information is highly suspect. The normative guideline of universalizability/reversibility to insure conflict resolution also comes into play. Simply put, would you think it fair, just, or equitable if someone made money at your expense by using information that you were prohibited from obtaining?

For all consequentialists and for nearly all deontologists, possessing accurate and full or at least adequate information is essential for making moral decisions. This is because of the role this information plays in the process of moral reasoning. But do we have any right to be given this information? Although it might be agreed that normal adult human beings have, in some sense at least, a "right of life," there is considerable controversy over most other alleged rights—including a basic right to full information. In any case, most theories of rights are rooted in some more basic theory about morality and moral reasoning. It will be useful to examine those theories even if there is a defensible "right to information."

Information and Consequentialism

The quality and quantity of information necessary to make reasoned decisions are pillars in the foundation of all schools of moral thought, but especially in utilitarianism. The theory of act utilitarianism was introduced and examined in Chapter 5. In addition, there is a related theory that is sometimes called *situation ethics.*

Situation Ethics and Utilitarianism

Situation ethics, which is actually a group of related theories, emphasizes the importance of basing one's moral decisions on detailed knowledge of each relevant situation. According to situation ethics, there are no absolute moral rules or principles; everything depends on a unique situation. If any rules are to be considered at all (and the various models of situation ethics differ on this), they serve merely as rules of thumb when limited time or limited information makes it impossible for the agent to study the particular situation at hand in sufficient detail.

It is easy to see how act utilitarianism can be considered as one variation of situation ethics. The act utilitarian urges us to choose whatever action will bring about the greatest balance of good over evil when everyone affected has been taken into account. Making such a choice, of course, is a difficult—sometimes impossible—undertaking. Since life is complex and the future is often difficult to predict, the most practical advice that the act utilitarian can offer is to try to choose that action which will maximize the good. This, in turn, means to try to determine (given all of the information available to you), which action is likely to lead to the greatest net good in the long run. This way of putting the matter makes explicit the role of information in theories of this sort. Whenever relevant information is lacking, the process of moral decisionmaking will be defective.

The Need for Adequate Information

So that we are perceived as providing accurate information, Habermas claims that we have the responsibility to validate our statements. This means offering to lay open for inspection the body of evidence from which we have drawn our conclusions. This disclosure covers all the information at our disposal that a reasoning person should consider relevant to the claim in question.

Habermas also projects a second responsibility onto us with respect to our claim. Simply put, we have to stand behind our claim apart from its grounding in a body of evidence. This implies an obligation to document our truthfulness or honesty. This documentation is validated by testing if the reason we have given the other person to justify our position appears consistent with the probable consequences accruing to us when we act upon our claim.

The key question is whether people in business will accept these responsibilities as foundations for whɛt constitutes adequate information.

Kant

Immanuel Kant, one of the eighteenth century's greatest philosophers, held that correct ethical thinking rested on what he called the *categorical imperative*. He stated this imperative in several different ways, although he claimed that each version was equivalent. The most well-known version of Kant's categorical imperative states as follows: "Act only so you can will the maxim on which you act to be a universal law." Perhaps the most plausible example given by Kant concerns a person trying to decide whether or not to make a promise to lie. That person could not will the maxim underlying the lying to be universalized since

> clearly any maxim about lying will have to include the rule of "lying in order to achieve something that depends upon the lie's being believed." Otherwise it would be pointless. But surely, to seek credibility by lying is not a policy that can be universally adopted! No rational agent can will that maxim as a universal law, for in its universal form it is self-contradictory.[7]

In other words, in the very act of lying the person wants or wills that the lie be accepted by others; but if such lying were practiced by everyone, promises would not be accepted—and thus there would be a "contradiction of will." The person would be simultaneously willing that promises be accepted and willing something that would inevitably prevent this.

How would Kant's view apply to the issues of information presented in this chapter? Since the lying-promise example just discussed would involve the giving of misinformation, one kind of application may already be clear. But to take a business-oriented example, consider the implications of Kant's theory for the product manager who is trying to decide whether to approve an advertising campaign. Suppose that the advertisements contain only statements that are literally true but that are nevertheless presented in such a way as to mislead the average reader. First, Kant would want us to identify the maxim on which this person proposes to act. This is frequently more difficult than Kant seems to have realized. For our present purposes, however, let us assume that the maxim involved is "let me mislead potential customers whenever doing so is likely to benefit me without serious risk of harm to me." Kant would probably concede that this maxim could theoretically be acted on by an individual—and in fact may well be acted on by many persons already in their day-to-day practices. But could it be willed to be a universal law without some sort of contradiction of will resulting? If everyone acted so as to mislead others when it would benefit themselves, it would not take long before misleading statements (whether in advertising or elsewhere) would be rejected by the public. But note that Kant would not simply say that such a consequence would be a bad thing in itself. His point would be that one would be simultaneously willing that the misleading advertising be accepted and willing something to make this impossible (or at least highly unlikely). Thus a contradiction of will would again result. This is the general approach to ethical dilemmas given by Kant.

Conclusions

Take into account Kant's views when you read the cases that follow this chapter. Some general questions will deserve consideration:

1. Does not an efficient business system operate best over the long term by encouraging a *caveat emptor* mindset?

2. Conversely, does an effective business system require total honesty or trust between buyers and sellers?

3. If not, what boundaries would you set in the following cases?

As you analyze the cases, reflect on the criteria for Discursive Communication that were laid out in the beginning of the chapter. Those criteria are that all the facts needed to resolve the conflict be available to the parties involved, and that the parties be honest with each other in their efforts to resolve the conflict. A final aspect to be drawn from the chapter is to determine whether nonmaleficence underlies the actions of the conflicting parties in the cases described. If so, then a resolution to the conflict may be reached to fulfill the last clause of our definition of ethics—to enhance societal well-being.

❖   Case Study 9–1   ❖

NESTLÉ

For three decades—from the 1970s through the early 1990s—Nestlé aroused widespread social ire for the marketing of one of its products. Ironically, most of the anger came from neither the purchasers nor the users of the product. The controversy centered on Nestlé's sale and distribution of baby formula in developing countries. Was the product worth Nestlé's defense? Perhaps not, if you consider that sales of formula in developing countries generated less than 1 percent of the firm's revenues.

The question is whether baby formula is appropriate for use in developing countries. A doctor in Venezuela associated deaths from gastroenteritis with bottle feeding. He commented that "a totally breast-fed baby just does not get sick like this." A physician at UCLA estimated that millions of babies suffered from malnutrition due to bottle feeding. The unsanitary conditions in some countries can make bottle feeding a risky practice.

Baby formula has been created to resemble mother's milk. It is based on cow's milk and lacks the antibodies of mother's milk that aid in the development of the child's immune system. When sold as a powder, it should be mixed with pure water and given in sterilized bottles. However, pure water and sterilization are often lacking. And illiteracy renders written instructions meaningless. The dangers of formula feeding have been dramatized by a Cornell nutritionist, who said: "Placing a baby on the bottle in the third world might be tantamount to signing the baby's death certificate."

Nestlé acknowledged that breast feeding is better than bottle feeding. Its educational materials have stressed that fact. But the company has challenged the claim that its infant formula causes infant death. Nestlé pointed to the fact that infant mortality was decreasing in a number of developing countries. This decrease, in Nestlé's view, was due in part to better nutrition, and baby formula contributed to the trend toward better nutrition.

The issue is an emotional one. It has gained the attention of health officials as well as social activists. Nestlé bridled at the criticism of some activists who had attributed the questionable marketing practices of Nestlé's competitors to Nestlé. Nestlé denied that it dressed salespeople in white to project a legitimate medical image. It denied that it gave free samples to mothers. Nestlé also denied that it advertised baby formula in developing countries.

Despite the firm's denials, a boycott was launched against Nestlé by a coalition of religious and social action groups. The boycott lasted for seven years until Nestlé agreed upon a selective distribution policy. The policy followed World Health Organization (WHO) guidelines that stated that baby formula in developing countries would be distributed only to children in need. Assessing which children were truly in need was a task left to local hospital administrators.

The boycott had its effects on both Nestlé's public image and its sales. Boycott organizers claimed over one billion dollars in lost sales, a figure that Nestlé disputed. There appears to be no doubt that Nestlé spent tens of millions of dollars fighting the boycott.

The controversy has not ended. Nestlé modified its distribution system and even removed the picture of babies from its label. These voluntary actions were taken even though the WHO guidelines have been incorporated into the law of only a handful of countries. But critics claimed that Nestlé indiscriminately sent large quantities of formula to developing-world hospitals. The source of the problem was that hospitals in some countries did not monitor their own requests for and use of the formula. Said Thad Jackson, a spokesman for Nestlé: "If a hospital comes to us and asks for supplies, under the WHO guidelines we have almost an obligation to provide them." Jackson added, "We recognize that no matter how hard we try, free samples can be abused. . .We can't impose our will on governments."

Critics answer that free distribution to hospitals should be stopped. Deliveries to those "in need"—and they believe that there are very few— should be through normal procurement channels. Reacting to an independent audit committee, Nestlé proposed a pilot plan for unilateral withdrawal of its formula from selected countries. As it did so, Nestlé wondered about the reaction of its competitors. Its major competitor would not commit to Nestlé's proposal to join in this withdrawal. When Nestlé withdrew its formula from Thailand, competitors had the market to themselves and took advantage of the opportunity.

Competitors view the worldwide $6 billion baby food market with acquisitive eyes. Those same competitors were the first to call public attention to customers' confusion over the labeling of Carnation's hypoallergenic baby food. The Carnation product was to be Nestlé's entry into the U.S. market. Nestlé's competitive problems, though, were of little concern to critics. They point out that after the first boycott, Nestlé had agreed to halt free distribution regardless of the actions of its competitors. In their eyes, Nestlé's withdrawal from selected developing countries was neither as far-reaching nor as quickly enacted as was needed.

Questions

1. What stage of moral reasoning would you attribute to Nestlé's critics? Why?
2. Is there a morally justifiable alternative to Nestlé's total withdrawal from the developing world market?
3. Suggest a resolution to this conflict that involves all the baby formula manufacturers. Demonstrate that each of the four normative criteria for lasting conflict resolution has been met.

Sources

Robert Ball, "Nestlé revs up its U.S. campaign," *Fortune* 97 (February 13, 1978), 80–83.

"Battling the bottle," *Journal of Commerce and Commercial* (August 7, 1989), 1A, 4A.

Betsy Bauer, Patrick Chu, and Paul Eisenstein, "Third World boycott of Nestlé called off," *USA Today* (January 27, 1984), 2B.

Laurie Duncan, "Group calls for resumption of Nestlé boycott," *Los Angeles Times* (October 5, 1988), IV-I.

Alix M. Freedman, "Nestlé to restrict low cost supplies of baby formula to developing nations," *The Wall Street Journal* (January 30, 1991), B5.

The Infant Formula Controversy: A Nestlé View (White Plains, NY: The Nestlé Company, 1978).

Leah Margulies, "Bottle babies: death and business get their market," *Business and Society Review* (Spring 1978), 43–49.

Rosalind Rachid, "Switzerland's Nestlé nurses its sullied baby food image," *Journal of Commerce and Commercial* (August 7, 1989), 1A, 5A.

"Renewed boycott of Nestlé is urged by advocacy group," *The Wall Street Journal* (October 5, 1988), 4.

❖   Case Study 9–2   ❖

Acid Rain

The sugar maple trees in Vermont are slowly dying. As a result, the state's maple syrup industry, worth over $15 million per year, is threatened. The threat stems from acid rain. Sophisticated analysis of chemicals in the air has pinpointed the source of the problem. The chemicals affecting the Vermont maples most likely originated from industries five hundred miles away in the Ohio River valley.

In the eastern forests of the United States, the chemical balance of trees is slowly being altered. At particular risk is the red spruce. Plant physiologists at Cornell University have traced the problem to the major elements in acid rain—nitric acid and sulfuric acid. These acids alter the spruce needles so that the trees cannot produce enough internal nutrients. This makes them vulnerable to freezing temperatures. The importance of these forests to our ecological system is quite simple: they store carbon. In doing so, they play an important part in controlling carbon dioxide in the atmosphere. The amount of carbon dioxide, in turn, is directly related to global warming.

Whether the issue is global warming or, on a smaller scale, the decline of Nova Scotia salmon, acid rain has caught the attention of environmentalists. Canadians in the eastern provinces feel particularly at risk from the air-borne chemicals emanating from the industrial midwest. Their concern was documented in two films—*Acid Rain: Requiem or Recovery* and *Acid From Heaven*. But when environmental groups in the United States attempted to show the films, they ran into an unexpected obstacle.

The U.S. Justice Department declared that the films were government propaganda. The Justice Department based its ruling on legislation from 1938 dealing with attempts to influence foreign policy. The films could be shown in the United States only after the following stipulations were met: (1) they were registered with the Foreign Agents Registration Act, (2) they were prefaced by a warning that registration did not imply U.S. government approval, and (3) a list of those ordering the films was given to the Justice Department. The Canadian Environment Minister reacted by wondering what had happened to the concept of freedom of speech.

Canadians were also unhappy with the U.S. participation in a joint study on the effects of acid rain. One Canadian environmentalist accused the United States of trying to manipulate the results. After one group of U.S. scientists in a joint project recommended more stringent controls over acid rain, they were reassigned to other duties. Their recommendations were not acted upon. Canadians also were displeased that the United States would not match their own decision to cut back on sulphur dioxide emissions.

The U.S. approach to the problem was to fund a ten-year study costing over half a billion dollars. The results became the determinants of the 1990 amendments to the Clean Air Act. The goal was to reduce sulphur dioxide emissions by 10 million tons a year by the year 2010. The first phase of the program in 1995 will affect 100 electric power plants. The second phase, beginning in 2000, affects another 800 plants. The cost of the cleanup has been estimated at $5 billion to $10 billion.

The Environmental Protection Agency (EPA) has established emission allowances for the utility companies affected. If a company cuts emissions below the prescribed level, it gains an allowance credit. It can then sell this allowance credit to another utility that has not met its prescribed level.

The costs involved could hinder a utility from meeting its mandated emission level. One utility in Ohio estimated the cost of the emission control at 15 percent of its current revenues. Another utility in Wisconsin estimated that a 10 percent rate increase would be needed for it to meet the costs. Still another in Virginia estimated a 40 percent rate increase. If smokestack scrubbers are used for the cleanup, the cost per single plant can run to over $100 million. In both Indiana and Ohio, utilities must submit economic analysis reports to state public utilities commissions estimating the effects of cleanup measures on the state economies. That is, the utilities need to evaluate whether the state coal industries which supply the utilities will be hurt. The United Mine Workers have estimated that 15,000 jobs will be lost. Coal from the Appalachian region tends to have higher sulphur content than coal mined in the western states.

Is the cleanup worth the price? One industry commentator stated that except for effects on the red spruce tree, there is no conclusive evidence that acid rain causes North American forests to decline. A government official questioned the cost of emission controls if the benefits were only in terms of marginal dollars received from cleaner lakes in the northeast. A congressman commented that the acid rain problem was "greatly exaggerated." He conjectured that once the president had agreed to support an acid rain bill, a convenient target had to be chosen, and that target was the electric utility industry.

Questions

1. Does a utilitarian approach to solving the acid rain problem best satisfy the criteria for resolving ethical conflicts?
2. Given both the definition of ethics posited in the book and the phrase *to enhance societal well-being,* present your definition of societal well-being as it applies to this case.
3. Is the use of the saleable emission allowance credit an example of Discursive Communication? Can you come up with a more ethically defensible solution?

Sources

"Acid rain conference held as Congress gives final approval to bill," *Public Utilities Fortnightly* (December 6, 1990), 47, 49.

Melinda Beck et al., "The bitter politics of acid rain," *Newsweek* (April 25, 1983), 36–37.

Laurent Belsie, "In Ohio Valley, coal equals jobs: and clean air bill worries many," *The Christian Science Monitor* (April 3, 1990), 7.

Fred Blazer, "Distrust across the border," *Maclean's* (March 7, 1983), 38–39.

Lori Burkhart, "EPA announces final acid rain rule," *Public Utilities Fortnightly* (November 15, 1992), 35–36.

Geoffrey Norman, "The acid rain wars," *Esquire* (March 1983), 241, 243.

Robert Pierre, "Scientists find how acid rain does dirty work," *The Atlanta Journal and Constitution* (December 6, 1989), A6.

Barbara Rosewicz, "Price tag is producing groans already," *The Wall Street Journal* (October 29, 1990), A7.

R. W. Scott, "Don't bet on it," *World Oil* (August 1990), 5.

William H. Smith, "Air pollution and forest damage," *C & EN* (November 11, 1991), 30, 31.

"Sugar maples sicken under acid rain's fall," *The New York Times* (May 13, 1991), A18.

Matthew L. Wald, "Industry way of clean-air bill," *The New York Times* (May 13, 1991), D1, D8.

❖   Case Study 9–3   ❖

T^2 MEDICAL

Thomas Haire and Tommy Carter, co-founders of T^2 Medical, Inc., met while they were employed by Baxter Healthcare. Armed with $100,000 and a sense of determination, they spent quite a bit of time laying the groundwork for their T^2 infusion therapy centers. These centers provide intravenous medication for patients outside the confines of a hospital.

A brief description of how T^2 has set up its centers is in order. T^2 recruits ten or more doctors in an area to start one of its centers. The doctors invest $100 each and provide a letter of credit. The doctors are encouraged to send their own patients to the T^2 center for care. T^2 staffs the center and sets the service fees. After the center is on its feet, T^2 buys it back from the doctors. The purchase price, paid in both cash and T^2 stock, is generous. In the case of one center in New York, each of the physician-investors was reported to have received the equivalent of $296,000 for his share of the sale back to T^2. An internal company memorandum summarized the T^2 growth plan: "A physician will be more likely to refer patients to the Corporation if the physician owns an interest in the Corporation." A study funded by the Congressional General Accounting Office verifies that doctors with a financial interest in a medical service do refer patients to that service more than doctors who have no stake in the service.

The firm's growth plan has been highly successful. In fact, T^2 was ranked as one of the ten most successful small businesses in the United States. That ranking by Forbes was based on the firm's return on equity. But even with strong returns and excellent growth prospects, the price of the firm's stock went down. The cause of the decline was a series of news reports that questioned the propriety of the firm's referral practices.

More than 2000 doctors in 37 states have had a financial interest in T^2 or in the therapy centers that the company manages. The question has been raised, though, about whether doctors should refer patients to medical clinics in which they have a financial interest. This is of questionable legality when those patients receive government-supported Medicare and Medicaid payments. T^2 claims that its physician-investors' referral of Medicare patients to company-owned centers is in no sense a violation of medical ethics or the law.

The company strongly advises its physician-investors against referring Medicare patients to T^2 centers that the doctors own. This assures that the doctors do not act in a way construed as violating the law. Medicare patients account for less than 5 percent of the company's business and are directed to T^2 centers that are company-owned rather than doctor-owned. Joseph Allegra of T^2 says that the firm only serves Medicare patients so as not to be accused of age discrimination.

There are critics both inside and outside the medical profession who have ethical problems with physician self-referral. One critic is former U.S. Surgeon General C. Everett Koop, who said: "Doctors referring their patients to facilities in which they have an economic interest is incompatible with all that professionalism in medicine stands for." He views the practice as akin to taking kickbacks. The American Medical Association agrees, but makes an exception when the service is an extension of the doctor's practice. And that is how T^2 views its centers—as an extension of its doctors' medical practices.

T^2 patients are apparently happy with the company's service. Ninety-five percent expressed satisfaction in response to a company-sponsored survey. T^2 claims that its doctors cannot abuse the treatment protocol because their choice of approved therapies is limited. T^2 also claims to save its patients money even though markups for drugs and professional service range from 100 percent to 400 percent. But critics wonder if cancer patients, a large portion of the T^2 business, would question the costs of the T^2 center treatment, given their unsettled emotional conditions. Approximately 10% of the nation's cancer specialists have invested in T^2.

Joseph Allegra, CEO of T^2, refutes the criticism of T^2 on three levels. With respect to quality of care, he claims that the care received at a T^2 center is "second to none." With respect to cost, he states that "T^2 is the lowest priced of national providers." With respect to ethics, Allegra states that the "relationship between T^2 and its physicians meets every ethical criteria of the American Medical Association."

The returns for the physician-investors in their T^2 centers have been lucrative, with many earning from $30,000 to $60,000 per year. Some doctors, however, have felt uncomfortable. One physician claimed he spoke for many "who have not been involved in these schemes" when he judged the T^2 physician–investor relation as "an unacceptable conflict of interest [that] is grossly inappropriate." Another physician who had invested in a T^2-affiliated company asked to back out of his investment. Upon personal reflection, he said that he had qualms about referring patients to a company from which he profited. Still another doctor had simply no problem: He asked T^2 to make out his checks to the state Council for Child Abuse. He said he didn't need the money.

Questions

1. Is societal well-being enhanced by the T^2 physician–investor relationship?
2. In terms of deontological versus consequentialist ethical theory, what would be the theoretical justifications for supporting and opposing the T^2 physician–investor relationship?
3. How would you suggest a resolution to the conflict which you identified in the previous question?

Sources

Joseph C. Allegra, "Newspaper distorted facts about physicians' firm," *Atlanta Constitution* (January 1993), A12.

Dow Jones News Service, "T^2 shares bear the brunt of debate over referrals," *Atlanta Journal and Constitution* (July 27, 1991), 5.

"Georgia medical concerns to cooperate with inquiry," *The Wall Street Journal* (June 25, 1992), B5.

Charles H. Mendenhall, "Thanks for the truth," *Atlanta Constitution* (December 21, 1992), A20.

Glen Ruffenach, "Medical firms' stocks plunge on probe news," *The Wall Street Journal* (June 26, 1992), B4.

Glenn Ruffenach, "T² Medical's dazzling prospects becoming tarnished," *The Wall Street Journal* (July 7, 1992), B8.

Steve Sternberg, "Doctor turns his T² checks into windfall for charity," *Atlanta Journal and Constitution* (April 22, 1993), D1, D7.

Steve Sternberg, "Rx for profit," *Atlanta Journal and Constitution* (December 13, 1992), A1, A8, A9.

Steve Sternberg, "T² recruited doctors to get lucrative referrals, memo indicates," *Atlanta Journal and Constitution* (April 22, 1993), D1, D7.

"T²: Medicine and money," *Atlanta Constitution* (December 15, 1992), A22.

Tom Watson, "In doctors' defense," *Atlanta Constitution* (December 21, 1992), A20.

"What it takes to be the best," *Forbes* (November 12, 1990), 242.

Notes to Chapter 9

[1]Jürgen Habermas, *Communication and the Evolution of Society,* trans. by Thomas McCarthy (Boston: Beacon Press, 1979).

[2]Ibid.

[3]G. J. Warnock, *The Object of Morality* (London: Methuen & Co., 1971), pp. 83–84.

[4]Ibid., p. 84.

[5]Ibid., p. 81.

[6]Ibid.

[7]Warner A. Wick, Introduction to Immanuel Kant, *Ethical Philosophy: Grounding for the Metaphysics of Morals,* trans. by James W. Ellington (Indianapolis: Hackett Publishing Company, 1983), p. xviii. First published in 1785.

Chapter 10

Environment

In the Orient, a dominating view equates the purpose of ethics—societal well-being—with the concept of harmony.[1] Harmony is to be sought with others and even with the natural environment. Societal well-being in the Far East is more allied to adapting to circumstances than it is to following objective ideas about what is right and fair. What it takes to bring about harmony in one set of circumstances or part of the world may not be viewed as appropriate in another. If we are inflexible in propounding our version of what is right and fair, eventual harmony between conflicting parties is unlikely to be attained. This observation brings us back to the focus on conflict resolution in our definition of ethics.

The desire for harmony leads us to the final step that Habermas believes is necessary for reaching consensus in communication. That step is to agree on an appropriate course of action to reconcile conflicting positions.[2] Conflict about business practices is almost inevitable. Many situations do not lend themselves to formal sets of rules and answers about correct procedures. In addition, more than one course of action may appear to enhance societal well-being, even when that well-being is broadly defined to include the widest group of people possible and the environment in which they live.

Taking our cue from the process of conflict resolution outlined in Chapter 7, we should be open to new ideas. If both parties are honest in their intention to reach consensus, they will rely strongly on logical reasoning when applying their personal ethical principles to a course of action. It may well be that the principles held by both parties in common can be represented by an entirely new position. Arriving at such a position entails attempts at Integrative or Discursive Communication, not Adversarial or Strategic Communication. The result is not necessarily a compromise, since compromise implies giving up something we hold dear. Too often, pride impedes our reasoning power, and we forget that more than one position can be derived from a commonly held principle.

Dealing with Others

We may believe that the moral rightness of our particular position should be perfectly clear to the other party. But it is not usually the case that our argumentative skills are so polished that we can educate the other party "up" to our level of understanding. In reality, empirical evidence seems to indicate that it takes at least ten hours of intensive communicative action to raise people's moral reasoning approximately one third of one of Kohlberg's stages. And this is accomplished only by a skilled negotiator involved in a process called *moral intervention.*[3] Moral intervention, in this context, represents an effort to induce a person to reason from what Kohlberg considers to be a higher stage of moral judgment.

Reaching a normative consensus with the conflicting party necessitates a commitment of time and thought. Time is needed to analyze alternative courses of action. Those actions then should be matched both against principles held in common and against the criteria of consistency and universalizability. Then the feasibility of each alternative has to be assessed.

Our mental commitment to conflict resolution should start when we focus on the other party's stage of moral reasoning. Surprisingly, few people will be willing to negotiate using postconventional (Stages Five and Six) reasoning. Instead, we have to negotiate using a level of reasoning that feels comfortable to them. Preconventional reasoners (at Stages One and Two) prefer to work with ideas about concrete actions and the results of those actions.[4] General rules, norms, and abstract maxims usually do not draw positive reactions from those at the preconventional level. In contrast, those who rely on conventional moral reasoning (at Stages Three and Four) ground most of their positions on social norms and formal societal rules. Norms and rules should provide the base for our negotiations with them.

These moral negotiations give us the opportunity to review how we adopted our underlying principles. Viable principles will withstand this introspective questioning. We do not wish to sacrifice our principles, but principles conveniently accepted from tradition rather than crafted by careful reasoning deserve close scrutiny. A suitable area for reviewing our principles concerns an issue that will affect the business world over the next decade.[5] That area of concern is the environment.

The Environment: A Growing Concern

To some people, concern for the environment is as sacred a subject as motherhood. To others, however, concern for the environment and the environmental movement have become code words for threats that business should resist. We encourage you to keep an open mind while you aim toward a deeper understanding of the subtleties involved in this controversy, rather than to take sides at the outset.

In some discussions of environmental issues, the debate seems to turn on whether or not the environment is sacred. Many environmentalists claim that the doctrine of the sanctity of the environment should be an essential factor behind our business decisions. Many businesspersons, on the other hand, say, "There is nothing sacred about the environment; it is a means to be used." Rather than taking a side in this sometimes bitter debate, we shall consider some of the points of commonality for both positions. These points may prove to be a basis for resolving some of the conflicts.

To begin, consider a word that holds prominence in discussions of environmental ethics: *ecology*.[6] The word is based on the Greek roots for "house" (*oikos*) and "study of" (*logos*). According to the original meaning of the term, ecology is the study of our house—in this case, our biological surroundings or environment. The science of ecology is especially interested in how what goes on in one part of our "house" influences and is influenced by what goes on in other parts.

As a science, ecology is intended to be *de*scriptive of what is as much as possible, rather than *pre*scriptive about what should be. We need normative or ethical thinking, then, to decide what we should do in the light of the facts that ecologists bring to our attention.

The starting point for such normative thinking about what should be is not too difficult to find. Virtually everyone, whether in business or not, has a legitimate interest in living in a relatively healthy environment. Other things being equal, no one would voluntarily destroy or pollute his or her living space. Some persons, of course, are imprudent—but this fact would hardly lead us to approve of imprudence as a virtue to live by.

The prevalence of imprudence in human life, however, is directly connected with what we consider the single most important concept in the field of ethics and the environment: long-range consequences. Whether one is primarily concerned with one's own good, the good of one's firm, or the good of the whole world, it seems clear that the long-term as well as short-term results of one's actions need to be considered. This is an elementary lesson that most of us learn repeatedly in the process of growing up.

From an ethical standpoint, however, the interesting questions arise not so much from imprudence but from situations in which the prudent behavior of one person conflicts with the prudent behavior, or at least the interests, of others.

There appears to be a natural progression or development in the criteria we use for deciding how to behave. We reflected on this development earlier by presenting Lawrence Kohlberg's stages of morality. It is only after individuals have reached the conventional level of development (Stages Three and Four) that they typically take an interest in any long-range consequences for themselves. In other words, genuine prudence occurs later than does short-term self-interest.

Environmental Harm

In the same fashion, a certain level of maturation is required before one can be aware of the effects of one's actions on others. At first, such an awareness will be limited to the present moment and will serve only practical ends: "Will this person give me what I want right now?" or "Will this person hurt me now in some way because of what I do?" Even when long-term consequences begin to be considered, egoism or self-interest remain the basic orientation. Only at a relatively late stage of development is it even possible for a person to entertain the notion that the well-being of another person should be considered to be valuable in and of itself. Some persons never reach this level of thinking about morality. Some reach it in thinking but fail to act on it in any consistent manner.

There are some, though, who demonstrate a level of concern and behavior that encompasses more than the well-being of other people. This latter group gives us the opportunity to explore the issue of the environment and ethics. Some in this group would claim that besides considering only the consequences of our behavior for all human beings we must also take into account the effects of our behavior on all other sentient beings as well—that is, on animals. Furthermore, some have gone on to suggest that we need to extend moral consideration even beyond sentient beings to nature itself. This possibility merits a brief exploration.

Aldo Leopold: "The Conservation Ethic"

Aldo Leopold's essay "The Conservation Ethic," first published in 1933, is a classic statement of the need for, and the basic principles of, environmental ethics.[7] Leopold begins his essay by pointing out some of the ways in which our ethical thinking has developed throughout history. Ancient Greeks, for example, were not shocked to hear stories of Odysseus killing the slave-girls he suspected of misbehaving. In those times, slaves were simply considered as property or objects. But over the centuries, ethical criteria have been gradually extended to the point where now it is a valid question to ask in what way(s), if at all, ethical criteria should be extended to the nonhuman world.

Garrett Hardin: The "Tragedy of the Commons"

Even if we stop short of extending ethical criteria to the nonhuman world, virtually all of us may be able to agree about certain concepts in environmental ethics. One such concept, the "tragedy of the commons," has been articulated by the contemporary biologist Garrett Hardin.[8]

Hardin asks us to imagine a pasture open to all—the sort of pasture typical of England in the past and the sort of shared public space that lent its name to places like "the Boston Common." Under such arrangements, each cattle herder will want to make as much use of the common pasture as possible. This means that each one will add to his or her herd of cattle at any opportunity. Grazing additional cattle on the common pasture will not add anything directly to the herder's costs—and individual herders will receive the entire benefit when these animals are sold.

The problem with this arrangement is that there is a biological limit to the number of animals who can survive by grazing in a particular pasture. This limit is referred to by ecologists as the "carrying capacity." Since the pasture is open for all to use, each cattle-herder will want to exploit it for personal gain. Eventually and inevitably, however, this will lead to overgrazing and the ruin of the pasture altogether. Hardin writes:

> Each man is locked into a system that compels him to increase his herd without limit—in a world that is limited. Ruin is the destination toward which all men rush, each pursuing his own best interest in a society that believes in the freedom of the commons. Freedom in a commons brings ruin to all.[9]

All of these persons are not necessarily totally selfish in their actions. It is just that a large component of self-interest does exist in most of us, regardless of our additional motives and concerns. Moreover, a healthy amount of this self-interest seems essential if individuals and businesses are to survive and flourish. What is needed is not the rejection of self-interest as such, but ways to keep the combination of freedom, temptation, and the limits on our natural (and other) resources from leading to disaster.

Enlightened Self-Interest

One feature of the tragedy of the commons deserves special mention. Up to a certain point, there is nothing wrong with adding another cow or steer to one's herd. It is only when the number of cattle approaches the carrying capacity of the pasture that a moral issue arises. This is also true of other things shared in common—our air and water, for example. If we live in relative isolation, we can dispose our garbage in a nearby stream without causing any difficulty since the chemical action of water, air, and sunlight will purify the stream again as it flows along. But problems arise when the capacity of the stream for self-purification is approached. This is why the pollution of the environment is a serious issue today but was not even a moral issue in frontier times. Today there are more of us and we live closer together. Furthermore, many business enterprises operate on a scale unheard of in earlier times, and some of our technologies produce highly toxic substances. Hence, it is a small wonder that questions are being raised today about business ethics in relation to the environment.

However, if our freedom to use the "commons" in our lives becomes restricted, we may begin to feel that our rights are being infringed upon. After all, do we not have a right to do as we please with what belongs to us?

We may find an answer to this dilemma if we combine Aldo Leopold's story of Odysseus and the slave-girls with Garrett Hardin's tragedy of the commons. What was once thought of as personal property—meaning that one could do as one pleased with it—can now be seen in a new light. Our thinking about ethics can evolve, and we can come to accept that limits exist on what we may morally do with what is "ours." In effect, the right to personal property entails the related responsibility to use that property reasonably so as not to cause physical harm to others.

Reflect on the final part of our definition of ethics: ethics aims "to enhance societal well-being." Should that phrase be extended to include the land, air, water, animals, and plants? Exactly what this might mean in terms of business practices is far from clear. That is an issue for you to evaluate as you consider the following examples. This line of thought does suggest, however, that individuals and business firms are not always free to treat their environment as they please. At the very least, they must take into account the long-term consequences of their actions.

An Example

In the "workplace environment," the following examples indicate where long-term consequences might result.

1. In one sense, management has a stewardship role with regard to the work environment. The work environment should allow workers to maintain their health (otherwise the company can rightly be accused of maleficence—and encouraging a Stage One worker reaction based on fear of losing jobs).

2. Health screening in some form should be used to prevent high-risk people from being exposed to unnecessary danger. (Health screening for AIDS, for example, can be used to help persons at risk avoid taxing their immune systems—an example of Stage Five or Six reasoning. Can the law give us some guidance—relying on Stage Four reasoning, which seeks to foster order in society?)

3. Health screening is also appropriate when employees are hired for potential long-term work and their continued presence is needed on the job—a Stage Two motivation grounded on anticipated profits for the employer.

4. In those cases where persons with high health-risk factors need or want a particular job and are willing to expose themselves to danger, is there a company ethic that can guide us—indicating Stage Three reasoning that stresses following customary moral values? It is here that some would suggest asking which course of action will most enhance societal well-being. But others will argue that there are some risks that society should simply not allow people to take, regardless of the people's willingness to do so. We would not argue for any one position. Rather, we suggest that the normative guidelines of feasibility and universalizability could provide the focal points for Discursive Communication in efforts to resolve conflicting views. The H & H Music case at the end of this chapter will give you an opportunity to resolve this conflict.

Rethinking the Principle of Liberty

It may be, however, that the temptations of short-term thinking and of focusing only on self-interest are so strong that Discursive Communication about the environment needs an agreed-upon starting point. Perhaps we also need to have detailed environmental law. This seems to be what we are experiencing in our century. And with this thought we come full circle to the issue of the letter versus the spirit of the law, which was the subject of Chapter 4. Ethical, legal, and practical issues are so intertwined that none of them can be studied in total isolation.

Once we accept ethical and legal restrictions on the ways we may act toward our environment, we will no longer be as "free" as our ancestors were to discard waste into water, land, and air. This fact is often lamented by business leaders and others, who point out that we live in what is supposed to be a "free" country. Some also claim that it is morally wrong or even self-contradictory to accept limitations on our freedom. Philosophers refer to this idea as the *paradox of liberty:* in order to preserve or protect our liberty, we may have to give up certain liberties. For example, to preserve our liberty to drive an automobile in safety, we have to accept limitations on our "right" to drive wherever and however we please.

The paradox of liberty does not imply that rights do not exist. It simply helps us realize that rights and liberties are not as absolute as they may sometimes seem. On the other hand, we may also see the emergence of new rights and liberties. In this spirit, some writers today have argued for a "right to a livable environment." This right, it has been argued, may be even more basic than many of our other rights because it is a necessary precondition of our being able to exercise those other rights. To survive and flourish, both individuals and firms have certain basic requirements, which obviously include "a livable environment." No business leaders dispute this; the controversies revolve around the details of what the minimum standards for such an environment might be and who should bear the costs of maintaining this environment.

Particular situations need answers, often immediately. Ideally, we would recognize that moral behavior may require a certain amount of reflection and choice. Taken to its logical end, this ideal behavior would rest, in Kohlberg's terms, on "self-chosen ethical principles. . .which are used to generate particular decisions."[10] The problem is that Kohlberg found very few people who reason consistently from a Stage Six perspective. Since few of us have arrived at a set of universal ethical principles, can we at least develop an approach to resolving ethical conflicts as we struggle from one problem to the next?

Synthesis

As you formulate your own approach to ethics, we believe there is much that can be helpful in the various theories we have introduced you to—the consequentialist and deontological approaches to ethics, along with Kohlberg's stages of moral development. At the same time, we need to warn you that there is often something troubling about such theories: they are frequently so lofty and abstract that we find ourselves at a loss to apply them to our lives. Here is Harvard philosopher Hilary Putnam's comment on this situation:

> One reason such arguments are always unsatisfying is that they always prove too much; when a philosopher "solves" an ethical problem for one, one feels as if one had asked for a subway token and been given a passenger ticket valid for the first interplanetary passenger-carrying space ship instead.[11]

We can imagine Putnam applying this thought to utilitarianism, to Kant's Categorical Imperative, to theories about absolute rights, and to many of the other views we have examined. But Putnam goes on to suggest a different way of looking at this situation, a way more in keeping with the rationale behind *Practical Business Ethics*. It is true, says Putnam, that we need to examine moral principles rationally,

> But the way *not* to solve an ethical problem is to find a nice sweeping principle that "proves too much," and to accuse those who refuse to "buy" one's absolute principle of immorality. The very words "solution" and "problem" may be leading us astray—ethical problems are not like scientific problems, and they do not often have "solutions" in the sense that scientific problems do. . . .I suggest that our thought might be better guided by a different metaphor—a metaphor from the law, instead of a metaphor from science—the metaphor of *adjudication*.[12]

Adjudication, of course, is what is done by judges in courts of law. And Putnam points to several features of the process of adjudication that we believe also apply to ethical decisionmaking: (1) adjudication involves a weighing of conflicting claims and of factual evidence, (2) under adjudication, any given court decision is provisional rather than "the last word," (3) there are typically "better" or "worse" adjudications of a particular dispute even when there is no one total solution, and (4) a sense of community and shared loyalties is required if the consensus that adjudication involves is to be successful.

There is a parallel between this adjudication process and the steps toward consensus building outlined by Habermas. Habermas's approach puts special emphasis on the fourth condition mentioned in the previous paragraph. He pays close attention not just to a consensus position but also to the norms and values underlying that position. He claims that the conflicting parties have the responsibility to justify verbally how their consensus position embodies their common norms.[13]

In synthesizing the work of moral communications scholars, we can map out a sequential negotiation process to meet the conditions that both Habermas and Putnam have put forward (see Table 10-1). But it takes more than following a negotiation process to resolve conflicts over ethical issues: it takes a frame of mind. Piaget set forth ground rules, similar to those mentioned by

Habermas, to facilitate resolution.[14] He believes that both parties to the conflict must do the following:

- Respect each other as equals.
- Share assumptions about what will be discussed.
- Share assumptions about how to proceed.
- Share possession of background information.
- Be willing to submit knowledge, assumptions, and values to scrutiny during the negotiations.

These are noble conditions, but are they realistic? We normally enter negotiations trying to win over the other side to our point of view. Each of us can point to frustration experienced in past negotiations. We have all met our share

**Table 10–1   Steps to Negotiating Conflicts
Over Moral Issues and the Obstacles Encountered**

Sequential Steps	Major Obstacles
1. Each party states a personal position on the issue	Miscomprehension Complexity of the issue
2. Each party presents reasoning as well as the underlying principles that validate the personal position	Held-back information Less than complete honesty
3. Each party paraphrases the other party's position, principles, and the reasoning that links them	Failure to empathize Organizational pressures/expectations
4. Each party explains why the other party's position conflicts with one's own personal principles	Adversarial rather than critical explanations Failure to look for similarities as well as differences
5. Each party explores: (a) alternative positions which do not violate the other party's stated personal principles or	Failure to abandon original position
(b) Each party explores for unstated principles that are mutually held. Then alternative positions are derived from the previously unstated principle(s)	Transformation of principles into ordered rules
6. Alternative positions are tested against four normative guidelines to resolve conflict so as to enhance societal well-being	Weighing cost vs. benefits Defining universalizability from narrow perspective
7. Implementation of appropriate alternative agreed-upon position	Failure to inform affected parties Inability to transform new positions into implementable steps

of Stage Two, shortsighted, ethical egoists. Did they change either their moral stance or negotiating position after being exposed to our opinion? Probably not. But that was the past and this is the present. This text has presented you with the tools to negotiate a satisfactory resolution to moral conflicts. It is your job to put these tools to use.

Your Ethics

In the Introduction to this text, we listed a series of objectives. The text itself provides only the tools to accomplish these objectives. It is up to you, the reader, to use these tools to attain the objectives. At some time in the past, you may have made the comment, "That's unethical!" when you heard of something that had been done. The comment was probably made with force if the practice in question affected you personally. In a business setting, it is reasonable to assume that someone in the future will direct that same comment toward one of your actions.

If this text has done its job, you will be more than able to defend and explain your behavior. That will be the case if our fifth and sixth objectives have been realized. Those goals, in brief, were that you would *integrate moral competence with managerial competence, and that you would develop and be capable of articulating exactly what you believe your moral responsibility to be in business situations.*

As you decide on appropriate courses of action to resolve conflicts, you will most likely try to optimize the benefits for all involved. These benefits do not exist in a vacuum. Ethical conflicts in business occur within both a social and a physical environment. It is within these environments that a consensus position must evolve from commonly held principles.

It is one thing, though, to decide on an appropriate course of action and another to implement it. James Rest[15] advises isolating the following impediments when making ethical decisions:

- transformation of goals into operations.
- timing difficulties.
- physical obstacles.
- distractions.

He then cautions that to overcome these impediments, you should outline a sequence of actions so that you will not lose sight of your goals. This sequence is similar to the process of communication described in Table 10-1. The timing of these sequential steps is as important as the steps themselves. But what may be the prime prerequisite for implementing a course of action is that you have the courage and ego strength to act on your convictions. You will have to work around impediments and through frustrations to resolve the ethical problem. There will be a strong temptation to arrange a quick-fix solution as other aspects of your job demand your attention.

Rarely will you have all the information you need when you make and implement those decisions. Perhaps you will develop a feeling for what is right and wrong. It is difficult, though, to explain and justify that feeling when your actions conflict with someone else's concept of what is ethical. If you use the filtering criteria that we have posited in this book—making reasoned, consistent, universalizable, and feasible decisions—you will be better able to handle ethical dilemmas and criticism. It is up to you, however, to adopt your own ethical principles. Your options—the deontological or consequentialist theories and the stages of moral reasoning—have been discussed in previous chapters. Each approach has its benefits as well as its weaknesses. After finishing this tenth and last chapter, it is time for you to make that choice. With the principles you choose, can you arrive at an appropriate answer to these issues in the following cases? Ask yourself these questions:

1. Whose welfare should you consider when making a decision?

2. Under what conditions will your decision include the welfare of the environment?

3. What time span should you consider when evaluating the ethical implications of your act?

❖   Case Study 10–1   ❖

H & H Music

The worst of the AIDS crisis may be yet to come. The World Health Organization has estimated that the number of cases will have reached 5 to 6 million cases by the turn of the century. But as a populace, we have mixed emotions about the disease. Many cases of AIDS result from behavior that runs contrary to our moral precepts. Drug abuse, homosexual relations, and heterosexual promiscuity account for the majority of these cases.

Judgments about AIDS abound within our religious communities. One end of the spectrum of feelings is represented by Jerry Falwell, head of the Moral Majority. He conjectured that AIDS might be God's retribution for the sin of homosexual behavior. AIDS, he felt, was God's way of tempering the sexual revolution. Falwell's thoughts mirror those of many others.

At the other end of the spectrum are people who feel that charity is called for when confronting AIDS. Ben Patterson, writing in *Christianity Today*, stated: "It is not our job as Christians to make dying people feel worse. It is our job to give them hope and healing in the name of Christ." Patterson, like Jerry Falwell, puts words to the thoughts of many within our society.

The justice versus mercy approaches to treating AIDS have become points of controversy in business as well. The cause of the controversy, though, seems to be based more on pragmatism than on religious beliefs. This is due to the cost of treating the disease. For those who have tested HIV-positive, but who do not yet show symptoms of the disease, treatment with the drug AZT now can cost $2200 per year. AIDS activists protested Burroughs Welcome's original higher price for the drug, and the pharmaceutical firm cut its margins. But $2200 a year is still a lot of money. Even more formidable is the price tag for treating an AIDS victim—$75,000. It is these costs that are causing changes in the benefit packages that businesses offer to their employees.

This problem is probably best embodied in the actions of H & H Music, a musical equipment distributor employing approximately 150 people in Texas. John McGann, who had been with the firm for five years, told the company that he had AIDS. During the next year, H & H revised its health insurance plan. Among the changes was a reduction in lifetime AIDS benefits from $1 million to $5000. At the same time, H & H also changed its general healthcare plan to a self-funded plan with stop-loss (a cap) coverage.

McGann's coverage disappeared. Even with the disability payments he received from Social Security, his medical bills exceeded the money he had available to pay those bills. Thomas Stoddard, McGann's legal counsel, labeled H & H's action as offensive. Stoddard, a director of the Lambda Legal Defense and Education Fund that provided help to gay men, offered these thoughts: "What is offensive is that the employers singled out AIDS." He expressed his worries about the future: "A self-insured employer could decide leukemia is too expensive, or for that matter any type of cancers or any other illness." McGann sued H & H, claiming discrimination. Support for McGann came from a variety of sources, including the American Association for Retired People. That organization's attorney filed a brief in favor of McGann's position. His group of retired older Americans worried that similar medical plan changes could negatively affect them.

Mark Huvard, H & H's attorney, argued that the firm's health plan coverage was a type of welfare benefit. Such benefits have no vesting rights. He stated that the risk of AIDS claims presented too much of a risk for the company to bear.

The judge in the case ruled in favor of H & H Music. His explanation was as follows: "Defendants made changes in the plan because in past years the plan suffered serious financial losses. Defendants were faced with either dropping the plan altogether or making changes. The alterations were not made to discriminate against McGann or anyone who was diagnosed with AIDS."

An attorney for one state's AIDS task force offered some pertinent observations on the issue. He wondered how a firm was to balance employee needs with the need of the firm to survive. In his words: "It appears to pit all the macropolicy issues against one another; the crying social need to provide medical care for people who are seriously ill; the insurance industry's need to rate and price its products according to the risks involved; and the employer's need to remain competitive in a free-market economy."

Questions

1. Given your own ethical norms, how should a firm handle benefits for employees found to have a terminal illness?
2. If an employee contracted an illness by engaging in a practice that was contrary to societal norms, would this factor influence your answer to the previous question?
3. Contrast your position with either the Falwell or Patterson position mentioned in the case. Outline the communication appeals that you would use to reach a negotiated resolution with the person who holds the opposite view.

Sources

Paul Bock, "Religious responses to AIDS," *USA Today* (May 1989), 66–67.

"Employers can reduce benefits to AIDS sufferers, court rules," *The Atlanta Journal/The Atlanta Constitution* (November 27, 1991), A6.

Kim Foltz, "Burroughs Welcome Co. criticized for AIDS effort," *The New York Times* (November 15, 1990), D19.

Susan B. Garland, "Sure you can get sick—but not too sick," *Business Week* (December 3, 1990), 40.

Jerry Geisel, "Self-insurers can limit AIDS benefits: court," *Business Insurance* 25 (August 6, 1990), 1, 27–28.

Robert G. Knowles, "AIDS cost hikes spur tough employer choices," *National Underwriter* 94 (December 17, 1990), 19–20.

Jennifer Landes, "Employer wins 1st round in AIDS coverage lawsuit," *National Underwriter* 94 (August 20, 1990), 1, 4.

Amy Cockser Marcus and Alecia Swasy, "Cap on AIDS benefits wins legal round, " *The Wall Street Journal* (August 1, 1990), B2.

❖   Case Study 10–2   ❖

PACIFIC LUMBER

A lumber mill worker in Cloverdale, California, learned just how serious some environmentalists could be in their efforts to save forests. A log with an embedded steel spike hit a saw next to his workstation. The damaged saw flew apart. One piece of the saw slashed the worker's face, smashed his teeth, and took away part of his jaw.

Dave Foreman, who founded the movement Earth First that protested the logging operation in certain western forests, explained the purpose of tree spiking. It was to dissuade the lumber firms from cutting down the forests. It was not to injure the lumberjacks.

Members of Earth First have been involved in blocking roads used for hauling lumber. They have chained themselves to logging equipment and tree spiking. Foreman has drawn analogies between the tactics of his groups and the efforts of Revolutionary War patriots, Civil War abolitionists, and civil rights activists. His rationale is simple: "We're breaking the law for a higher ethical ideal."

Foreman is a committed environmentalist. His attitude toward environmental activism was strongly influenced by a government recommendation to open up millions of acres of wilderness area for logging. Foreman had worked for over a year on the U.S. Forest Service investigation leading to the government recommendation. He claims that he tried to bring about change within establishment rules to no avail. It was time to throw a monkey wrench in the gears of a system that appeared to show little respect for nature. In his words: "Grizzly bears and 1,000-year-old redwood trees are seen as things, property, with no standing under our laws."

A key target of Earth First's activities was Pacific Lumber. Of particular interest to the group was Charles Hurwitz, the financier who had led the takeover of Pacific Lumber. Hurwitz viewed Pacific Lumber as an asset-rich, debt-free firm. He acquired a large block of Pacific Lumber stock for a price above the traded market price. He then offered to buy more at even a higher price. Shareholders who said that they would be loyal to the old management sold out. Said one member of the old management team: "We found out that shareholder loyalty is worth about a quarter point per share."

Hurwitz addressed Pacific Lumber employees who feared change under new management. He promised to live up to merger agreement conditions dealing with wage and benefits. But in no uncertain terms, he pointed out who was now in control: "There's a little story about the Golden Rule. Those who have the gold, rule."

To meet the debt payments for the leveraged buyout, the new management pursued two strategies. The first was to cannibalize part of the company's accumulated pension funds. The second was to increase logging operations. The firm stated that it would double its usual logging rate until the year 2005. Part of Hurwitz's logging plan was to clear cut acres of old redwoods. The retail market price of lumber from these old trees was extremely high. And Pacific Lumber had logging rights to the largest privately owned redwood forest in California.

Environmentalists were angered, for they saw the redwoods as a national treasure. They initiated a lawsuit to stop the cutting. Also opposed to the logging were the Sierra Club, the Wilderness Society, and over forty members of Congress. Pacific Lumber officials were disturbed. They noted that even though they planned to cut 3000 acres of redwoods, there were 76,000 acres of old-growth redwood protected within California public preserves. They also resented the fact that most of the protesters were outsiders who had no appreciation of the economic factors of life in logging areas. Industry representatives feared that additional environmental restrictions would result in the loss of 40,000 more jobs and an annual revenue drop of over $1 billion by the year 2000.

Pacific Lumber wanted logging treated fairly and without emotional interference by outside sources. Hurwitz's position on logging, as it appeared in a newspaper article, stated: "It is a clean nontoxic production process that does no damage to the environment. It is renewable, provides clean air and water and wonderful wildlife habitats."

Questions

1. Describe, in terms of the information provided in this case, just what you believe constitutes societal well-being—the third component in our definition of ethics.
2. Try to identify Dave Foreman's and Charles Hurwitz's stages of moral reasoning.
3. Detail a resolution to this conflict that would satisfy both Earth First and Pacific Lumber.

Sources

Jack Anderson and Dale Van Atta, "Tree spiking: an ecoterrorist tactic," *The Washington Post* (March 5, 1990), C20.

Bill Bartol and Lynda Wright, "Eco-activist summer," *Newsweek* (July 2, 1990), 60.

Peter Hong and Dori Jones Yang, "Tree huggers vs. jobs: it's not that simple," *Business Week* (October 19, 1992), 108, 109.

Michael Parrish, "Western environmentalists' enemy no. 1," *Los Angeles Times* (August 19, 1990), D1, D15.

Susan Reed and Lorenzo Benet, "Eco-warrior Dave Foreman will do whatever it takes in his fight to save mother earth," *People* (April 16, 1990), 113, 115, 116.

Ellen Schultz, "A raider's ruckus in the redwoods," *Fortune* 119 (April 24, 1989), 172, 173.

Mark A. Stein, "Plan to log redwoods hits a buzz saw of opposition," *Los Angeles Times* (January 27, 1990), A1, 16, 17.

Mark A. Stein, "Redwood summer: it was guerrilla warfare," *Los Angeles Times* (September 2, 1990), A3, 34, 35.

Mark Walters, "California's chain-saw massacre," *Reader's Digest* 135 (November 1989), 144–149.

❖ Case Study 10–3 ❖

PETA

New York City has been called the fur capital of the world. But wearing fur in New York may not prove to be a pleasant experience. Being accosted by animal rights activists in the streets of large cities has become a common occurrence. A spokesperson for the People for Ethical Treatment of Animals (PETA) explained the group's strategy. It was to move away from trying to evoke sympathy for animals and toward "stigmatizing people who wear furs as callous and self-indulgent."

Splashing paint on fur coats, showing pictures of trappers killing fur-bearing animals and of caged animals in freezing conditions are tactics used to embarrass owners of fur coats. The tactics seem to be effective because the largest furriers have reported declining sales. However, the issue with the activists concerns more than fur coats. It is about the right of animals to live. According to PETA's literature, "animals need not suffer for human beings to flourish."

PETA is not a small group. It claims over 300,000 members and has annual revenues of over $5 million. Founded in the early 1980s by Ingrid Newkirk and Alex Pacheco, the organization has challenged the use of animals by both researchers and business concerns. The rationale for PETA's existence comes from the author Peter Singer in his book *Animal Liberation*.

Singer's position is that all animals who can feel pain should be treated as equal to humans. The fact that we, as humans, differ from other biological species "cannot be a morally relevant criterion." He further states that this species equality "is a moral idea." His argument is grounded in the evolution of species: in the evolutionary chain, we appear closely related to the apes. Does the fact that we have reached a higher stage of evolution give us the right to abuse other species—even for the best of motives?

Singer particularly questions the use of animals in laboratory experiments. He condemns that use as "speciesism," a prejudice akin to racism. With this rationale, PETA filed suit to bar euthanasia of monkeys at Tulane University's Primate Center. Lawsuits are not the only means of protest that animals rights activists have chosen. A series of thefts of laboratory animals has been reported across the county. In Irvine, California, 250 animals were taken from a lab; similarly, in Arizona, 1200 animals were stolen from an animal research facility. Other break-ins have occurred in Maryland and New York. The destruction of research data resulting from animal experiments has gone hand in hand with many of the animal "liberations."

One security expert commented on the aggressive behavior of animal rights activists: "In attempting to preserve the rights of animals they are depriving us of our rights—the right to be safe from terrorism and crime." That expert claims that groups such as the Animal Liberation Front (ALF) have humanitarian motives but use violent means to attain their goals. Among those means are bombing and arson, in addition to disrupting business, destroying records, and stealing animals. PETA press releases often quickly follow break-ins attributed to ALF.

The animal rights activists defend their actions by calling attention to the types of research being conducted on animals. They question the army's injuring of goats so that battlefield surgery techniques can be perfected. They also question whether abandoned dogs should be tortured so that medical instrument salespeople can understand and explain suturing techniques by using live animals instead of models. Nor do they accept the explanation from the fur industry that animals such as minks are raised on ranches in decent conditions rather than inhumane ones and, like cattle, are legitimately used for human consumption.

Medical organizations have a more serious complaint about the tactics of the animal rights activists. Their concern is perhaps best embodied in ALF's actions against John Orem, a researcher in Texas who was investigating Sudden Infant Death Syndrome (SIDS). ALF stole five cats used for sleep research and research data from Orem's lab and caused $50,000 worth of damage caused during the break-in.

After the break-in, PETA filed a complaint against Orem's lab with the National Institutes of Health. The complaint was about violations of animal protection laws. Another animal rights group claimed that Orem's work was not important to SIDS research.

An inspection of Orem's lab by the National Heart, Lung and Blood Institute vindicated Orem. The inspection team not only commended Orem but condemned the "illegal acts of violence, vandalism and character assassination." Orem himself worried about the future of medical research if the animal rights activists continued their tactics.

Questions

1. Under what circumstances, if any, do animals have a right to life?
2. What stages of moral reasoning seem to be depicted by Peter Singer and John Orem?
3. Prepare a short position statement to resolve the conflict between PETA and the furriers. Test that position against the four guidelines for a lasting resolution of conflict.

Sources

Robert M. Bleiberg, "Animal worship—II," *Barron's* 69 (November 13, 1989), 9.

Elizabeth A. Brown, "Furor over fur coats heats up," *The Christian Science Monitor* (January 17, 1990), 2.

John R. Cole, "Animal rights and wrongs," *The Humanist* 50 (July–August 1990), 12–14, 42.

Sneed B. Collard III, "Reforming animal rights," *The Humanist* 50 (July–August 1990), 10, 11, 49.

Kenneth L. Feder and Michael Alan Park, "Animal rights," *The Humanist* 50 (July–August 1990), 5–7, 44.

James Kersch, "Animal rights groups step up attack on furriers," *The New York Times* (November 27, 1988), 50.

Edward L. Lee II, "Violent avengers," *Security Management* 33 (December 1989), 40–42.

Christopher Meyers, "People for the ethical treatment of animals, 325,000 strong, assumes influential controversial role in fierce national battle," *The Chronicle of Higher Education* (October 10, 1990), A21, 28.

Susan Okie and Veronica Jennings, "'Rescued' animals killed," *The Washington Post* (April 13, 1991), A1.

Peter Singer, *Animal Liberation* (New York: Avon Books, 1977).

Rod Smith, "California animal rights proposals show how out-gunned agribusiness is," *Feedstuffs* (December 16, 1991), 16, 19.

Notes to Chapter 10

[1] Boye Lafayette De Mente, *Japanese Ethics and Etiquette in Business* (Lincolnwood, IL: NTC Business Books, 1988).

[2] Jürgen Habermas, *Communication and the Evolution of Society*, trans. by Thomas McCarthy (Boston: Beacon Press, 1979).

[3] Marvin W. Berkowitz and John C. Gibbs, "Measuring the developmental features of moral discussion," *Merrill-Palmer Quarterly* 29:4 (1983), 399–410.

[4] Habermas.

[5] Ronald E. Berenbeim, *Corporate Ethics: Research Report No. 900* (New York: The Conference Board, Inc., 1987).

[6] Some of the material in this introduction is based on Chapter 7, "Ecology," in John Granrose, *Perspective on Ethics* (Athens, GA: Georgia Center for Continuing Education, 1981), pp. 75–84.

[7] Aldo Leopold, "The Land Ethic," *A Sand County Almanac* (New York: Ballantine Books, 1970), pp. 237–264.

[8] Garrett Hardin, "The tragedy of the commons," *Exploring New Ethics for Survival* (Baltimore: Penguin Books, 1973), pp. 250–264. First published in *Science* 162 (December 13, 1968), 1243–1248.

[9] Hardin, p. 254.

[10] Ann Colby et al., *Moral Stages and Their Scoring* (Cambridge: Harvard University Center for Moral Education, 1980), Part I, p. 25, Table 2.

[11] Hilary Putnam, "How not to solve ethical problems," The 1983 Lindley Lecture (Lawrence, KS: University of Kansas Department of Philosophy, 1983), 3.

[12] Putnam, pp. 4–5.

[13] Habermas, p. 5.

[14] William M. Kurtines, "Sociomoral Behavior and Development from a Rule-Governed Perspective: Psychosocial Theory as a Nomadic Science," in William M. Kurtines and Jacob L. Gewirtz (eds.), *Moral Development Through Social Interaction* (New York: John Wiley & Sons, 1987). Marvin W. Berkowitz, Fritz Oser, and Wolfgang Althof, "The Development of Sociomoral Discourse," in William M. Kurtines and Jacob L. Gewirtz (eds.), *Moral Development Through Social Interaction* (New York: John Wiley & Sons, 1987). Jürgen Habermas, *Communication and the Evolution of Society*, trans. by Thomas McCarthy (Boston: Beacon Press), p. 19.

[15] James Rest, *Moral Development: Advances in Research and Theory* (New York: Praeger Publishers, 1986).

GLOSSARY

Act Deontologism The type of deontologism which denies that rules are fundamental in making moral decisions. (The opposite of act deontologism is rule deontologism.)

Adjudication The function performed by judges in a court of law—deciding based on situational characteristics the rightness or wrongness of an action.

Beneficence The ethical principle which holds that one should produce the greatest net balance of benefit over harm, the ideal being to do no harm and do only good. Note that beneficence can also be thought of as a disposition or character trait as well as a principle.

Coercive Power The type of power that is based on a relationship between persons in which one has the ability to hurt or punish the other.

Consequentialism The ethical theory which holds that the consequences (either actual or probable) are the sole factor determining whether something is right or wrong. (The opposite of consequentialism is deontologism.)

Consistency The requirement that the various beliefs and principles a person holds should not contradict each other, and that a person's beliefs are in harmony with his or her subsequent behavior.

Conventional Level of Moral Thought The type of moral thinking that is characterized by mutual interpersonal expectations, relationships, and interpersonal conformity.

Customary Morality The type of morality that obtains legitimacy from customs, traditions, or societal norms. (The opposite of customary morality is reflective morality.)

Deception All or some of what is said or implied, verbally or nonverbally, is false. In addition to falsehoods, there may be concealment of relevant facts about the issue in question.

Deontology The type of ethical belief claiming that obligations or duties form the basis of right and wrong.

Descriptive Ethics Accounts provided by social scientists of the moral beliefs and theories held by particular groups of people. Such accounts are intended as factual claims rather than as value judgments; that is, they describe rather than prescribe behavior.

Discursive Communication   A stage of ethical deliberation between two or more parties involving an explicit understanding of the facts and principles underlying the other parties' position, and an effort to establish a shared ground based on mutually accepted facts and principles.

Equity   The condition where some type or degree of equality exists between two or more parties.

Ethical Egoism   The ethical theory which claims that the morally right thing to do is whatever produces the greatest balance of good over evil consequences for the actor or agent.

Ethics   A set of normative guidelines directed toward resolving conflicts of interest, so as to enhance societal well-being. Also, the branch of philosophy that studies such guidelines.

Existentialism   The ethical stance that one's free and independent decision is the criterion of something being morally right or wrong. In this sense, existentialism is a type of act deontologism.

Exploitation   Taking advantage of another for personal reward.

Feasibility   An ethical guideline used to determine whether an action is doable, practical, and realistic.

Firmism   A restricted consequentialist theory of right and wrong that holds that the results for the firm are the sole factor determining whether an action or practice is morally acceptable.

Imperfect Procedural Justice   Where the justice of the procedure is agreed upon, but for various practical reasons it is impossible to achieve perfectly just results.

Justice   A process or an end by which individuals receive what is considered as their fair due. (Note the definitions of Marxist, Meritarian, and procedural justice.)

Legalistic   Applies to situations in which laws function in ways that are objectionally rigid, inflexible, and lifeless.

Legitimate Power   That type of power which is held by individuals because of their role in formal, interpersonal relations.

Letter of the Law   The interpretation of legal codes according to their strict written form.

Marxist Justice   The view of justice that is based upon the premise "From each according to his abilities, to each according to his needs." Marxist justice advocates the equal distribution of goods regardless of merit.

Meritarian Justice   The view of justice which holds that the good things in life should be distributed in accordance with the merit of the recipient.

Meta-Ethics   Concerned with the philosophical analysis of the meaning and justification of the concepts and principles put forward by normative ethics.

Mixed Deontologism   The view that consequences are one factor but not the only one determining the morality of an action. (The opposite of mixed deontologism is pure deontologism.)

Monistic Rule Deontologism   The deontological theory of ethics which holds that there is one and only one fundamental rule in ethics. (The opposite of monistic rule deontologism is pluralistic rule deontologism.)

Moral Intervention   An effort to induce a person to reason from a higher stage of moral judgement.

Moralistic   Connotes that morality itself can be practiced in a way that leads to disharmony rather than harmony in a person or society.

Morality   Human institution or practice of guiding our behavior by rules or goals that are in some way related to human welfare.

Mutuality   Two parties treating each other as ends in themselves and taking an active interest in the ends or goals of the other.

Nondeception   An ethical principle of conflict resolution based on the necessity of honesty and straightforward-ness in communication.

Nondiscrimination   The ethical princi-ple which holds that one should show no special favor to one person or group.

Nonmaleficence   The ethical principle that one should abstain from deliberate and unjustified harm to others (as well as to oneself). (Note that nonmaleficence could be considered a disposition or character trait as well as a principle.)

Normative Ethics   The systematic attempt to formulate and defend the-ories about what is right, good, or oblig-atory. (Normative ethics is contrasted with meta-ethics and also with descrip-tive ethics.)

Ordinary Communicative Action   Ethical discussion stance focused on the speaker and his or her views, and not on the listener and his or her position.

Paradox of Liberty   In order to maintain freedom, certain restrictions, laws, and limitations of true freedom must exist.

Perfect Procedural Justice   An arrange-ment where goods can be divided equally among concerned parties, and where the nature of that division is a tendency toward equality as it is in the best interest of all parties concerned.

Pluralistic Rule Deontologism   The type of rule deontologism which holds that more than one rule is fundamental in morality. (The opposite of pluralistic rule deontologism is monistic rule deontologism.)

Postconventional Moral Reasoning   The level of ethical deliberation that is free of captivity to coercion, reward, group pressure, or law. Postconventional deci-sions are made with the interests of both the individual and others in mind.

Power   The ability to get someone to do something that he or she otherwise would not do.

Prima Facie Duties   Described by philoso-pher W. D. Ross, these are factors that must be considered in assessing right and wrong. A prima facie duty is an actual duty in life, providing that it is not overridden by a conflicting prima facie duty. According to Ross, the prima facie duties include fidelity, reparation, gratitude, justice, beneficence, self-improvement, and nonmaleficence.

Psychological Egoism   The theory in descriptive ethics which claims that all human behavior is ultimately motivated by self-interest alone. (The descriptive theory of psychological egoism is often held in conjunction with the normative theory of ethical egoism.)

Pure Deontologism   The view that con-sequences have nothing to do with the morality of an action.

Pure Procedural Justice   The type of jus-tice that is based on procedures which are claimed to be justified in themselves rather than because they bring about the best possible consequences when applied.

Pure Rule Deontologism   The type of rule deontologism which holds that conse-quences have no relevance to ethics.

Rational   Appeals to the reasoning abil-ity of human beings.

Reasoning   An ethical guideline focus-ing on rational thought in the resolu-tion of conflict.

Reciprocity   Two persons using each other for their own ends by trading favors.

Referent Power   The type of power that is based on respect for knowledge or values.

Reflective Morality   The type of moral-ity that appeals to conscience, reason, or to some principle which includes thought. (The opposite of reflective morality is customary morality.)

Reversibility   The ethical principle that advocates the consideration of the ques-tion "Would we want others to do to us what we propose doing to them if our positions were reversed?"

Reward Power   The type of power that is based on the ability of one party to bestow financial or other benefits on another party.

Rule Deontologism   The type of deontologism which holds that using rules is fundamental in our moral decision-making. (The opposite of rule deontologism is act deontologism.)

Situation Ethics   Emphasizes the importance of basing one's moral decisions on detailed knowledge of each relevant situation. (Both act deontologism and act utilitarianism would be types of situation ethics.)

Spirit of the Law   Interpretation of legal codes according to the underlying principles that originally spawned the law.

Strategic Communication   Ethical discussion stance bluntly directed toward obtaining agreement, even if there is no consensus.

Teleology   The type of ethical theory which claims that whether or not an action is morally right or wrong depends completely on the consequences or results of that action (or of a rule which dictates that action). Also known as consequentialism.

Universal Consequentialism   Takes into account all consequences of an action, regardless of the person or group to whom they occur, to be relevant to one's ethical judgement. (Universal consequentialism is also known as utilitarianism.)

Universalizability   An ethical guideline claiming that taking the moral point of view requires that we be willing to allow others to do the same types of things we consider morally acceptable for ourselves.

Utilitarianism   The ethical theory which holds that the right thing to do is whatever will lead to the greatest good for the greatest number.

Values   Those principles or goals that are actually worthwhile, good, or desirable, as distinguished from those merely thought to be so.

INDEX